I've Been Here
All the While

AMERICA IN THE NINETEENTH CENTURY

Series editors
Brian DeLay, Steven Hahn, Amy Dru Stanley

America in the Nineteenth Century proposes a rigorous
rethinking of this most formative period in U.S. history.
Books in the series will be wide-ranging and eclectic, with
an interest in politics at all levels, culture and capitalism,
race and slavery, law, gender and the environment, and
regional and transnational history. The series aims to
expand the scope of nineteenth-century historiography by
bringing classic questions into dialogue with innovative
perspectives, approaches, and methodologies.

I've Been Here All the While

BLACK FREEDOM ON NATIVE LAND

ALAINA E. ROBERTS

PENN

UNIVERSITY OF PENNSYLVANIA PRESS

PHILADELPHIA

Published by
University of Pennsylvania Press
Philadelphia, Pennsylvania 19104-4112
www.upenn.edu/pennpress

Printed in the United States of America
on acid-free paper

2 4 6 8 10 9 7 5 3 1

A Cataloging-in-Publication record is available
from the Library of Congress
ISBN 978-0-8122-5303-0

For all the dearly departed members of the Roberts
family, but especially for Travis Roberts. You were
the family historian long before I was born, and
this book would not be what it is without your
remembrances. Thank you for safeguarding this
knowledge for us all and for being so generous
with your time. I wish you were here
to see our family story finally told in print

I feel so fortunate to have been born into a
story so rich I can barely believe it at times.
I know that I was gently led to this scholarship by
my ancestors, and I hope that I have done justice
to their stories and to the stories of the millions
of African, African American, and mixed-race
people who shared similar experiences

Contents

Introduction

WHEN MY GREAT-GREAT-UNCLE Eli Roberts described his family's arrival as enslaved people in Indian Territory (modern-day Oklahoma) from the Mississippi Chickasaw homelands in the mid-1800s, he detailed a world distinct from that which they had left. The fertile, green grasses of Mississippi metamorphosed into red and brown clay, and the southern pathways that had become crowded with white settlers clamoring for land were suddenly wide-open spaces occupied predominantly by Indians and Black people. In his childhood western home, he recounted to an interviewer with the Works Progress Administration in 1937: "It was wild tribes of all kinds, animals, hogs, cows—everything was wild. We wore shirts and they were woven. We made moccasins out of buck skin. There weren't any bridges. There weren't any typewriters. We had stage routes, trails, and no newspapers. The country was all open Indian lands. Just one store and post office, plenty game and fish, and no homesteaders. We had lots of horse racing, but no medicine, and no settlements."[1]

Soon, however, this western space began to resemble the southern homelands that its Native settlers had been forced by the U.S. government to leave behind. The Chickasaw, Choctaw, Cherokee, Creek, and Seminole Nations (also known as the Five Tribes) had brought their slaves, their distaste for foreign American oversight, and their proven adaptability to Indian Territory. The wealthy citizens of these Indian nations rebuilt their plantations larger than before, increasing their cotton production, cultivated by an enslaved populace that grew to make up approximately 14 percent of Indian Territory's total population by 1860.[2] It became evident that slavery was now both economically and socially important within the Five Tribes right as the United States saw the 1830s period of plantation expansion shift into the 1850s skirmishes that became known as "Bloody Kansas."[3] As white Americans argued over Black humanity and the spread of slavery, the Five Tribes were swept into analogous disputes that sparked discord and challenged their notions of race and kinship. In the war that followed, both white and Indigenous slaveholding societies fractured. After their ideological and martial involvement in the Civil War, Indian nations, too, experienced a Reconstruction period. Like their white southern counterparts, they resisted emancipating and enfranchising their former slaves until the United States' intervention compelled them to do so. But for Indian nations, this federal intervention represented a combination of the American obsession with the spread of slavery in the West and a fixation on the seizure of western Indian land.

It is this connection between North American slavery, Black freedom, and settler colonialism that constitutes the nucleus of this book. What do I mean by "settler colonialism"? Scholars from a number of disciplines have traditionally defined "settler colonialism" as the exploitation of a region or country's resources and labor, plus the forcible resettlement of Indigenous peoples and their replacement by settlers who then move onto their lands and rewrite history in an effort to erase the longevity of their presence, and often their very existence. Because throughout the Americas, Africa, Australia, and the Pacific Islands the settlers who have put these practices into motion have, for the most part, been white, settler colonialism also involves an element of racial ideology, specifically the idea that white dominion in political, social, and economic systems and control over land is natural and logical.[4]

In Indian Territory, I identify settler colonialism as a process that could be wielded by whoever sought to claim land; it involved not only a change in land occupation but also a transformation in thinking about and rhetorical justification of what it meant to reside in a place formerly occupied by someone else. This means that, in my definition, anyone could act as a "settler," despite previous status as, say, a slave or a dispossessed Indian, as long as they used this process—composed of rhetoric, American governmental structures, and individual action—which may have aided in their efforts to acquire land or protection but which ultimately served the goals of spatial occupation and white supremacy: the dual nature of settler colonialism.[5] Power did not emanate from only one person or governmental agency. Rather, these settlers appealed to tribal agents, the secretary of the interior, various governmental commissions, the president of the United States, and so on. Together, these sources of power made up the settler colonial state.

The settlers I follow are members of the Five Tribes (especially Chickasaws and Cherokees), Indian freedpeople (Black people once owned by members of the Five Tribes), and Black and white Americans. These overlapping waves of settlers employed particular iterations of settler colonialism to justify their claims to the land in Indian Territory, and hence to privileges of citizenship or communal belonging. The terms I use for people of African descent throughout this book are a mixture of historical creation and historians' interventions. Freed African Americans were often referred to as "freedmen" in their own time (for instance, the governmental agency charged with helping them to acclimate to freedom was called the Freedmen's Bureau). In the same historical moment, the U.S. government referred to Black people owned by Native Americans, and their descendants, as "Chickasaw freedmen," "Cherokee freedmen," and so on, to differentiate their histories of enslavement from those of Black people in the United States and to categorize them for the purpose of resource distribution. I use "Indian freedpeople" as a gender-neutral catchall to refer to formerly enslaved women and men from all of the Five Tribes.[6] Though today the descendants of Indian freedpeople identify, for the most part, as African American, here I largely refer only to those people of African descent who lived in the United States as "African American" to call attention to their nationalities. Indian freedpeople were part of the Indian nations they were connected to, and, as such, I believe that calling them "African American" is anachronistic.

In many ways, Eli's life experiences embody the complexities of my definition of settler colonialism and the key arguments of this book. Throughout the United States, enslaved people of African descent owned by whites were used to till and tame the land that was stolen from Native Americans, becoming coerced participants in the process of settler colonialism. Eli's enslavement would eventually serve a similar purpose. He and thousands of other enslaved people of African descent who lived within the Five Tribes were the product of an eighteenth-century American goal to "civilize" Native peoples by encouraging them to take part in capitalistic endeavors, including chattel slavery.[7] When the United States' Indian policy changed in the early nineteenth century, the Five Tribes' qualified adoption of "civilization" was not enough to stop them from being displaced by impatient white settlers, and they, along with the Black women and men enslaved in their nations, were coerced into moving westward. Though there were Indians such as the Comanches, Caddos, and Plains Apaches already living in Indian Territory, once the Five Tribes arrived, they, along with enslaved people like Eli, tended this land that had been forcibly taken from other Native tribes. In doing so, they formed a connection to their new homeland, and in order to protect their claim to it, they turned to the process of settler colonialism: the Five Tribes urged the American government to help them safeguard their property (settlements, cows and horses, enslaved people) from the raids of western Indians, and they rhetorically situated themselves as more "civilized" than the former occupants of their land. They would be only the first wave of settlers to construct such a dichotomy to justify their fitness to occupy the land.

As it did in the United States, the Civil War forced a reckoning with slaveholding in Indian Territory and provided American politicians an excuse to disavow their own treaties and once more demand land cessions from Native peoples, including the Five Tribes. Eli and other Indian freedpeople benefited from this project of dispossession, receiving forty-acre allotments of Indian land (the same forty acres that has long since echoed in African American culture) through the Dawes Severalty Act. In the process, Indian freedpeople became the only people of African descent in the world to receive what might be viewed as reparations for their enslavement on a large scale.[8] To solidify their hold on their new assets, Indian freedpeople, and subsequent waves of Black and white Americans who arrived in the 1880s seeking new beginnings, utilized this same process of settler colonialism to claim land through the U.S. government and articulate a right to dispossess their spatial forebears.

Though these historical actors may not have truly believed that the American government should hold the power to police their land claims or that white people were the superior race, they engaged with the settler colonial process in an effort to realize their own visions of freedom. For the Five Tribes, this meant the freedom to rebuild after the trauma of Removal; for Indian freedpeople and African Americans from the United States, this meant the freedom of ownership after lives of enslavement; for white Americans, this meant the freedom from hierarchical communities that offered them no economic advancement. For all of these groups, Indian Territory became the ground upon which they sought belonging.

"Belonging" is a term that many scholars have used as a sort of all-encompassing way to reference community, kinship, social welfare, or citizenship, at times respectively or all at once. The term resists a firm interpretation, as it is tied to the emotional connections of people in the past. And yet a desire for belonging shaped historical events, and so I deem it necessary for examination. Though I use "belonging" throughout my narrative to refer to the community ties of all my historical actors, I most often use "belonging" throughout this book to signal that the Black and mixed-race characters in this story did not always seek citizenship, the legal conveyance of certain rights and privileges upon a person by a state. Rather, they often clung to kinship networks and natal communities in locations where citizenship was an impossibility in order to possess land.[9] Chickasaw freedpeople, like members of my family, were offered no tribal membership by the Chickasaw Nation after emancipation. And here lies the importance of examining belonging in this period: even without the prospect of tribal citizenship, Chickasaw freedpeople stayed within the nation, demonstrating that, for them, kinship ties and generational connections to the space of

Indian Territory were often more important than political rights, insofar as they allowed them to stake a claim to the land.[10]

This importance of land broadens the idea of Reconstruction that has been put forth in much historical scholarship: that Reconstruction revolved predominantly around the pursuit of political rights by people of African descent.[11] What if we looked at Indian Territory as a space where a different sort of Reconstruction project occurred, one that allowed for the successful pursuit of land, and it was *this* undertaking that influenced Black people's decisions and experiences?[12] It is true that, constrained by institutional and individual racism as well as by the crushing poverty of newfound emancipation, Black settlers did not have access to the same economic and social resources that white settlers possessed. But Indian Territory was a space upon which people of African descent projected their hopes and dreams of successful land claims. In their letters to Indian and white officials in Indian Territory and the United States, as well as in their communications to the U.S. Congress, Indian freedpeople and African Americans from the United States expressed a sense of ownership of Indian land and a willingness to take whatever steps were necessary to gain and maintain access to it, a key part of their sense of belonging in their respective all-Black or mixed-race communities.

At the same time, formal citizenship was also important to this story of the West, as Reconstruction saw Black and Indian citizenship negotiated in dynamic relation to each other in both Indian Territory and the United States.[13] Textbooks, films, and both academic and popular works of history that consider American Reconstruction have primarily defined the era in terms of the U.S. government's efforts at reconciling the northern and southern regions of the country, torn asunder by the issue of slavery. This concern now ostensibly settled through emancipation, federal and state governments attempted to incorporate free African Americans into their polities to a degree through laws, fragile promises, and military support, while at the same time placating white people who had previously owned these same freedpeople. Whether characterized as a period in which African Americans and their supporters unfairly penalized the South or as a period in which Republicans truly tried to change the racist foundations of their government and society only to eventually capitulate to white southerners and Democrats, the standard narrative has focused on Black and white Republicans' legislative and grassroots struggles for political power, and the principal protagonists of Reconstruction have thus largely remained only white or African American.[14]

Reconstruction, though, was not solely a project designed to force southern states to recognize the freedom and rights of African Americans. Republicans wielded their power in the West as well, and the inclusion of the Native peoples and people of African descent located in Indian Territory in our narrative of this period demonstrates that settler colonialism must be connected to our analysis of the period. This brings me to the second part of my argument. When Eli, his parents, and his siblings received their land allotments, the nineteenth century was nearly over, and what the average person thinks of as "Reconstruction" had long ago ended.[15] Considering the allotment of Indian land to Indian freedpeople expands the timeline of Reconstruction from 1863–1877 to 1863–1907 and demonstrates that in Indian Territory, Native Americans' national conversations about Black and Indian citizenship were directly connected to *American* conversations about Black and Indian citizenship.[16]

In the Civil War and Reconstruction eras, white politicians debated the dimensions of African American rights and citizenship.[17] These conversations joined those they had about Native Americans: whites assumed they would soon conquer the West, forcing Native Americans to become American citizens. At the same time, within the Five Tribes, Indian leaders began to strategize about how to subvert forced absorption into the United States and also how they could preserve slavery and sovereignty.[18] When the United States forced them to free their slaves, the Five Tribes then found ways to keep people of African descent from fully accessing tribal membership. The emancipation and enfranchisement of Indian freedpeople that culminated in their receipt of land was the result not of Indian nations' decisions but of progressive Americans wrestling with the question of Black citizenship and fulfilling Black freedom and advancement within Indian nations in a way that they would not in their own country. This both violated Native nations' sovereign right to define their own tribal membership and provided Indian freedpeople with rights they would not have obtained otherwise. At the same time that the United States was broadening its definitions of citizenship, the Five Tribes were narrowing theirs.[19] In Indian Territory, previous inclusive definitions of tribal membership that revolved around ideas of adoption, shared history, and extended kinship became racialized and limited to a small number of citizens who would have access to tribal lands and monies.

"Citizenship" was by no means an established concept in the nineteenth century, and its boundaries remain contested to this very day. In the nineteenth century, states, the federal government, and Indian nations loosely defined it piecemeal, through property rights, wealth, ancestry, and access to voting. This excluded poor whites, recent immigrants, and most former slaves to varying degrees.[20] During Reconstruction, federal, state, and tribal citizenship became solid legalities only as a result of grassroots efforts, constitutional amendments, and legal suits brought by people of African descent, Native nations, Chinese and white immigrants, and Indian freedpeople.[21] With Reconstruction in Indian Territory, tribal citizenship became essential to determining who had access to what resources.[22] Putting the debates about Black and Native citizenship in Indian Territory and the United States into conversation with one another reveals how these dialogues both fed off disagreements over increasing migration and settlement in the West and the manner and degree of federal intervention in local definitions of societal membership.

As Indian land was allotted by the U.S. government to make room for white settlers, Creek, Cherokee, Seminole, and Choctaw freedpeople received their land, along with the ability to vote, hold office, and serve on juries, decades after Jim Crow laws had stymied much of the progress of their southern counterparts.[23] American agents took pains to ensure that all Indian freedpeople were able to access their land, with varying success, up to 1907—a use of federal force in the West to ensure Black progress long after the military had pulled out of the South.[24]

After Indigenous land holdings were divided and distributed through the Dawes Act, after "surplus" lands in Indian Territory were opened to

American settlement and became Oklahoma Territory, and after the Five Tribes unsuccessfully launched protracted negotiations with the United States, the lands that made up Indian Territory became part of the state of Oklahoma in 1907. At this point, Black progress no longer seemed to concern the federal government. Oklahoma statehood brought discriminatory legislation and white political power that disintegrated tribal governments and the Indigenous kinship practices that allowed for an acceptance of Black inclusion. This change did not occur overnight. It settled in slowly, first with land theft and lynchings in the quiet, rural spaces of Eli Roberts's Oklahoma, then with concerted racial violence in urban centers signaling its destructive arrival.

In 1921, the Tulsa Race Massacre was just such an event: an effort by white Oklahomans to destroy the economic success that people of African descent, many of whom were Indian freedpeople, had found through the oil and mineral resources on their land allotments. The division and allotment of Indian land made Indian Territory into a space where Indian freedpeople, whites, and African Americans could imagine, respectively, a homeland, a fresh start, and a racial paradise. African Americans and Indian freedpeople created all-Black towns and neighborhoods, such as "Black Wall Street," the Greenwood district of Tulsa, whose names still conjure images of nineteenth-century Black self-determination and coalition. After statehood, efforts by white Americans to forcibly take the economic and social control that landownership had brought people of African descent culminated in two days of mass murder and terror, the extent of which is still being discovered.[25] Not until perhaps the civil rights movement of the 1950s and 1960s would we again see American governmental intervention on behalf of people of African descent. Although 1907 marked the end of U.S. intervention in Indian Territory on behalf of Indian freedpeople, and thus the end of this expanded Reconstruction, my story ends in 1921, with the cruel reverberations of this removal of support for Black property ownership. Settler colonialism and Reconstruction shared the same end: white Americans and their rights and goals were now the U.S. government's only concern. This is why the interconnected series of migration, displacement, and seizure that begin in the 1830s with the Five Tribes' large-scale removal to Indian Territory are necessary to help us understand the trajectory of this western space and the importance of the multilayered claims made on land in the nineteenth and early twentieth centuries. The aggregation of Reconstruction and settler colonialism allowed for all of these possibilities but for only one ultimate ending.

The titular utterance, "I've been here all the while," represents both words spoken verbatim by numerous Indian freedpeople as a means to denote their long-held connections to Indian Territory and the sentiment that each wave of settlers in the West took on. Land, kinship, and migration were mediums through which people of African, Native, white, and mixed Afro-Native descent navigated and claimed this new space.[26] In post–Civil War Indian Territory, white and Black women and men moved in to occupy and claim land upon which Native peoples still resided, and ideas of belonging and citizenship within America and within Indian nations were constructed simultaneously. Reconstruction's promise allowed people of African descent to be part of this continued settlement and displacement, part of this continuous reimagining of Indian Territory.

This book tells a broad history of Reconstruction but also uses my family's stories to represent the excavation of Chickasaw freedpeople's history and, more broadly, the experiences of the portion of the African Diaspora enslaved and freed within Indian Territory. I tell this story, a unification of Black, Native, and white narratives, not only as a historian but also as a descendant of all four peoples: white settlers, Indian freedpeople such as Eli, African Americans from the United States, and Native members of tribal nations. On the one hand, it fills me with pride to think of the resilience of my Chickasaw and Choctaw forebears, who took a forced passage to a new land and turned it into an opportunity to create politically strategic and economically successful nations. And I feel honored to possess the rare legacy of historical Black landownership on the Roberts side of my family. I know that my ability to visit Ardmore, Oklahoma, and see the church that my father's family built in the 1890s and the gravestones that sit above the resting places of my ancestors is one that is foreign to many people of African descent; their histories of enslavement made opaque the communities in which their families lived, worked, and died.

As I wrote this book, though, I realized that my joy at these two inheritances came at other people's expense; that the land that allowed the Chickasaws and Choctaws to become two of the wealthiest and most influential tribes in Oklahoma came from other Native peoples who previously had lived upon it; that the land that allowed my family and hundreds of others in Indian Territory to become Black property owners was part of the broader theft of Indian land that also led to the loss of much Native sovereignty, culture, and language.

I characterize the different protagonists that populate my book as settlers because my perspective as their descendant has helped me to see how their freedoms and opportunities were begotten by impeding the freedoms and opportunities of others. The sources I've analyzed demonstrate that my ancestors' involvement and investment in this settler colonial process made their lives subtly easier and helped them survive. They were in difficult circumstances—forced migrations across oceans and across lands—but they were not forced to use the specific language and actions they chose. Though they were limited by their circumstances, as we all are, they actively chose their path in the midst of a myriad of difficult decisions. If we looked at just *this*, would it not be clear? Would we not consider them settlers? Reconciling divergent histories has granted me another way of looking at these peoples and places: as a heightened example of how oppressed people can oppress *other* people—no matter how trite that may seem.[27]

This complex history is not an exotic, peripheral story; rather, it is central to our understanding of America today. Expanding our narratives of Reconstruction to incorporate Indian Territory and the framework of settler colonialism is essential to an understanding of U.S. history: we must see western Indian nations as important spaces in which the convergence of race, belonging, and citizenship paralleled, and was connected to the sociopolitical realities in the United States.

CHAPTER 1

The First Settlers of Indian Territory

ELI ROBERTS REMEMBERED how the human landscape of Indian Territory had changed over his time spent in the West in the 1800s. "Walker
Martin was the only white man in the settlement. He lived near where
Caddo Creek empties into the Washita River. He moved here from Atoka,
where he had operated a large grape press. . . . Uncle Charlie Henderson
was the next settler in this country. He established a store on the Washita at
the location which was later known as Dresden. Before Henderson's store
was established, the negro settlers carried their grain to [Chickasaw] Governor Harris's mill at Mill Creek [at the southern point of the Chickasaw
Nation]."[1] Eli's narrative illustrates, among other things, a progression of
settlement in Indian Territory: The Five Tribes came along with their Black
slaves, and for years only they populated the region, along with a number
of other Indian tribes, until they were followed by white and Black settlers from the United States, whose intermittent encampments gradually
became towns and businesses.

Accepted wisdom about westward migration might have us believe
that centuries-old Indigenous inhabitance of western lands gave way to a
steady stream of white settlers who changed the racial landscape of North
America in one fell swoop. In reality, the various movements and removals of Indigenous peoples from the Southeast due to white invasion meant
that the first western settlers were often Native Americans who migrat-

ed to spaces other than their homelands, where they encountered other tribes—longtime enemies, other displaced peoples, and groups who had long called this land home. Native peoples adjusted their oral histories and survivance strategies to incorporate their new surroundings as they had done for millennia, crafting stories that told of successful migrations and learning about the food and herbs of their new homes.

As they were forced westward, the Five Tribes' experience in Indian Territory was different from the other Indigenous migrations occurring around them. The Chickasaw, Choctaw, Cherokee, Creek, and Seminole Nations sought to use the settler colonial process to cast themselves as civilizers of their new home: they used the labor system that Euro-Americans insisted represented sophistication—chattel slavery—to build homes, commercial enterprises, and wealth, and they portrayed themselves as settlers in need of protection from the federal government against the depredations of western Indians, which, the Five tribes claimed, hindered their own civilizing progress.[2] Moreover, they followed their physical appropriation of Plains Indians' land with an erasure of their predecessors' history.[3] They perpetuated the idea that they had found an undeveloped "wilderness" when they arrived in Indian Territory and that they had proceeded to tame it. They claimed that they had built institutions and culture in a space where previously neither existed.[4] The Five Tribes' involvement in the settler colonial process was self-serving: they had already been forced to move once by white Americans, and appealing to their values could only help them—at least at first. Involvement in the system of Black enslavement was a key component of displaying adherence to Americans' ideas of social, political, and economic advancement—indeed, owning enslaved people was the primary path to wealth in the nineteenth century. The laws policing Black people's behavior that appeared in all of the tribes' legislative codes showed that they were willing to make this system a part of their societies. But with the end of the Civil War, the political party in power—the Republicans—changed the rules: slavery was no longer deemed civilized and must be eliminated by force. For the Five Tribes, the rise and fall of their involvement in the settler colonial process is inextricably connected to the enslavement of people of African descent: it helped to prove their supposed civilization and it helped them construct their new home, but it would eventually be the downfall of their Indian Territory land claims. Recognizing the Five Tribes' coerced migration to Indian Territory as the first wave among many allows us to see how settler colonialism shaped the culture of Indian Territory even before settlers from the United States arrived.[5]

Though the Cherokee "Trail of Tears" has come to symbolize Indian Removal, the Five Tribes were just a handful of dozens of Indigenous tribes who had been forced to move from their eastern homelands due to white displacement. This displacement did not begin or end in the 1830s. Since the 1700s, Indian nations such as the Wyandot, Kickapoo, and Shawnee began migrating to other regions to escape white settlement and the violence and resource scarcity that often followed.[6] Though brought on by conditions outside of their control, these migrations were "voluntary" in that they were most often an attempt to flee other Native groups moving into their territory as a result of white invasion or to preempt white coercion, rather than a response to direct Euro-American political or legal pressure to give up their homelands.

The majority of nineteenth-century Native migrations, though, were a result of direct white coercion. White settlers moving in from Georgia, Alabama, and other states began illegally occupying the Five Tribes' land on the eastern side of the Mississippi River and requesting state and federal support to do so. Despite a Supreme Court ruling, *Worcester v. Georgia*, which upheld the Cherokee Nation's right to their lands (and therefore other Indian nations' same right), the support of the states for white settlers' occupancy of tribal lands led President Andrew Jackson to rebuke the court's decision. Through the Indian Removal Act, which pushed for removal treaties with Indian nations and for forcible evacuation by the U.S. military if necessary, Jackson insisted on the resettlement of the Cherokees, as well as the Choctaws, Creeks, Seminoles, Poncas, and Chickasaws, among others.[7]

Removal was devastating emotionally and physically for the Five

Tribes, but it was not an immediate change in their lives; rather, tribal members moved gradually, with complete migration occurring over a period of nearly a decade. Native peoples were compelled to leave their homes, their buried loves ones, and many of their belongings.[8] Even before the passage of the Indian Removal Act in 1830, trauma brought on by the expectation of removal permeated the lives of Native peoples. Cherokee woman Cornelia Chandler remembered that as her people were rounded up to begin their move, "the people were hunted like cattle. [Federal soldiers] went through their homes, ripping open the feather beds, destroying the [beehives], and making the country as desolate as possible. Many tried to hide from them."[9] Sarah Harlin was a young girl when her people, the Choctaws, were forced to leave their homes in Alabama. She came to Indian Territory by steamboat and then by wagon with a twelve-person party. Along the way, a baby in their group died, and its mother was overcome with grief. Sickness threatened to derail their journey, their meat spoiled, and three of their horses died.[10] If this was the journey of a family who, according to Harlin, "was thought in those days as well fixed, having a good wagon, fat horses, plenty of provisions and covering," then what heartache and misadventure must those poorer than Harlin have faced? The destitute would likely have had little food of their own and would have been forced to subsist solely on the rations meted out by soldiers to them "as if they were cattle."[11] The poor, the sick, and even the expectant mothers, if they stumbled or slowed down on their journey, "were shoved on, kicked and commanded to proceed on."[12]

The majority of women and men in the Five Tribes faced only one extreme removal, from the Southeast to Indian Territory.[13] But other Native peoples, such as the Lenape, faced multiple land dispossessions and migrations. The Lenape, also known as the Delaware, are originally from the East Coast and had been forced west into Ohio and western Pennsylvania in the 1750s by British colonists. In the 1830s, the Lenapes' Trail of Tears had taken them to Kansas, but in the 1860s, as Americans moved further West, the Lenape once again migrated. This time, they signed a treaty agreeing to settle among the Cherokee Nation in Indian Territory.[14] These layered migrations, removals, and dispossessions impacted Native American nations in a number of ways. Native peoples have long established their connection to the lands they occupied through their origin and morality stories and through medicinal, food, and spiritual traditions that utilize plants and animals indigenous to the area.[15] The Five Tribes' connection to the land in their pre-Removal homes had been further bolstered by the fact that, as farmers, they lived on the produce and resources the land provided for themselves and their livestock. Thus, Removal meant that the Five Tribes were not only physically uprooted but also spiritually uprooted. They had to find ways to relate to and claim their new homeland as their own in order to reestablish their nations economically, socially, politically, and spiritually—in other words, to find a new sense of belonging. The settler colonial process they chose to use to accomplish this was the same process that had forced them to leave their original homes—only this time, the Five Tribes were the settlers.

When the Five Tribes arrived in Indian Territory, there were a number of other Native peoples already living there. Some, like the Plains Apaches, Comanches, Wichitas, Yuchis, and Kiowas had long used Indian Territory as an occasional residence and hunting ground. Others, like the Quapaws and Osages, had moved from their homelands and farms to Indian Territory as a result of dwindling resources, pressure from settlers in surrounding regions, such as Texas, and forced treaties.[16] They saw the Five Tribes as intruders, and this shaped their reactions to them: members of these western nations often raided and killed members of the Five Tribes. These Indians' use of horses brought by Spanish explorers provided them with a great advantage over other tribes, and they saw that they could easily use their speed and agility to raid and war on agricultural peoples.[17]

Neither white Americans nor the Five Tribes considered most of the western tribes to be civilized. Americans believed early on that "emigrant Indians" such as the Five Tribes would need to be protected from the "erratic tribes to the west and north of them."[18] In describing the Five Tribes' exodus to the West, John C. Calhoun, then secretary of war, wrote in 1825 to President John Quincy Adams that, in removing tribes such as the

Cherokee, Chickasaw, and Choctaw, the U.S. government should "protect the interests" of both themselves and the Indian tribes. He emphasized that moving West would bring these "more or less civilized" Indian nations into contact with Indian tribes "of discordant character."[19] The western tribes' lack of American-style government and refusal to engage in capitalism and permanent property ownership rendered them uncivilized in the eyes of white Americans, whereas the Five Tribes' receptiveness to these practices made them allies—at least relative to other western Indians and when they weren't competing for land with white Americans.[20] As for the Five Tribes, even before their official move, they were wary of these Native peoples they found so different from themselves.[21] In 1824, a Cherokee delegation rejected removal on the basis that it would force them to "wage war with the uncultivated Indians" west of the Mississippi.[22] As a young man, Peter Pitchlynn, a future chief of the Choctaw Nation, visited Indian Territory in 1828 on a scouting mission. Looking to identify lands acceptable to serve as his tribe's new home, Pitchlynn encountered some of the Native peoples who would eventually become his neighbors. Of meeting these Plains Indians, he wrote in his journal, "You never saw such a people in your life. Their manners and action are wild in the extreme. They are in a perfect state of nature and would be a curiosity to any civilized man."[23] Clearly, neither the Cherokee delegation nor Pitchlynn identified with the Native peoples already living in Indian Territory and, in comparison to themselves, they found them to be uncivilized.[24]

These leaders' views are important because they shaped the policies of their nations and show that they were well aware of the language and characteristics the American state used to denote civilization. However, Pitchlynn and a number of Cherokee leaders are not necessarily representative of the average member of the Five Tribes. As well-educated men from wealthy, well-connected families, their worldviews had been heavily shaped by the civilizationist policies preached at the schools they attended and by the white people they befriended. Records for common Native peoples are few and far between. Yet it was these ordinary tribespeople who felt the wrath of the western tribes the most. Unlike the wealthier Indians in their tribes who had a significant amount of property, when these ordinary people's livestock were taken or killed, they went hungry; when their lone slave was kidnapped, they lost their only source of capital. From the arrival of the Five Tribes in Indian Territory through the Civil War, Indian agents regularly reported receiving letters from tribal members complaining about the theft of goods by "wild Indians" and appealing to them for stability.[25] I will note that not every tribal member had negative experiences with western tribes. Edward Nail recalled that after his grandfather came from Mississippi to Indian Territory in 1835, he lived in the western part of the Choctaws' territory. He did not fence the ranch where his "fat" cattle roamed. Yet, according to Nail, the Comanches who "camped near his house, were peaceful."[26]

But many members of the Five Tribes had various reasons to harbor ill will toward western Indians: they may have suffered from raids or vandalism, or they may have truly felt they were morally and intellectually superior to them.[27] It is possible that tribal leaders were thinking, in part, of the effects raids had on their members when they spoke of western Indians. But the Five Tribes went beyond mere ethnocentrism or retribution when they involved themselves in the settler colonial process, using the language and methods that their ally, the United States, had created to dehumanize western Indians, in order to call for an American military presence in the region to erase southern Plains history and land claims.

After moving to the region and immediately experiencing crop and animal raids by various western tribes, members of the Five Tribes and tribal representatives demanded that the United States build forts in Indian Territory to protect them and to monitor those they called the "wild tribes." The United States was often slow to send troops to help the Five Tribes, as they wanted to reserve this power for their own (white) settlers. To build a case for the help they wanted, the Five Tribes reported every skirmish and theft perpetrated by western tribes, going so far as to submit claims for the losses they suffered and to contemplate retaliating with violence.[28] They used language that created a dichotomy between themselves and their foes, comparing themselves, as "civilized people," to white Americans, and jux-

taposing their "civilized" nature with the savagery of the "wild Indians."
Cherokee Chief John Ross called Indian Territory the "wilderness of the
West," a term borrowed from the white conqueror lexicon denoting Indian
nonuse or misuse of land, and Indian inhumanity.[29] Ross used language he
knew the U.S. government would understand and relate to, language that
exploited Americans' fear that barbarism would inhibit the expansion of
their civilized "empire of liberty," in the words of Thomas Jefferson.

The Five Tribes' complaints resulted in the creation of Fort Washita in
1842, which fulfilled the United States' promise written into the Indian Removal Act to "cause each tribe or nation to be protected, at their new residence, against all interruption or disturbance from any other tribe or nation of Indians, or from any other person or persons whatever," though the
violence certainly did not stop altogether.[30] The U.S. government's promise
to protect them from "domestic strife and foreign enemies" also sometimes came in the form of brokering meetings between the Five Tribes
and various western groups, organized to quash animosities and agree to
peace; these agreements worked only temporarily.[31] Whether the United
States intervened militarily or diplomatically, the Five Tribes' rhetoric allowed and enabled Americans to treat them as the injured settler parties
whose claims were protected by the might of the American government,
and the western Indians as trespassing marauders.

Creating an observable difference between themselves and other Indian nations was part and parcel of the Five Tribes' settler colonial process
because it allowed them to appeal to white Americans, upon whom the
Five Tribes depended for protection and resources as promised in their
Removal treaties. White Americans had also experienced the wrath of
western Indians; many Arkansas Territory forts were initially built to protect white settlers from them. Despite a military presence, white settlers
suffered numerous attacks on their possessions and their persons. In this,
their experiences mirrored those of the Five Tribes, sometimes directly.
For example, in 1838 an Indian agent reported that the Comanches had
killed white Americans as well as several members of the Five Tribes and
other peoples in Indian Territory.[32] The Five Tribes' calls for protection,

which used language such as "wild" and "uncivilized," tapped into white Americans' empathy through shared fear and shared thought about how civilized people acted. Therefore, white Americans could more easily identify with the Five Tribes' complaints, seeing themselves in their struggles, both attempting to civilize the West. U.S. Indian agents even referred to the Five Tribes and other Indians pushing into Indian Territory as those who would "colonize" this space, literally labeling them colonizers, just as they labeled themselves.[33]

In putting the other Indian nations in the category of "wild" and unlike them, the Five Tribes could think of and portray themselves as the rightful inhabitants of Indian Territory. Putting forth the idea—originated by Euro-Americans—that the "wild tribes" had not properly taken advantage of the land in Indian Territory, the Five Tribes would use the tools of civilization, agriculture, and animal husbandry to banish the wilderness and introduce development. This is exactly how the Five Tribes would later depict their experiences in Indian Territory.

The Five Tribes not only physically displaced other Indian nations in Indian Territory; they erased the history of southern Plains people and drafted a new history of Indian Territory. For example, in 1855, the Chickasaws built their council house, a sixteen-by-twenty-five-foot log house. Here, the Chickasaws rewrote their constitution and took their first actions as a sovereign national legislature, under the first Chickasaw governor, Cyrus Harris. Although the log house was quickly replaced (within the next year or so) by a brick iteration, the log house serves a particular purpose in the pantheon of Chickasaw public history. In 1911, the *Wapanucka Press*, an Oklahoma-based newspaper, interviewed someone (presumably a representative of the Chickasaw Nation) about the story of the log house's origins. The paper reported, "Slaves of the Chickasaws toiled in the dense oak forests cutting down the finest trees and hewing them into shape.... Thick undergrowth was cleared from a knoll ... paths were cut from bottom meadows."[34] Rough-hewn and surrounded by overgrown foliage, the log house is meant to evoke the idea that the Chickasaws encountered a "wilderness" in early Indian Territory. The reader is meant to believe that, as civilizers, the Chickasaws shaped this wilderness into the modern space that it became. This idea of "civilization" is based on Euro-American colonizers' ideas of advanced societies. The Cherokee Nation alleges on its website that "upon earliest contact with European explorers in the 1500s, Cherokee Nation was identified as one of the most advanced among Native American tribes."[35] Although the Cherokees were asserting their longevity as a people and their pride in their culture, here they use a European measurement of their merit. These examples make quite clear that remnants of the Five Tribes' settler colonial process remain to this day.

In the nineteenth century, the Five Tribes succeeded at crafting a perception of difference. The western Indians certainly saw them as settlers. The special agent to the Comanches reported that they were angry that tribes such as the Creeks and Choctaws "have extended their occupation and improvements to the country heretofore used by themselves as a hunting ground," expressing that they saw the Five Tribes as unlawful settlers, just like whites, and themselves as the dispossessed indigenous peoples of the region.[36] The Comanches had seen their former hunting ground as perfectly suited to their needs; now, they saw the Five Tribes' improvements in the service of civilization as impediments to their livelihood and used violence to strike back at the interlopers. On the other hand, to the Five Tribes and to Americans, the Comanches' very use of a "hunting ground" was evidence of their barbarism.

Though the Five Tribes accomplished their goal of drawing parallels between their and white Americans' need for protection as civilizing settlers in the West, the United States was slow to build forts, to provide arms and ammunition, and to remove interlopers from their lands, and even when they did, this failed to solve the Five Tribes' issues with the Plains tribes.[37] So the Five Tribes sought another strategy that would stimulate peace yet still allow them social superiority: unity. Upon the Five Tribes' arrival in Indian Territory, the United States alternated between military force and peace meetings in their efforts to get the western tribes (both those "indigenous" to the region and those new to the area) to stop "harassing" the Five Tribes. In 1830, for example, Peter Chouteau, U.S. Indian agent to the Osage, forced a meeting between the Osage and the Western Creeks and Cherokees to settle animosities stemming from the Osages' thefts and raids. The meeting resulted in a peace treaty.[38] After several years, leaders of the Five Tribes wanted to take up this mantle of mediation, and they asked the American government for permission to hold an annual grand council.[39] This allowed the Five Tribes the opportunity to hold authority over other Native peoples within the territory, to be seen by the United States as interlocutors and mentors in civilization in the region, and to amass respect among the western tribes that they hoped would lessen raids and violence within their own national boundaries. After the Civil War, this council transformed into the foundation of a sort of pan-Indian identity, as the Plains Indians were replaced as the Five Tribes' key enemy by a greater evil: mass white invasion.[40]

Along with the work of erasure and rhetorical justification, the Five Tribes performed the work of actual settlement. Individually, from the 1830s to the 1860s, the Five Tribes rebuilt their nations, strengthened their governments, and crafted new foundational narratives that incorporated the importance of migration to identity and belonging. The Cherokee, Creek, Choctaw, and Chickasaw Nations already had origin stories and folktales that spoke to the centrality of migration to their existence. They had long ago established that when they moved physically they brought with them their social customs, institutions, and identities. This made it easier—though not effortless or without trauma—for the nations to frame removal to Indian Territory as the continuation of established customs.[41]

The Chickasaws, the tribe situated on the most western portion of "settled" Indian Territory, continued to experience severe raiding by western tribes through to the Civil War but still managed to put into place a highly successful cotton trade and the makings of a standardized education system. The Cherokee Nation also suffered violent strikes but was able to advance its social, political, and economic cachet to the point where the period from 1846 to 1860 is often referred to as their "Golden Age." The *Cherokee Advocate* became the first newspaper of Indian Territory in 1844, and the Cherokees built over 100 schools, including elementary schools and two institutions of higher education, where youths learned the Cherokee syllabary. Wealthy white settlers nearby sent their children to Cherokee seminaries, and Cherokee children had a higher literacy rate than their white counterparts.[42] The Choctaw Nation revised its constitution, establishing a bicameral legislature and a Supreme Court, and allotted $18,000 per year to education.[43] An 1842 school law established six academies reserved for different segments of the population, including future (male) national leaders, female students, and male students.[44] At the same time, members of the Creek Nation had trouble adjusting to Indian Territory's disparate climate, finding it vastly different from the water- and timber-rich environment they had departed from. Disagreements over moving meant that the tribe migrated more incrementally than any of the other Five Tribes, leaving them with little consensus to nation-build and depleted strength to fight off raids.[45] The Seminoles did not have full self-governance, nor their own lands, until 1856.[46]

The labor of enslaved women and men was crucial to the Five Tribes' economic and social success in Indian Territory. Enslaved people helped build schools, government buildings, newspaper offices, and individual homes. Because of the forced removal of slaveholding Indian nations, slavery and its effect on legislation and societal norms were rooted in the culture of the West long before "Bleeding Kansas." Preserved through family lines and nourished by increasing dividends, Black chattel slavery had been an element of life in the Five Tribes for decades by the time of the Civil War. Europeans had introduced Native Americans to the transatlantic slave trade as both victims and participants as early as the 1490s. Though a form of Indigenous involuntary labor and captive-taking existed before European contact, Native bondage was neither transgenerational nor racial and hereditary before the eighteenth century.[47] White Europeans persuaded Native Americans to enslave members of other Indian tribes using their method of slave-trading, which focused on the accumulation of captives for sale, and thus for profit, rather than for population augmentation.[48] Indigenous peoples across North America were sent to places as far away as the Caribbean to work as slaves. A great number died due to tropical diseases or onerous labor.[49] Indian slavery was largely phased out in the early to mid-eighteenth century in favor of increased Black chattel slavery.[50] Indians quickly changed with the times, and, by the 1750s, some owned African slaves.

The Five Tribes, to varying degrees, adapted the institution of slavery to suit their own needs beginning in the late 1700s and intensifying in the early 1800s. Along with the institution of slavery the Five Tribes also adopted other parts of American "civilization," such as Euro-American clothing, agriculture, political language, religion, and economic structures in ways that benefited them, while retaining aspects of their own culture.[51] As in the United States, the majority of people in the Five Tribes did not own slaves. Yet, Indian elites created an economy and culture that highly valued and regulated slavery and the rights of slaveowners. Chickasaw planters exported an estimated 1,000 bales of cotton in 1830; this cotton was picked and processed by enslaved Black women and men.[52] Comparatively, in 1826 the state of Georgia produced 150,000 bales of cotton.[53] In the 1840s, ten cotton gins operated in the Choctaw Nation.[54] In 1860, about thirty years after their removal to Indian Territory from their respective homes in the Southeast, Cherokee Nation members owned 2,511 slaves (15 percent of their total population), Choctaw members owned 2,349 slaves (14 percent of their total population), and Creek members owned 1,532 slaves (10 percent of their total population). Chickasaw members owned 975 slaves, which amounted to 18 percent of their total population, a proportion equivalent to that of white slave owners in Tennessee, a former neighbor of the Chickasaw Nation.[55] Slave labor allowed wealthy Indians to rebuild the infrastructure of their lives even bigger and better than before. John Ross, a Cherokee chief, lived in a log cabin directly after Removal. After a few years, he replaced this dwelling with a yellow mansion, complete with a columned porch.[56]

The Five Tribes' nineteenth-century legislation demonstrates that, like their southern counterparts, they believed in the detailed regulation of enslaved people's lives. The Chickasaws restricted the assembly and movement of slaves, creating patrols and a pass system.[57] The other four tribes respectively prohibited enslaved people from learning to write and read, from singing hymns, and from sitting at the same table as their owner.[58] They also instituted constraints on land improvements and weapon ownership.[59] However, slave owners had the ability to disregard these laws as they chose. For instance, some slaveholders were willing to educate their slaves because it benefited them. Slaves on some larger plantations were put into positions of leadership and tasked with running their owners' businesses in their absence—positions that required the ability to read, write, and perform mathematical equations.[60]

One of the most important laws in the Chickasaw, Choctaw, Cherokee, and Creek Nations was the prohibition of interracial sex between Native and Black peoples.[61] In practice, these laws were often ignored and rarely enforced, as evidenced by the number of mixed-race children born to enslaved Black mothers in all of the Five Tribes. American tribal agents consistently remarked on the interracial mixing that occurred within all of the nations and observed that the Choctaws seemed to have the smallest population of mixed-race persons.[62] It is worth noting that there was no such Indigenous ban on interracial sex between whites and Native people. Laws against interracial sex, combined with Cherokee, Creek, Chickasaw, and Choctaw laws that criminalized Blacks' use of communally owned land to build houses or barns and that forbade citizens of the Five Tribes from freeing their former slaves and from hiring these freed slaves, created a racial underclass: Black and mixed-race people who lived and persevered within these Native spaces in spite of laws created to stifle their access to tribal membership, upward mobility, and community.[63] By this time in the nineteenth century the Five Tribes, formerly matrilineal, had begun recognizing bilateral kinship; refusal to acknowledge children born of Black mothers and Native fathers as fellow tribespeople was adherence to tradition but also evidence of the creation of a new, legally sanctioned, racially based system of exclusion and hierarchy. However, there are pointed examples where mixed-race people *were* able to overcome discriminatory legislation and prejudice to be seen as kin and play important roles within the Five Tribes.

Charles Cohee Sr. was a man borne by a Chickasaw father and a Black, enslaved mother. He served as an official interpreter for the Chickasaws and was described as mixed race, with "Indian-like" features, such as "quite strait" hair. While Cohee was not legally defined as a member of Chickasaw society, he exercised the mobility and autonomy of a free person and was well-respected by Chickasaw leaders. After his death, his son, Charles Cohee Jr., took up his mantle.[64] The Beams family, descended from a white owner and his slave woman (later wife), whom he eventually freed along with all of their children, lived in the Choctaw Nation. The Beams patriarch had been married to a Choctaw woman before his Black second wife, and thus his mixed-race Black and white children made their home with Beams's mixed-race white and Choctaw children (the product of this first marriage), first in the Mississippi Choctaw Nation and then in the Indian Territory Choctaw Nation. While the Beams children were able to live unmolested for several years after the death of their father, they faced a number of attempts on their freedom from Choctaw half-siblings and relatives, as well as other Indians and whites. Though in Indian Territory some Beams children had married Choctaw spouses, as free Blacks they had a price upon their heads; several of the Beams children or grandchildren were kidnapped or murdered, and the others spent the rest of their lives hiding from slave catchers or fighting in court to prove their free status.[65] In the Creek Nation, a number of people of African descent had been freed by their owners and some owned businesses such as boarding houses, stores, and blacksmith shops.[66] In the Cherokee Nation, an example made famous by historian Tiya Miles is that of the mixed-race children of Shoeboots, a Cherokee war hero, and Doll, an enslaved Black woman. A number of Doll and Shoeboots's children were recognized as Cherokee citizens through special acts of government. However, Miles makes clear that Shoeboots's acclaim was likely the cause of the nation's recognition of his children and of his interracial marriage.[67] The flexibility that allowed exceptions to the rule such as these would largely disappear in all of the Five Tribes after the war.

Nonmixed Black people, both free and enslaved, had varying experiences within these nations. Moses Lonian, the slave of a Cherokee man named Louis Ross, said that Ross "had not been a very kind master to his slaves. He whipped my father and several other of his slaves."[68] On the other hand, Mary Grayson, the slave of a Creek family, remembered: "We slaves didn't have a hard time at all before the War. I have had people who were slaves of white folks back in the old states tell me that they had to work awfully hard, and their masters were cruel to them sometimes, but all the Negroes I knew who belonged to Creeks always had plenty of clothes, and lots to eat, and we all lived in good log cabins we built."[69]

One can find both positive and negative experiences cited by enslaved people in all of the Five Tribes, but there are far fewer recollections available from Black people who navigated the nations as free people before universal emancipation by American treaty in 1866. This in itself betrays the rarity of people of African descent who successfully overcame the strict hierarchy imposed within these nations. Not until the postwar period would this small number of free Blacks become a large free population whose designation as "freedmen" of their respective Indian nations was solidified through the Dawes allotment process.

Many of the laws I have mentioned here have not referred to the Seminole Nation. This is because the Seminoles were unique in that their desire to engage in the institution of slavery differently than the chattel model was, in part, what led to their very existence. In the eighteenth century one of the reasons the Creek Nation split into two, creating the Seminole Nation, was disagreement over how, and to what extent, Indigenous ways should steer the future of the tribe. Slavery was a substantial facet of this debate. Hence, while the Seminoles legally owned slaves, they treated them differently from the other Indian nations. The Seminoles' treatment of Black slaves meshed more with former Indigenous captivity practices than with those of the chattel slavery model introduced by white Euro-Americans.[70] People of African descent owned by Seminoles lived apart from their owners and were able to cultivate their own agriculture and possess their own livestock—making restrictive Black Codes unfeasible. While this put the onus on the enslaved to provide for themselves in addition to giving a tribute to their "owners" on a regular basis, for the most part these Black people experienced relative autonomy.[71]

While the Creek and Seminole Nations were the only tribes to experience such a drastic struggle related to tradition and slavery, the other nations found that they, too, had to carefully negotiate these issues. In the Cherokee Nation, division over slavery was representative of estrangement in the tribe over adaptations to other Euro-American norms dating back to Removal.[72] The Keetoowah Society, which had existed for several decades before the Civil War, was the most influential tribal faction to protest the Cherokees' adoption of slavery. The group's core beliefs highlight the complexities of nineteenth-century Native life: while the Keetoowahs saw chattel slavery as a negative effect of Euro-American influence, their spiritual beliefs included aspects of Christianity.[73] The Choctaw and Chickasaw Nations did not seem to have had antislavery factions that wielded power and influence, though some Choctaws did feel that the practice of owning slaves had led to lazier generations because enslaved peoples now performed labor practices formerly carried out by Native peoples themselves, such as agricultural work and animal husbandry.[74] Overall, it does not seem as if the issue of slavery would have led to a civil breakdown in any of the Five Tribes as it did within the United States; rather, it seems to have been accepted as an important part of elite economic success. The Five Tribes did not count on the United States' struggle over the institution of slavery becoming their own.

The United States' struggle with slavery had begun decades before— many would argue it began with the very founding of the nation.[75] Throughout the late eighteenth and early nineteenth centuries, a number of northern states had begun to outlaw slavery or introduce gradual emancipation laws, and southerners feared this trend would continue until the federal government took their right to own slaves away from them. White abolitionists, most often motivated by religion, and African American abolitionists, motivated by their own experiences of slavery, used moral, religious, and practical appeals (trumpeting the benefits of free labor and invoking their fear of a southern "slave power") to plead their case on regional and national levels.[76] White abolitionists' attitude toward slavery in Indian nations, though, was more ambivalent. Although abolitionists found themselves on the opposite side of the Five Tribes with regard to slave ownership, many of these same white men and especially white women supported Native American causes—first in their struggles against Removal, and then against further postwar encroachment into their new western homes. For white abolitionists, the Five Tribes' adoption of chattel slavery was proof that, as "civilized" peoples, they should not face displacement, for they had obediently followed Americans' guidelines for acceptance.[77]

The Five Tribes had engaged in the process of settler colonialism in order to stake a legitimate claim to Indian Territory land and foster a new sense of belonging. But now their presence in and connection to the West and their successful adoption of Black chattel slavery would prove to be their downfall.

White and Black Americans were divided over whether slavery should follow western expansion, but they were united in the belief that western expansion was necessary: for wealthy whites the West represented an untapped market, and for poor whites and African Americans the West represented a space of opportunity and freedom.[78] White desire for land was the impetus behind Indian Removal, which led to the explosion of plantation slavery. Now, as white American politicians argued over this institution that had so shaped the nineteenth century, they knew that, once again, western expansion would require contending with Indian nations.[79] Native land served as the literal foundation of negotiations over slavery and states' rights, making the Civil War an important marker in the expansion of settler colonialism and the transformation of the process that would become Black Reconstruction.

The Five Tribes leaders' affinity for Black slavery and its economic benefits was known to the Confederacy. In fact, Albert Pike, who would go on to become a Confederate brigadier general, had a long-standing relationship with the Choctaws and Chickasaws, having served as their lawyer and advocate from the 1830s on. Pike's familiarity with the tribes in Indian Territory won him the position of Confederate envoy, in which he used his knowledge of the tribes' grievances with the United States to convince them to join in the southern rebellion.[80] Pike won a portion of all of the Five Tribes over to the Confederate faction, but these Indian people were really fighting for their own causes—chief among them the ability to maintain autonomy and residence on their new homelands in Indian Territory and the preservation of treaty rights and guarantees that were of the utmost importance to all of the Five Tribes.

On June 11, 1861, Cyrus Harris's address to the Chickasaw Legislature explaining his reasoning for allying with the Confederacy appeared in Tennessee's *Nashville Union and American*, a mouthpiece of the Democratic Party.[81] In his address, Harris very clearly laid out the reasons he believed the Chickasaw legislature should back his determination to ally with the Confederacy. Harris identified the "dissolution of the United States of North America" as cause to air his (and his nation's) grievances with the United States: primarily that the government was not regularly paying the Chickasaws their annuities from the sale of their southeastern homelands and that with the Civil War under way the government had withdrawn their soldiers from Indian Territory, leaving the Five Tribes relatively defenseless in the midst of western tribes and roving Confederates. Indian Territory bordered Arkansas and Texas, two staunch slave states loyal to the Confederacy, and Texans were already making plans to invade and plunder Indian Territory.[82]

Both of these items (annuity receipt and military protection) had been guaranteed by treaty and yet were not being carried out. The Union had even refused to supply the Chickasaws with guns so they could defend themselves, instead destroying those weapons the army could not carry off. This was a crucial snub, as marauding Texans and nearby western tribes had threatened the Chickasaws from the outset of their residence in Indian Territory. Now the presence of adjacent Confederate troops in the spring of 1861 added to the fears of Chickasaw citizens, particularly those living in the Leased District, which lay at the border of Indian Territory and land claimed by other Indian tribes.[83] Thus, defense of their land and the ability to maintain safe residence on their land was a chief concern for the Chickasaws and for all of the Five Tribes, and this shaped their reactions to the Civil War.

In his address, Harris, a staunch slaveholder, used the language of the southern Confederacy, calling the Union alternately "the Lincoln Government" and "the present Government at Washington." With this language, Harris rebuked the legitimacy of the Union government, as did the Confederacy, but he did so in service of tribal sovereignty, arguing that this so-called governmental "dissolution . . . leaves the Chickasaw Nation *independent*."[84] This independence, in Harris's mind, allowed the Chickasaws the freedom to ignore American treaty stipulations (just as the U.S. government was doing) and also to make an alliance with the Confederacy if they wished. The Confederacy, through their envoy, Albert Pike, offered to rectify all of Harris's grievances if the Chickasaws supported their bid to subdue the Union.[85]

While Chickasaw tribal leadership thought the best route to protecting their land was to ally with the Confederacy, Cherokee Chief John Ross thought the opposite—that his nation must show its loyalty to "the people of all the states" by staying neutral during the war. In exchange, Ross hoped the United States would stay true to its treaty promises, including a Removal treaty clause that would allow for a Cherokee "delegate in the House of Representatives of the United States"—a provision that has yet to be realized.[86] Yet Ross felt that in order for the Cherokees to "maintain their own rights unimpaired, and to have their own soil and firesides spared from the hateful effects of devastating war," his nation must observe "non-interference with the people of the States."[87] This view was unpopular, and when Ross left the nation to go to Washington, DC to plead his case to the federal government (or to fearfully abandon the Cherokees, depending on who you ask), members of his nation chose sides, the Confederacy or the Union—doing what *they* thought was best to protect their land and sovereign nation.[88] The *Evening Star*, a paper with a Unionist slant, published Ross's letter to his fellow Cherokees. Clearly, Americans on both sides of the war were interested in, and affected by, the alliances chosen by Indian nations.

Some members of the Five Tribes, like Ross, went to great lengths to choose no alliance at all. They were so intent on not being involved in the conflict, either for ideological reasons or for fear of wartime violence, that they fled their nations. The 1863 Census of the Southern Refugee Indians in Kansas and the Cherokee Nation shows that 225 Chickasaws, 2,070 Cherokees, 3,078 Creeks, 728 Seminoles, and 370 Yuchis, among other Indians, took refuge in either the Cherokee Nation or the state of Kansas in an effort to flee from the war.[89] These refugees, especially those in Kansas, were "without shelter, without adequate clothing, and almost destitute of food."[90] While parts of the Cherokee Nation and Kansas served as spaces of asylum for some Indians, the Chickasaw Nation served as a protector of Indians sympathetic to the Confederacy and to slavery. Mary Grayson, a former slave of Creek Indian Mose Perryman, recalled her owner moving into the Chickasaw Nation during the war. After all his male slaves ran off to fight for the Union or to join the pro-Union Upper Creeks, Perryman told his remaining slaves that he was moving them to "a place where there won't no more of you run away."[91] Several other Creek families accompanied Perryman to the Chickasaw Nation. Once there, Grayson observed that, in her opinion, the Chickasaws "didn't treat their slaves like the Creeks did. They was more strict, like the people in Texas and other places."[92] Perryman's journey into the Chickasaw Nation indicates that slaveholders felt safe within Chickasaw country in this divisive period.[93]

Feeding on the distrust, speculation, and fear of the Five Tribes, the Confederacy offered them all of the conditions they craved: protection, annuities, representation, and a guarantee that they would never be forced to become citizens of the Confederacy nor move from Indian Territory—instead they would be able to maintain their independent governments and stay in their new homelands indefinitely.[94] These were the magic words for the Five Tribes: reassurance about their land claims and political autonomy with a voice on a transnational level. This was crucial because even shortly after forcing Indian nations to move to Indian Territory, white Americans' hungry eyes never strayed far from western lands. The United States had sprung up from its eastern beginnings enthusiastic to widen its grasp on

North American geography. The annexation of Texas, followed by the Mex-
ican-American War, were its first forays into expansion over the borders
of a non-Native nation. But that did not mean Americans were done with
Indian land in their quest to fulfill Manifest Destiny. In the first few years of
the 1830s, white Arkansans had begun preparations to seize the land Choctaws had only just taken possession of in Indian Territory. An October 8,
1835, issue of the *Arkansas Gazette* advertised the future sale of lots in the
town of Van Buren, Crawford County, an area bordering the Choctaw Nation's new boundaries in Indian Territory.[95] And an advertisement claiming
that extensive territory would be for sale "subject to the extinguishment of
Indian title" ran once a week for three weeks in the *Nashville Republican,
Louisville Public Advertiser, Cincinnati Whig,* and *New Orleans Bulletin.*[96]

This information makes the Five Tribes' decision to ally with the Confederacy considerably more comprehensible: the possibility of being made
to vacate their new homes was real, and white Americans (or Unionists,
anyway) had shown themselves willing to disregard treaty promises. From
the Five Tribes' standpoint, the Confederacy's rational and legally guaranteed overtures were far more favorable than the very real threat of being
overrun by Texans, rogue Confederates, or other Indian nations in the fog
of war. The Five Tribes had fought hard—physically and rhetorically—to
claim Indian Territory as their own, and they weren't about to let it go.
While the Five Tribes' new allies were some of the same southerners who
had pushed them off their original southeastern homelands, these new allies had at least not yet defaulted on their new promises as the U.S. government had. The Union was now threatening two foundations of the Five
Tribes' societies and cultures: land and slavery. Prior to 1861, most white
slaveholders would have happily displaced the Five Tribes from any land
they set their eyes on. But with the common causes of maintaining slavery
and averting federal oversight, the Five Tribes and southern Confederates
overcame their fraught histories to fight together.

During the war, Indian men put their bodies on the line to fight for
their land and tribal elites' right to continue their practice of Black enslavement, and, as in the United States, members of all tribes served on

both sides of the war. The Chickasaws had the lowest number of men in Union service.[97] Unlike Indian units raised for the Union, Indian Confederate units served only in Indian Territory, as was negotiated by the Five Tribes. Indian Union regiments served mainly in Indian Territory as well, but also took part in several battles in Missouri and Arkansas, most recognizably in the December 1862 Battle of Prairie Grove.[98] Fourteen battles were fought in and around Indian Territory. The Choctaw and Cherokee Nations were hit the hardest, as three battles took place in the Choctaw Nation (Park Hill, Boggy Depot, and Fort Gibson) and eight battles in the Cherokee Nation (Round Mountain, Chustenahlah, Caving Banks, Locust Grove, Cowskin Prairie, Fort Wayne, Park Hill, and Honey Springs). The largest battle fought in Indian Territory was at Honey Springs, and the Confederate loss there was a turning point in the war. Honey Springs was a unique battle in that white troops were a minority of the fighting force, with African Americans and Native Americans composing the bulk of the Confederate and Union armies.[99] Black men enslaved in the Five Tribes, like African Americans in the United States, were involved in the Civil War both through their owners' involvement with the Confederacy and by their own desire to fight for the Union. William Blue and fifty-six-year-old Solomon Abram, both slaves of Chickasaw Indians, ran away to serve in the Union Army, whereas Henry Shannon and Frank Poleon were hired out by their owner, a captain of a Chickasaw Confederate company, to haul forage for Confederate soldiers.[100]

As American politicians contended with the war, the Five Tribes' fears of displacement and governmental deception were legitimated, and 1862 was a landmark year for the beginning of the federal government's plans for encroachment. Only a year after the start of the Civil War, American legislators began scheming to take western Indian land under the guise of punishing Indian disloyalty. After the defection of the Five Tribes, Senator James H. Lane of Kansas proposed a Senate inquiry into "the propriety and expediency of extending the southern boundary of Kansas to the northern boundary of Texas, so as to include within the boundaries of Kansas the territory known as the Indian Territory."[101] The year 1862 also marked the start of a project approved by the federal government to survey Indian land. For surveyor Thomas Spence, it was the Chickasaws who had "the most lovely and picturesque portion of the Indian Territory," which, according to him, was "destined to develop great mineral riches; vast coal fields underlie the sandstone strata . . . and in many places are large and extensive beds of iron ore." He also specifically mentioned salt, tar, water, and oil springs.[102] Thinking of possible exploitation not just by corporations but also by individual settlers, Spence observed, "near Fort Washita and Fort Arbuckle are most eligible and beautiful tracts of country adapted to rain-growing, stock-raising, and herding on the grandest scale." Whereas Indian Territory was previously meant to function as a repository for as many Native people as possible, to separate them from the white population and force them to reside on largely undesirable land, Indian Territory was increasingly viewed as an alluring beacon to white Americans, particularly for its natural resources.

In his report for the year 1862, the secretary of the interior described sympathy for the Five Tribes' situation during the war, writing, "In no part of the country have the sufferings and privations endured and the sacrifices made by loyal citizens on account of their fidelity to their country, exceeded those of the loyal Indians of this [southern] superintendency."[103] But in the same year, the secretary's own superintendent of Indian Affairs wrote that because the Five Tribes had made treaties with the Confederacy and had "braves or warriors in arms against the United States government," the U.S. government was absolved from "its obligations under treaty stipulations."[104] He then remarked that "the making of new treaties with all those tribes at an early day will be indispensable."[105]

The unwillingness of white Americans to agree en masse that the Five Tribes' land—and, indeed, all Indian land—was off limits after they had created treaties that made this very promise demonstrated that the Five Tribes were right to fear for their landownership. When the Confederacy lost the war, the Five Tribes lost guarantees of slavery, land claims, and political representation. Soon they would find they had lost even more. Most Native peoples in the far West had little recourse against removal and white settlement, save for war.[106] But the Five Tribes had lobbyists, tribal members with law degrees and higher education, and access to governmental channels that these other Indian nations did not have. Their capital and position as "civilized" nations allowed them a degree of influence on policy, and in a time of peace, reformers and friendly politicians may have questioned attempts to disregard treaty promises to land in Indian Territory.[107] But after the war, the U.S. government withheld from the Five Tribes certain items—namely annuities from the sale of their homelands—and made other demands in surrender negotiations, the most extreme of these being land cessions and the emancipation and enfranchisement of their slaves. As with the Mexican–American War, during the Civil War the process of armed conflict served as a way to bring manpower and resources into a space in which Americans had no legitimate sovereignty. Once in place, these new frameworks of American sovereignty and settler colonialism became entrenched in their new environments.

The American government's treatment of the Five Tribes was far worse than that of white former Confederates. Though many southerners expressed anger and a sense of victimization at the federal occupation that characterized the Reconstruction period, soldiers and supporters of the Confederate government actually experienced very few repercussions from their coup.[108] During negotiations at Appomattox, the Union guaranteed Confederate officers and soldiers immunity from prosecution for treason and allowed cavalry and artillery men to keep their horses.[109] President Andrew Johnson offered general amnesty to southerners except for a group of prominent Confederates, whom he required to submit individual petitions for amnesty. In addition, Johnson required rebellious southerners to pledge oaths to "support, protect, and defend the Constitution of the United States, and . . . pledge to support all laws and proclamations concerning the emancipation of slaves." Presidents Lincoln and Johnson were eager to forgive Confederates and begin the reconciliation of the North and South. While the Confederacy had lost, its former citizens were now, once again, Americans. This meant that it was the responsibility of the federal government to join the two halves of the country into a unified nation. Southerners thus held a trump card in their negotiations over possible sanctions—their appeasement was necessary to move forward.

On the other hand, the U.S. government was not afraid to anger Indians, who were neither voters nor citizens.[110] The U.S. government could afford to consider Indian nations "conquered peoples" because their support was not necessary for the restoration of the Union. The neutralization of Native Americans and tribal sovereignty in Indian Territory and the far West that had begun with various removals of Indian nations would continue with the Treaties of 1866, the surrender and peace treaties between the United States and the Five Tribes. The difference in the United States' treatment of the Five Tribes and of former Confederates is important because it speaks to the way western Indian land figured into American reconciliation. Almost as a peace offering, the United States could offer the possibility of settling on western land to white southerners. American politicians' treatment of Native peoples with regard to land cessions and reservation policy told white Americans that, even without slavery, the United States would expand fruitfully. This promise of self-sustenance was particularly enticing for poor, rural southerners who had never been able to own slaves, but who had nevertheless fought and died for a slaveowners' rebellion.[111] After the war, the U.S. government would use its peace treaties with the Five Tribes to continue its expansionist mission, forcing land cessions, ending slavery in Indian Territory, and distributing land parcels to Indian freedpeople, forevermore uniting these themes of Black slavery and freedom and Indian land.

In September 1865, delegates from all of the Five Tribes met at Fort Smith, Arkansas, with a delegation from Washington, DC, that included Dennis N. Cooley, the commissioner of Indian affairs.[112] After this preliminary meeting where potential treaty terms were laid out, delegates met again, this time in Washington, DC, from November 1865 to April 1866, for the final treaty negotiations. All of the Five Tribes acknowledged in writing that, because of the agreements they had made with the Confederate States during the Civil War, previous treaties made with the United States would no longer be upheld, thus prompting the need for a new treaty and an opportunity for the United States to fulfill its goal of wrenching more land from Native Americans' grasp.[113]

Under the guise of punishment for the Five Tribes' disloyalty, the United States' main demands were: (1) the land cession of the leased district (a portion of land formerly set aside on the Five Tribes' land holdings for the use of southern Plains tribes); (2) the allowance of railroads to pass through their nations; (3) the allowance of any intermarried white to be deemed "a member of said nation"; (4) the survey and allotment of all of their tribal held land; and (5) the emancipation of their Black slaves and the extension of citizenship and land.[114] The Five Tribes did have the ability to negotiate some of these terms and were able to slightly decrease

FIGURE 1. Holmes Colbert in 1866. Holmes was a member of the wealthy and influential Choctaw Colbert family who owned Eli Roberts and other members of my family. He played an important role in the Treaty of 1866 negotiations. Salley Carr Collection. Courtesy of the Oklahoma Historical Society.

the amount of their land cessions, as well as completely eradicate some of the United States' stipulations. For instance, the Chickasaws and Choctaws negotiated a treaty without a clause accepting their guilt, allowing them to declare that they had been forced into a Confederate alliance by American desertion.[115] All of these items would irrevocably change life in Indian Territory. The cession of the leased district would further destabilize the lives of the non–Five Tribes Indian nations who lived in Indian Territory. Railroads would bring more white settlers and white businesses, driving out many Indian businesses and bringing more land speculators. The enfranchisement of intermarried whites would yield more marriages of opportunity and white influence in tribal affairs.

~

Through their use of the settler colonial process and the use of enslaved labor to build social, economic, and political capital, the Five Tribes have become so synonymous with Oklahoma that, nearly 190 years after they arrived in the region, most Americans think they are indigenous to the state. This is, of course, not the case. The Five Tribes and other Indian nations were forced by state pressure and individual white settlers—the settler colonial process working against them—to remove to Indian Territory from lands they had lived on for at least hundreds of years so that white Americans and slaveowners could profit from their mineral-rich soil. To survive and prosper, they situated themselves as settlers, like white Americans, in an only moderately successful attempt to leverage their relationship with the United States against the Indians who lived in Indian Territory before them. In attempting to use the American government as a mediator in their issues with the western tribes, the Five Tribes were not unique; since European contact Native people had used alliances with various colonial powers to wage wars against enemies or to gain protection from them. What was different in this context was the *language* used by the Five Tribes, which portrayed these other nations as uncivilized by *Euro-American* measurements that had essentially become their own—or which they, at least, were willing to use for rhetorical effect. This was an

essential part of the settler colonial process. Eventually, the Five Tribes'
attempt to distinguish themselves from other Indian tribes would come
to naught, for the majority of whites would lump them together with their
less "civilized" brethren for politically and economically expedient purposes—uncivilized Indians couldn't hold claims to land.

The Five Tribes' rise and fall as settlers accepted by the American government in Indian Territory was strongly connected to their use of enslaved labor to "tame" the land. Their adoption of the institution of slavery
allowed them to cast themselves as civilizers like whites, who had encouraged their acceptance of *this* institution. But the Five Tribes did not realize
that only white Americans could truly possess all of the rights and privileges of the settler colonial process, which includes the right to make the
rules about what constitutes civilization—first to embrace slavery, then to
eradicate it. When the Confederacy conceded, the Five Tribes, who still
held enslaved people in bondage, lost their perceived status as civilizers
of the West, and as their slaves were freed and white and Black Americans
flocked to Indian Territory, the Five Tribes would also lose a considerable
amount of their land.

CHAPTER 2

Emancipation and Intervention

N ED THOMPSON'S GRANDFATHER was born a slave in Alabama, and when his Creek owner journeyed to Indian Territory to scope out land for possible removal, Thompson's grandfather followed. He and his owner crossed the Arkansas River southwest of Fort Smith on horseback, then went southeast of Checotah, due northwest to North Fork, and then south.[1] Enslaved people of African descent were part of the initial surveyance of potential removal locations, the dangerous trek that brought the Five Tribes to Indian Territory, and the construction of new homes and new governments once their new homeland was established. As such, they experienced the same emotions Native people did—disillusionment, homesickness, and fear—in addition to the feelings that stemmed from the precarious nature of enslavement. A number of people enslaved by the Chickasaws were newly purchased, as the Chickasaws had sold their lands and improvements in the Southeast to fund goods, wagons, and other resources for the trip.[2] As movable property, the Five Tribes considered enslaved Black people an ideal way of transporting capital to the West. Thus, these Black people dealt with separation from their families and communities at the same time that they faced a long, hard trek and an introduction to an unfamiliar land. But soon many of these people of African descent would come to call the land in Indian Territory their home—and they would fight to maintain a connection to this home.

Although enslaved women and men arrived in Indian Territory at
the same time as their Native owners, they would not have their chance
to invoke their claims to this space until after emancipation. When that
occurred, the Five Tribes' former slaves, who had toiled alongside their
owners in their physical and rhetorical overhaul of Indian Territory,
used the settler colonial process to situate themselves as worthy settlers
and to encourage the intervention of the American settler state in Indian
Territory on their behalf. Like the Five Tribes, Indian freedpeople's actions were in the service of enlisting American protection and assistance
in their struggles to take possession of Indian Territory land already
claimed by others and to realize either community belonging or tribal
citizenship.

The same Treaties of 1866 that punished the Five Tribes as disloyal to
the Union and stripped their status as settlers also served to inaugurate the
second wave of settlers: Indian freedpeople. The Five Tribes' alliances with
the Confederacy during the Civil War had offered a unique opportunity:
the chance to acquire Indian land under the pretense of punishing disloyalty. The war served as the perfect storm of opportunity and justification.
After the end of the war, the politicians who steered the Reconstruction
of the United States were not only concerned with bringing together the
North and the South; having settled the issue of whether slavery would follow the expansion of the nation, for them Reconstruction also meant ac-
celerating this encroachment onto western Indian lands. Once again signaling the intermingling of slavery and settler colonialism, to Republicans
the emancipation and enfranchisement of enslaved Black people in this
part of the West was necessary, as Indian Territory must reflect the new
racial environment of the United States, which would soon be in possession of the territory. The allotment of Indian land under Reconstruction
would create independent land holdings for Native peoples, as was the
American way, but would also make room for white and Black settlement.
Indian Territory would become a proving ground for Reconstruction in
more than one way: first as a space where Republicans could provide the
equality and free land to people of African descent that was unfeasible in

the United States, and second as a demonstration of the difficulties of non-white inclusion into the American populace.

Indian Territory from the 1860s to 1907 is a rare place and moment in time in which people of African descent formerly enslaved by the Five Tribes—Indian freedpeople—were mobilized and legitimized by the U.S. government, converted into settlers precisely because this project of land settlement carried the goal of unseating Native peoples from their land and therefore from their tribal sovereignty. During this prolonged Reconstruction period, the U.S. government used the Dawes Commission, a federal bureau set up to carry out the allotment of Native American land outlined in the Treaties of 1866, to also advocate for Indian freedpeople.[3] I reconstruct this story primarily through the lens of the 1890s remembrances of Indian freedpeople as told in their testimony to the Dawes Commission, illustrating the importance of this U.S. governmental body in my recasting of the Reconstruction timeline.

~

The land allotment system that the Treaties of 1866 laid out was eventually implemented through the 1887 Dawes Act.[4] The Dawes Act was designed to break down the traditional communal landownership practices of Indian tribes throughout the United States. American legislators accomplished this by dividing formerly commonly held land into land allotments assigned to individual, nuclear families. Many white and Indian politicians and reformers believed that land allotment would positively affect Indian tribes and usher them on the road to complete assimilation by converting them, according to one historian, into "docile believers in American progress."[5] Land allotment and the focus on the nuclear family were intended to destroy tribal sovereignty, extended kinship ties, and Indigenous ideas about wealth and individualism. At the same time, land allotment made possible the maintenance of the communities that Indian freedpeople had constructed. Once lands were no longer held communally and under tribal sovereignty, they could be opened up to the more important settlers: white Americans. In this way, Indian freedpeople served as the leverage through which the American government widened its hold in Indian Territory. Granting land allotments to Indian freedpeople allowed the U.S. government to access and extract larger portions of Native land and to interfere in tribal governance on Indian freedpeople's behalf.

A council of three white men, the Dawes Commission determined who belonged on the rolls of each tribe and who therefore could or could not claim an allotment of land from the tribe's common holdings.[6] Henry L. Dawes, commission chairman and architect of the act, was a politician who served in various positions, from district attorney for the western district of Massachusetts to U.S. senator of Massachusetts. The two other original members of the committee, Archibald S. McKennon and Meredith H. Kidd, were both lawyers and former military men.[7]

Indian freedpeople used the structure of the Dawes Commission to voice and justify their connection and claim to Indian Territory land and wrote to tribal agents and the Department of the Interior, portraying themselves as more hardworking and civilized than their former owners. However, they also signaled their intentions to fight for their place in the West in a subtler way—through their movement during and after the war. By staying in or consistently returning to Indian Territory in the face of violence, unstable resource acquisition, and uncertainty about their rights, Indian freedpeople communicated that their ideas of belonging focused on inclusion in their own communities, defined by kinship and landownership. For most Indian freedpeople, the U.S. government's mediation was the only way to accomplish and maintain this.

The importance of land to African Americans in the nineteenth century has been embodied in the phrase "forty acres and a mule." While this expression is still used today to refer to the lost promises of equality and upward mobility in the Civil War and Reconstruction eras, it originated as an actual plan put forth by General William T. Sherman during the Civil War to provide land for African Americans in a specific region of the United States.[8] Legislation supporting this agenda did not come to fruition, leading to generations of sharecropping and economic deprivation. Land represented the opportunity for self-sufficiency and a place of one's own, rare concepts for newly freed people.[9] But to take the experience of Indian Territory's freedpeople seriously is to consider a post-emancipation world in which land redistribution to former slaves was not an unfulfilled promise but a reality. As the war ended and white and Black Americans agitated on the ground and looked to the federal government to take the next steps to recognize African Americans as equal citizens under the law through legal and political reform, people of African descent within Indian Territory looked to another aspect of their lives for fulfillment of the promises of freedom: land and community.[10] We generally think of the experience of African Americans after the Civil War in relation to (U.S.) citizenship and political rights, since in the absence of land redistribution these were the claims available to them.[11] But for Indian freedpeople, actions taken by the secretary of the interior, his agents, and the Dawes Commission represent the last form that Reconstruction took in the West: the federal government's intervention on behalf of Indian freedpeople, through which they obtained the greatest symbol of the era's promise: land.

In telling this story of Black Reconstruction in the West, I seek to rectify a representation of freedpeople in Indian Territory that has long skewed in favor of the larger Indian nations, particularly the Cherokees. Therefore, many of the individual stories in this chapter are from Chickasaw freedpeople, whose specific circumstances represent an extreme case of marginalization among Indian freedpeople, one which demonstrates how a subset of the African Diaspora thought about belonging and land. Foremost among the differences between Chickasaw freedpeople and other Indian freedpeople was the issue of citizenship. Emancipation was unique in the Chickasaw Nation because Chickasaw tribal leaders, unlike their counterparts in the other Five Tribes, never offered freedpeople citizenship.[12] Slaves of Chickasaw Indians were freed by their owners and immediately presented with a choice: continue to live within the boundaries of the Chickasaw Nation without the protections or privileges of citizenship or migrate into the United States.[13] At the same time, throughout this chapter, I also include glimpses of the ways in which Creek, Cherokee, and Choctaw freedpeople navigated war, freedom, and Reconstruction.[14]

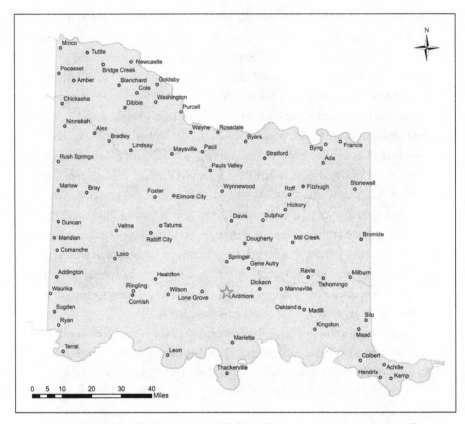

FIGURE 2. Map of the Chickasaw Nation Tribal Jurisdiction Area. 1,000,000. Generated by Boris Michev, 2020, using ArcGIS 10.7 [GIS software] (Redlands, CA: Environmental Systems Research Institute, 1992–2020) Courtesy of the University Library System, University of Pittsburgh.

As in the United States, each individual enslaved person in Indian Territory experienced emancipation differently. Some freedpeople were on their own because they had run away or their owners had gone to war, and they heard through informal information networks the news about their freedom through the Treaty of 1866.[15] Most freedpeople, however, were told by their owners. Chickasaw freedwoman Dora Willis recollected, "We were all down there with the old Boss: the old Boss sent for all the old colored people to bring the children; to bring every child in the quarters up to the boss's house. He puts a man on the gallery by the name of Dr. Warner and he reads a paper to the darkeys, and he said you are all as free as I am."[16]

Kiziah Love, another Chickasaw freedwoman, had a reaction that has long echoed in Black history. Love would later say that (because she was glad to be free) she "clapped [her] hands together, and said, 'Thank God Almighty, I's free at last!'"[17] This particular phrase persists in popular culture and African American spirituals and reminds us that though their owners were Native, not white, people of African descent in Indian Territory shared the same sentiments as their Black counterparts in the United States.

In the Cherokee, Creek, and Seminole Nations, Indian freedpeople were able to enjoy most rights available to Native tribal members soon after emancipation.[18] For example, Cherokee freedpeople could participate in local and national elections, though they were rarely elected to influential offices.[19] In the Creek and Seminole Nations, freedpeople did hold higher offices, serving as judges and members of the tribal supreme court.[20] As non–tribal members, Chickasaw freedpeople could not serve on juries or vote and were vulnerable to racial violence and poverty. In addition, the Chickasaws and Choctaws enacted legislation akin to the U.S. "Black Codes," which set certain wages for ex-slaves and attempted to force freedpeople to find employment under Indian tribal members—though my family's experience and those of many Chickasaw freedpeople demonstrate that these laws were not uniformly enforced.[21]

Because of their lack of citizenship and the anti-Black legislation present in the nation, Chickasaw freedpeople were the group most dependent on the United States to enforce the provisions of freedom, rights, and land laid out in the Treaty of 1866. Choctaw freedpeople would later be adopted as tribal citizens, but their experiences right after the Civil War were more akin to those of Chickasaw freedpeople than any of the Black members of the other Five Tribes. Chickasaw and Choctaw freedpeople solicited aid from the secretary of the interior and the U.S. government even before the creation of the Dawes Commission; the United States answered this call

because assisting these freedpeople and, indeed, all Indian freedpeople in
their pursuit of land and rights in the West furthered the American goal of
separating Native people from their land.

As slaves, African Americans were praised for their hard work, and
pseudoscientists claimed studies showed that they were biologically more
capable than whites of performing long, arduous labor.[22] But with Reconstruction, white supremacists weaponized the other half of this stereotype:
that without white owners, Black women and men would give in to their
idle natures. Even Republicans believed this racist stereotype to an extent,
enforcing policies that aimed to ensure African Americans signed labor
contracts, even if these agreements were exploitative, returning Black people to roles in which they were essentially subservient to whites.[23] The language used by Indian freedpeople was meant both to combat this thinking
about the African American work ethic and to contrast themselves with
Indians, who had long been stereotyped as lazy for not engaging in agriculture (patently false for many Native peoples) and for hunting, which
was still seen as a nonproductive, lazy pastime by whites.[24]

When Dennis N. Cooley, commissioner of Indian affairs, Colonel Ely
S. Parker, special commissioner, and Elijah Sells, superintendent of Indian affairs for the southern superintendency, insisted that land allotments
for former slaves be included in the Five Tribes' Reconstruction treaties
(the Treaties of 1866), these men created the structure that allowed Indian
freedpeople the opportunity for land ownership. This decision came from
the top of the bureau responsible for United States–Native American relations: the Department of the Interior. The secretary of the interior at the
time of the treaties was James Harlan, a former senator and an appointee
of President Lincoln. As a senator, Harlan was placed on the Senate Committee on Indian Affairs, where he advocated against policies of extermi-
nation, instead supporting "paternal kindness," in essence, a mixture of
civilizationist policies and nonviolence.[25] As a congressman, Harlan had
not joined with his fellow Republicans Thaddeus Stevens and Charles
Sumner to fight for land to be given to former enslaved people in the
United States. Unlike these two Radical Republicans, Harlan did not sup-

port Reconstruction as an "executive prerogative" for the southern states. But interestingly enough, he had no issue with forcing Reconstruction through the treaty process for the Five Tribes in Indian Territory.[26] This reflected his paternalistic views of Native Americans and also his beliefs about the rightful use of land.[27]

Harlan believed that land should be opened up to small, independent farmers, rather than to wealthy slave owners. This is why, as a senator, he had advocated for the Homestead Bill.[28] The Homestead Bill would provide free or low-cost land to any applicant willing to take up residence upon it. In 1860, Harlan had argued that the great prosperity it would bring to the West would increase "value for all the property already in the possession of the citizens [present in the West]."[29] The bill lacked the votes needed to overcome President Buchanan's veto and would not pass until two years later, with a Republican majority in both houses and Lincoln as President.[30] Harlan may have looked at the distribution of land to Indian freedpeople—certainly a group that represented the exact opposite of wealthy slave owners—as an extension of the Homestead Bill.[31] This would serve the purpose of helping the former enslaved take care of and provide for themselves instead of relying on others, a Republican maxim.

The Treaties of 1866 that Secretary Harlan championed essentially applied the principles that would be enshrined in the Thirteenth, Fourteenth, and Fifteenth Amendments to Indian Territory, before the Fourteenth and Fifteenth Amendments were passed in the United States (in 1868 and 1870, respectively).[32] Thus, Republicans' mission to enfranchise and empower African Americans in the United States encompassed people of African descent in Indian Territory. In the case of Indian Territory, without the impediments they faced in the United States—white discontent and state intervention, most notably—Republican ardor for change was not tempered by moderates of their own party or by reluctant Democrats or reluctant Indians (who had no congressional representation). They were able to dictate provisions to the Five Tribes that fulfilled Republican Reconstruction objectives for egalitarianism, such as emancipation and enfranchisement, and also to give people of African descent in Indian Territory one thing they would never receive in the United States: land. The land cessions in these treaties were a clear violation of Indigenous sovereignty.[33] And yet, this violation gave people of African descent the freedom and rights they may otherwise never have attained in the Five Tribes without U.S. intervention. This was a rare moment when settler colonialism worked in favor of Black people, as it had decades earlier for the Five Tribes when they sought to lay claim to Indian Territory after their forced removal.

For reasons unexplained in any documentation, land distribution as defined in the Treaties of 1866 varied by tribe. The Chickasaws and Choctaws were to provide former slaves 40 acres each, anywhere they chose within each nation; the Cherokees provided them 160 acres each, in the Canadian district of the nation; the Seminoles were to "permit" their former slaves to "settle" in the nation; and the Creeks would allow their former slaves "an equal interest in the soil." The United States would survey communally held land and divide it up into individual allotments.[34] Neither the documents chronicling the discussions surrounding the Treaties of 1866 nor the *Congressional Globe* indicate how discussions of providing Indian freedpeople land originated or whether these discussions occurred in tandem with discussions about former enslaved people in the United States. Surprisingly, neither Stevens nor Sumner seemed to reference these other freedpeople in their writings or their speeches to the U.S. Senate.[35] For Indian freedpeople, the path to land went from an idea in the mind of the secretary of the interior to being written into the Treaties of 1866 to being solidified and carried out in the Dawes Act. Still, American politicians were aware of the process of land distribution being formulated for and carried out in Indian Territory for Indian freedpeople.

During a February 23, 1867, Senate session discussion about using funds to pay for damages that Chickasaws loyal to the Union had suffered, Senator James Rood Doolittle of Wisconsin mentioned that the $300,000 payment for the Chickasaw and Choctaw Treaty of 1866 land cessions was to be used for the benefit of the Chickasaw and Choctaw's formerly enslaved people, who were supposed to be "adopted as citizens of the tribe, and each to take part of the lands of the tribe."[36] He then went on to say that "this reconstruction in that Indian Territory under the superintendence of Hon. Mr. Harlan, is, I think, a very good pattern of what might be done in the reconstruction of the Union."[37] Though Senator Doolittle was referencing the fact that loyal and Confederate Choctaws and Chickasaws now (supposedly) lived "side by side together" postwar as an example to follow, he was also lauding the provisions made for Indian freedpeople, as he had long campaigned for homesteads for African Americans.[38]

After the secretary of the interior had made the decision to include land allowances for freedpeople in the Treaties of 1866, various tribal agents and American politicians made comments about the way they thought land allotment should be executed. Tribal agents such as John Sanborn proposed that Choctaw and Chickasaw freedpeople be placed on land tracts that were "the most fertile in the Territory, as the Freedmen are the principal producers."[39] Sanborn also urged the Choctaws and Chickasaws to provide their former slaves with their own land tracts, which he felt "would result in the rapid development of the country, the civilization of the Indian tribes, and induce peace and good feeling on the part of all."[40] In 1873, Agent Albert Parsons reported that "many of the freedmen have doubtless made improvements on the lands which they and their fathers occupied but not possessed." In 1874, Commissioner Edward P. Smith wrote that the freedmen were "orderly, industrious, and eager for the education of their children, and yet are obliged to expend their labor upon farms to which they have no title, and which once well improved are not infrequently taken from them."[41]

This thinking, that Indian freedpeople were harder workers than Native Americans and that giving Indian freedpeople land would improve conditions for everyone in Indian Territory, was common among Indian agents. At times, Indian agents even made statements it is almost impossible to imagine their counterparts in the Freedmen's Bureau making. During postwar negotiations with the Five Tribes, John Sanborn conveyed to Secretary Harlan his opinion that "the Freedmen are the most industrious, economical, and in many respects, the more intelligent portion of the pop-

ulation of the Indian Territory."⁴² Although it was acceptable to favorably
compare people of African descent to Native people, who were viewed as
inferior to whites and in possession of valuable land Americans wanted, it
would have been inconceivable for Sanborn to make the same comparison
between African Americans and whites, for this would endanger the status of his own country and the racial disparity in landownership. This was
the way the settler state functioned: it used nonwhite people against each
other to craft arguments that would benefit itself; if Indians were lazy, it
made sense for Indian freedpeople to have some of their land, which they
would make better use of.⁴³

   In comparison to Indian freedpeople's industriousness, U.S. Indian
agents frequently alluded to or blatantly labeled Native Americans as lazy.
The language used by John H. Eaton, the superintendent of Indian affairs,
in an 1830 report was typical. Eaton remarked that the U.S. government's
priority should be to "turn [Indians] to industry," for "labor is never an acceptable pursuit to [them]."

   Instead, he felt they were only interested in "war and the chase [hunt-
ing]." He went on to say, "Their indisposition to manual labor, so peculiarly the characteristic of an Indian, causes [them] to select the poorest
grounds, because of the ease with which the timber is felled and cleared
away. The exceptions which exist to this are principally amongst those of
mixed Indian blood, whose habits have been improved, and whose minds
have been cultivated."⁴⁴

   Eaton's sentiments conveyed the belief that Native Americans were in-
herently apathetic and that only European ancestry was the reason behind
some Indians' diligence. These beliefs were shared by most Indian agents
and by many Americans. Though these sentiments were expressed in letters and reports written to other whites, no doubt these Indian agents also
expressed them to and around Indian freedpeople, thus inadvertently giving them a template to use when they wanted something from the United
States. When remembering the labor of his family after the war, Blain Holman, a Chickasaw freedman who had long lived in the Choctaw Nation,
linked his family's industriousness or, rather, lack thereof to their ties to

Native peoples. Holman recalled that his family had amassed only a "small farm of about five acres, [because] at that time the Indians did not have anything but small farms, and of course the freedmen were reared among them, so they didn't work like they should but just raised enough corn to make their bread."[45] Intimating that Native Americans did not work in an enterprising American way to create wealth, instead only looking to survive, Holman suggested that Indian freedpeople were capable of working harder, "the way they should," if they were only given the right model and opportunity. From Holman's perspective, then, land allotment to Indian freedpeople was not a benevolent gesture by the U.S. government but rather a way to put Indian land into the hands of people who were more like the ideal American frontier settlers—productive and diligent—and who would competently help develop these lands.

Indian freedpeople's entrance into the settler colonial process saw white politicians legitimately expressing a desire to help them. A number of Dawes commissioners recognized the exploitative sharecropping occurring in the Chickasaw Nation and urged the Department of the Interior and the Chickasaw government to recognize the necessity of including freedpeople in the land allotment process. These commissioners voiced their thought that the Dawes Act could serve as a way to help the freedpeople of the Five Tribes. Reflecting a sympathetic view of Chickasaw freedpeople's situation, the 1894 Dawes Commission annual report argued:

> They [the Chickasaws] now treat the whole class [Chickasaw freedpeople] as aliens without any legal right to abide among them, or to claim any protection under their laws. They are shut out of the schools of the tribe, and from their courts, and are granted no privileges of occupancy of any part of the land for a home, and are helplessly exposed to the hostilities of the citizen Indians and the personal animosity of the former master. Peaceable, law-abiding, and hardworking, they have sought in vain to be regarded as a part of the people to whose wealth their industry is daily contributing to a very essential portion.[46]

By providing Chickasaw freedpeople and, indeed, all Indian freedpeople with land, the Dawes Act would fix these issues of exploitation and exclusion—or so the commissioners thought.

Even American newspapers claimed to empathize with Indian freedpeople. In 1870 the *New York Times* reported that in Indian Territory, "The reality of bondage remained. Their former masters became their enemies. There was no longer the motive to tend them as useful animals. Equality created hatred, born of jealousy." Focusing on the plight of Chickasaw and Choctaw freedpeople, whom he considered the most legally and politically "disabled," a *Times* reporter advocated for American intervention because, though they "considered themselves full citizens of the nations with whom their lives have been passed, and, [regarded] the Territory as their proper home," when Chickasaw and Choctaw freedpeople gathered in attempts to seek political and social rights from their respective nations, the Indians "tore down the printed [meeting] notices, and threatened the lives of any who should venture to attend; and they actually did arrest one colored man."[47] This reporter could likely recognize prejudice and inequality in Indian Territory because former slave owners were Indians, rather than whites, and this criticism of Indians contributed to the stereotype that they were uncivilized and savage. Would he have written the same piece about whites' treatment of African Americans in the United States? It seems unlikely.

It is perhaps no wonder, then, that Indian freedpeople actively engaged in the settler colonial process by frequently writing to the Dawes Commission and to the respective Indian agents for their nations with the assertion that they were ready and willing to help them take possession of land they were owed and would work judiciously.[48] At times, Indian freedpeople even directly addressed the U.S. Congress in a bid to stress their dire circumstances and prompt American intervention in Indian affairs. In a March 1870 memorial, a written request presented in person asking that Congress take some specific action (or refrain from taking some specific action), James Ladd, Richard Brashears, and N. C. Coleman, representatives of a large group of Cherokee, Chickasaw, and Choctaw freedpeople, beseeched Congress to aid them in their quest to live peacefully and equitably within the Indian nations they called home. Acknowledging that during and shortly after the war some of them had sought to leave these nations, they emphasized that by this point in time they were "less than ever inclined to leave our native country, and more than ever claim protection from the government, equal rights with the Indians, and a speedy throwing open of the Territory to white settlement." Why were these freedpeople turning to the U.S. government for help in this regard? They claimed that the United States "[has] the power and the will to redress our grievances as well as the *right*, notwithstanding all 'treaties,' so called, of which so much only is kept by our late masters as suits their convenience, we trustfully turn to you to afford us the destined relief, and to secure to us those rights to which we claim to be entitled as men, as citizens of the United States, and natives of the Indian Territory."[49]

There is much to unpack here. Indian freedpeople wanted protection from the violence perpetrated against them by Native people, and they wanted access to the rights equal to tribal citizens granted to them by the Treaties of 1866. Yet, in order to obtain these goals, they referred to themselves as American citizens—likely seeing this as a way to prompt government action. These women and men were not naïve; as many had been owned by whites before belonging to Native owners, they knew white Americans were not saints. In their quest to live on the land that had become so important to them, to which they considered themselves "native," they touted American intervention as the country's moral and legal right. By putting their faith in the settler colonial process to change their status and improve their circumstances, these Indian freedpeople demonstrated their dissatisfaction with tribal governance and their willingness to renounce tribal sovereignty and Native claim to land if it made possible their *own* claims to land and rights.

Just as in the United States, many Indian freedpeople fought for recognition of their changed status from their former enslavers. But these freedpeople were not representative of *all* Indian freedpeople, as there were others who were content to live without agitating for rights and who rejected the arrival of white settlers and the eventual transition from In-

dian Territory to the United States. Creek and Seminole freedpeople especially seem to have been relatively content with their experiences in the
nation after the war. When discussing the plight of the freedpeople within
other nations, John Sanborn wrote that "the Freedmen of the Seminole
and Creek tribes believe that the National laws and customs of their tribes
are sufficient for their protection," and this seems to have continued to
be the case through the remainder of the nineteenth century.[50] These Indian freedpeople would experience an extended period of reconstruction,
where they were able to enjoy rights and peaceful landownership equal to
those of Seminole and Creek Indians until Oklahoma statehood in 1907.

   But for those not in the Creek and Seminole Nations, letter writing
was another way Indian freedpeople used the settler colonial process to
signal their approval of U.S. intervention in tribal matters. In 1899, Indian
freedman R. H. McDuffie wrote that he was in possession of a section of
land that he wanted for his Dawes allotment, but an Indian had moved
onto it and claimed ownership. The Indian man then gave a white settler
permission to live on the land rent-free for five years, and this man subsequently told McDuffie to move.[51] William Love faced a similar issue. Love
had lived on a piece of land for 26 years, improving upon it and preserving
it for his eventual allotment selection. During this period, he had leased
a portion of this land to a Black family from Texas. However, when their
lease was up, they refused to leave the land and were no longer paying rent.
Love asked that the commission "please take notice to this matter at once,"
and signed his letter, "your honorable servant."[52] Freedpeople even wrote
to the Dawes Commission to resolve disputes among *themselves*. Frances
Grayson asked the commission to recognize her allegation that since 1870
the land she had lived on and improved in the Chickasaw Nation "[had]
always [been] known by everybody as [her] place." She sought assistance
in her disagreement with her brother-in-law, who was trying to "deprive
[her and her husband] of the place."[53] In writing to the Dawes Commission
about their problems, Grayson, McDuffie and Love claimed the land they
lived on as their own. They recognized that the Chickasaw Nation would
do nothing to enforce their claims and thus turned to the entity willing to

do so: the U.S. government. As Cherokee freedwoman Eliza Whitmore later recalled, "The slaves who belonged to the Cherokees fared much better than the slaves who belonged to the white race, for the reason that the Indian slaves . . . could settle on Indian land, and . . . they gave us an equal right with them in land drawings. The United States government forced them to do this, I have been told."[54]

Whitmore, like most Indian freedpeople, recognized that her chance to acquire an allotment in Indian Territory had come from the United States, not the Cherokee Nation or any of the other Five Tribes. Though their connection was to Indian land, Indian freedpeople maintained a connection to American institutions, such as the Dawes Commission, because they saw them as the benefactors of this land and themselves as beneficiaries of the settler colonialist goals that had motivated the United States' actions. Freedpeople showed their commitment to settling in Indian Territory by maintaining their residence there, despite difficulties in finding food, jobs, and other resources, and by creating communities that provided them with material goods, educational opportunities, and places of worship—all of which contributed to their sense of belonging within the space of Indian Territory. The Dawes Act, a product of American intervention into tribal societies, both helped and hindered these communities.

After their emancipation, my family lived in the eponymous Robertsville. Robertsville's origins reveal the relationships sustained between Native Americans and their former slaves. As my second cousin and family historian Travis D. Roberts remembered being told by one of his uncles as a young child:

The Indians made an agreement with Grandpa Jack that from
some place he could get on his horse, and ride in any direction
in a day—North, South, East, West. And that was his land. And
Grandpa Jack [ended up having] a lot of land. His land went
all the way to the Red River and it went all the way across the
mountains, to Davis. Now, that wasn't in no writing or anything.

That's just what the Indians gave to him. . . . And of course he had
that for a long time. And then the Dawes Commission came . . .
and when they did that, they took all the land that Grandpa
Jack had, and he could only have about forty acres of what he
had previously had. So that's how he ended up with the farm [in
Robertsville].[55]

On this piece of land, my family developed and nurtured a connection
to a space within the Chickasaw Nation, sanctioned through an informal
agreement. Other freedpeople related that they, too, were told by Indians
within their tribe that they could settle informally. Charley Moore Brown,
a Choctaw freedman, said that his "father and mother just picked out a
place in this Choctaw Nation that was suitable to do some farming on,
and were permitted to settle on this land." His family raised various crops,
with corn forming their main form of subsistence, which they used to
make bread and other foods. Brown remembered that "there were hardly
any white people in the Choctaw Nation when I was growing up."[56] Nellie Johnson's Creek owner combined news of emancipation with an offer
for his former slaves to "take up some land for our own selves, or just stay
where we is, if we want to."[57]

It makes sense that the Five Tribes might try to "kill two birds with one
stone": By allowing some Indian freedpeople to settle on certain remote
western lands, they distanced themselves from people of African descent
and implemented a buffer between themselves and the "wild Indians" they
so feared. Travis's story also reveals that American interference did not
always solve Indian freedpeople's issues; some Indian freedpeople, who
had informal land agreements, actually *lost* land with the bureaucratiza-
tion of land settlement implemented through the Dawes Act. For most
Indian freedpeople, federal bureaucracy was the only thing standing between them and landless poverty, but for my family it was the opposite.
Case in point: Jack Roberts's chosen home once encompassed much of the
land upon which Ardmore, Oklahoma, one of the most oil-rich regions in
the United States, now sits.

Jack Roberts's *new* farm, on land allotted by the Dawes Commission, formed the backbone of the Robertsville township. Located about 3 miles east of Springer, Oklahoma, Robertsville was populated by the Roberts family and their spouses and friends, many of whom were mixed-race former slaves of some of the largest Chickasaw and Choctaw families, including the Loves, Stephensons, and Colberts.[58] About fifteen to twenty families lived and farmed together, raising cows and chickens and operating a general store.[59] Neighbors would buy items on credit and pay for them when the crop came in.[60] The general store also functioned as a communal gathering place, and the store ledger contained not only the accounts of customers but information about land allotment policy and monies gathered to send representatives of the Chickasaw freedpeople community to Washington, DC, to discuss their plight with Congress.[61] Though the community was not well-off, its members were able to provide some accoutrements of a lower-middle-class upbringing. For instance, in 1919, Jack Roberts purchased from the Wisconsin J. I. Case Company a case threshing machine, which helped with the family's agricultural undertakings.[62]

The community raised money for institutions that helped strengthen its identity and sense of belonging. The freedpeople within Robertsville constructed the Calvary Baptist Church with their own resources around the turn of the century. Ned Roberts served as its first pastor.[63] Indian freedpeople's religious beliefs had originated most often from their time spent as enslaved people of whites before coming into Indian nations or as interpreters for their Indian owners.[64] Many African Americans made Christianity their own, and it became an important facet of their lives, serving as both a sanctuary from hardship and a communal activity.[65]

A school was the second important institution the community came together to build and fund. The Chickasaws did not provide any financing for the education of their freedpeople, but this was not for lack of desire on the part of Chickasaw freedpeople.[66] In 1873 the U.S. agent to the Choctaws and Chickasaws wrote that the freedpeople were well satisfied in "improving farms and accumulating property" but not in "the want of any educational opportunities for them."[67] In September 1887 when a group of Chickasaw freedmen, including Dick Roberts, Mack Stephenson, and others from Robertsville and surrounding freedpeople communities, traveled to Washington, DC, to proclaim their desire to live in the Chickasaw Nation, they also voiced their desire for "school privileges."[68] Through community commitment, Robertsville residents succeeded around 1890 in constructing what *Oklahoma's Orbit* writer Marie Garland described as "the first Negro school in the Chickasaw Nation."[69]

In a 1971 profile of the school, Dawes Academy, Garland characterized it as being "closely interwoven" with the history of the Calvary Baptist Church. Soon after its founding, Dawes Academy had two stories with classrooms, a dining room, a kitchen, and a teachers' and girls' dormitory (a boys' dormitory was located in an adjacent building).[70] The oldest living student at the time of Garland's article, George Roberts, recalled his father, Jack Roberts, paying one dollar per month for his tuition, approximately 27 dollars per month today.[71] This price would have been a feasible, but not insignificant, amount for Jack, demonstrating the importance he placed on education for his son. Although Dawes Academy has gone down in history as a "negro school," its student body was more diverse than this categorization suggests. There is no existing roster, but one student mentioned in Garland's article was Tom-Pee-Saw, a man part Cherokee and part Choctaw.[72] Another former student was B. C. Franklin, the father of noted African American historian John Hope Franklin and an esteemed lawyer in his own right.[73] In a discussion of the school in his autobiography, B. C. recalled learning Latin and algebra.[74] Though Chickasaw freedpeople bore the brunt of the financial burden of providing for the school, the U.S. government did pay the salaries of at least one of the Dawes Academy teachers, as demonstrated by the quarterly mandatory reports the Dawes Academy administration sent to the superintendent of schools in Indian Territory in Muskogee, Indian Territory.[75] The United States intervened to help in the education of Indian freedpeople because education was one component of establishing settlement and civilization.

The Choctaw Nation established and funded thirty-four schools for their freedpeople, but the disparities between their schools and those for Choctaw children were substantial.[76] Religious orders played a large part in the creation of education facilities for Indian freedpeople. In 1886 the Presbyterian Board of Missions for Freedmen established a boarding school to train Choctaw freedpeople to be teachers.[77] The American Baptist Home Mission Society provided funds to both the Choctaw and Chickasaw freedpeople to build and run schools.[78] The Cherokee Nation devoted three of its fifty-nine schools to the children of Cherokee freedpeople, and the disparity in number of schools continued throughout the nineteenth and early twentieth century, into statehood.[79] The Creek and Seminole tribes provided for the education of their former enslaved people in a manner commensurate with that of Creek and Seminole children, with the Creek Nation funding eight neighborhood schools for Creek freedpeople.[80]

It must be reiterated, though, that whenever possible, freedpeople built, funded, and ran their own schools. Education was one of their dearest goals for their children, and they recognized its potential to lift up people of African descent in this new world free from enslavement. It was this potential that scared racist Indians, just as it did racist whites. A missionary doctor arriving in the Chickasaw Nation at a school for freedpeople reported that he had been warned, "If anybody went to teach those [n-g-rs] at Fort Arbuckle, they would kill him."[81] In addition, the Five Tribes worried that freedpeople were receiving more attention and resources than they were. Some Creeks complained that the Creek Agency was located in an area surrounded by freedpeople, and that it should instead be located in an area where Creek women and men lived. Their request for the agency's move was denied.[82] Like many former Confederates, the Chickasaw and Choctaw leadership saw the federal government as an entity that was now run by whites unfairly sympathetic to the needs of Black people, and they were not the only Indians who felt this way. In an 1874 article, the *Cherokee Advocate* disagreed with the secretary of the interior that Indian freedpeople were "the most industrious and useful portion of each nation, and are without the rights, privileges and immunities of citizens, and in securing the wealth possessed by said nations they have done as much as the average Choctaw or Chickasaw." Instead, the *Advocate* argued, "the whole effort is an attempt of sympathy, excited by an exaggerated representation of the condition of the freedmen in those nations to establish a community of property in the public moneys and domain of those Indians."[83] The tide had turned: no longer did the Five Tribes merit help and attention; rather, it was their former slaves who had become the vanguard of the American settler state.[84]

The establishment of churches and schools symbolized the determination of Indian freedpeople to create their own communities in the face of threats and violence during this liminal period in which they waited to be adopted as citizens of Indian nations and find out whether they would receive land they had applied for. Both their land and their citizenship depended on the Five Tribes and the United States upholding their treaty promises to them. These schools and churches formed the crux of communities that emphasized Black autonomy, allowing Indian freedpeople to create Black spaces within Indian nations. Aside from Robertsville, Chickasaw and Choctaw freedpeople coalesced in Bailey and Tatums. Bailey had a post office from 1892 to 1932, and Tatum, within the same county as Robertsville, was incorporated in 1896.[85] Most of the inhabitants of Fort Coffee, a town north of the first Choctaw Nation capital, Scullyville, were Choctaw freedpeople.[86] Residents grew their own produce, hunted small game, processed sorghum into molasses at various mills, and either sharecropped or worked for white or Black large-scale farmers. Women in the community served as midwives and used plants and herbs for medicinal purposes.[87]

In the Cherokee Nation, many freedpeople formed communities in the Illinois and Cooweescoowee districts, whereas others formed communities and townships along the Neosho River in Kansas.[88] The town of Foreman was founded by Cherokee freedman Zack Foreman, who served in the Union army during the war. Foreman would go on to become a successful businessman and one of the wealthiest members of the Cherokee Nation. Many of the residents of Foreman had, like Zack, been owned by members of the Gunter family. By the 1890s, Foreman had an African Methodist Episcopal Church, a Masonic Lodge, a post office, a general store, and a cotton gin.[89] In the Creek and Seminole Nations, freedpeople were subject to the same allowances as Creek Indians: they could settle in any part of the nation not already occupied, and if they could cultivate the land, it would remain under their individual control."[90] In the other tribes, this arrangement was primarily an option only for Indians, not freedpeople. Although Creek freedpeople formed several towns, chief among them North Fork Colored, Canadian Colored, and Marshalltown, there was little strict segregation in the nation, so Black and Native peoples often attended the same churches and purchased items from the same general stores.[91] The Creek Nation would also house a number of the famed all-Black towns founded by African Americans from the United States upon land allotments owned by Creek freedpeople.

My great-great-grandmother Josie Jackson's story demonstrates just how important these towns were as spaces of community, both before and after the Dawes Commission process legitimated Indian freedpeople's land holdings. Josie spent the majority of her time from the 1880s to 1890s on the move. She would later tell the Dawes Commission that she had been in Indian Territory just as often as she had been in Texas during this period. She completed this constant circular migration so that she could work in Texas for a white family, bring her wages back for her daughter, and see her family and community.[92] Josie was one of thousands of Indian freedpeople who spoke to the Dawes Commission in the nineteenth and early twentieth centuries.

From 1887 to 1905, the Dawes Commission sent out fliers and newspaper advertisements alerting Native women and men, their intermarried white spouses, and the former slaves of members of the Five Tribes that the commission would set up a tent at a certain location within the region and that applicants were to appear there at a certain day and time. These locations were not necessarily chosen for ease of access or convenience. The stakes in the Dawes process were high: land or per-capita payments were available to those who could prove their residency in the Five Tribes during the period directly after the war and into the 1880s. While this led to a number of false applications, Indian and freedmen assistants to the Dawes

FIGURE 3. Josie Jackson with her brothers. Courtesy of Travis D. Roberts.

Commission largely rooted these out. In order to testify to her attachment
to the Chickasaw Nation, Josie traveled to the town of Muskogee within the
Creek Nation. People of all the Five Tribes were to make their way there to
provide their initial testimony. The commission employed several freedpeople and several Indians of each specific tribe to serve as interlocutors
and verifiers of information, kinship relations, and neighborhood dynam-
ics; however, these people did not have the final say in the commission's
decisions. While an individual Indian nation could dispute specific applications or decisions, the Dawes Commission and the secretary of the interior
were the ultimate arbiters.

One requirement for an allotment was the ability to prove one's residence in the Chickasaw Nation's territory through the Civil War and up
to the time of enrollment, which began in the 1890s for Chickasaw freedpeople. Because the commissioners knew Josie had lived in Texas, they
were suspicious of her. However, Josie's success in her case tells us that the

commissioners were assured by her constant returns. Instead of choosing to permanently reside with her daughter in Texas, where she already possessed a job and could find better economic opportunities, Josie journeyed repeatedly to the Chickasaw Nation, returning to visit her daughter, her mother, and her half-sister, Jennie Davidson.[93] The trip from Dallas to Ardmore currently takes nearly four hours by car. For Josie, it would have taken around forty hours walking, or two days of fourteen-hour stagecoach rides, to cover the 120 miles. During this journey through a desolate landscape, she would have faced bandits, makeshift roads that were impassable in bad weather, and the threat of rape or murder.

Josie did not attempt to move her family from Indian Territory to Texas, where they would have enjoyed the benefits of Reconstruction-era amendments, civil rights acts, and federally protected American citizenship. With no voter registration rolls in the United States at this time, Chickasaw freedpeople who traveled to and stayed within the United States could have voted alongside African Americans; they also could have settled in the rural or urban United States, obtained jobs, and lived out their lives. The Fourteenth Amendment did not establish a system for monitoring citizenship, and, unlike other immigrants who might be more easily identified as "foreign," Chickasaw freedpeople easily blended in with the African American population; they were not readily identified as Indian freedpeople.

Instead, Josie chose to maintain her connection to her family and to the land that constituted the Chickasaw Nation—a nation that did not offer her the opportunity for citizenship. Subjected to a number of humiliating laws and rejected by the Chickasaw community, people of African descent created their own kinship networks made up of friends, neighbors, and extended family members. For Chickasaw freedpeople, emancipation was not a moment but rather an ongoing experience that shaped their actions and movements for decades, through Reconstruction and Oklahoma statehood.[94] Those who, like Josie, chose to stay in the Chickasaw Nation inhabited a liminal space of neither citizenship nor total societal disconnection. Instead of pursuing citizenship, they opted for belonging—creating their own communities through the possession of land, the establishment of institutions, and the maintenance of kinship ties.

Chickasaw freedpeople's Dawes testimonies reveal that they prioritized maintaining their connection to Chickasaw land over starting over in the United States. Of the 1,523 Chickasaw freedpeople who formally testified before the commissioners, only 73 freedpeople reported having temporarily left the Chickasaw Nation.[95] Alice Bennett used narrative to illustrate her connection to the Chickasaw Nation. She described traveling to Texas as a young teenager to attend school and then as an adult to find a job. On one of these trips Bennett met her husband, married, and had children. Despite the significant amount of time she spent in Texas, for Bennett and her mother, Lizzie Douglas, the Chickasaw Nation was home.[96] When asked if she had gone to Texas to "make it [her] home," Bennett replied, "No sir."[97] Although she admitted that her daughter had been "out of the nation," Douglas emphasized that Bennett "had never made her home outside."[98] Bennett and her mother were successful in their applications for enrollment.

Chickasaw freedpeople were careful to distinguish between temporary travel outside the nation and renouncing their home in the nation. They viewed the nation as their permanent home, where their community helped them weather difficulties such as widowhood, violence, and poverty. Freedpeople who viewed the Chickasaw Nation as important to their identity were willing to go through great inconvenience to retain their connection to it and to help others do so. As Alice Bennett's story of traveling to Texas to attend school illustrates, Chickasaw freedpeople sometimes used their meager resources to send their children to schools in the United States. Yet, instead of moving to the United States to facilitate access to education, these families maintained their residence in the Chickasaw Nation while their children traveled back and forth, sustaining an itinerant lifestyle in an effort to one day be able to legally claim a piece of Indian Territory land.

When Josie and other members of my family spoke to the Dawes Commission, insisting on their desire and right to an allotment in Indian Ter-

FIGURE 4. Captain McKennon of the Dawes Commission enrolling freedmen at Fort Gibson with Secretary Jakaway standing by the table. Aylesworth Album Collection. Courtesy of the Oklahoma Historical Society.

ritory, they claimed space in the Chickasaw and Choctaw Nations both as a sentimental expression of the way they wished to exercise their freedom and as a practical acquisition of land that would allow them to provide for their families. For a former enslaved person, land signified independence, namely the ability to provide food and resources for one's family. But where did this land come from?[99] It came from the communal holdings of the Five Tribes; it came from land that was once part of a Native nation.

In creating their own communities, Indian freedpeople took ownership of land to which only their owners had previous legal claim but on which they had labored, lived, and died for decades. This was an act of belonging, of agency, of protest, of reclaiming what was previously not allowed to be theirs as enslaved persons.[100] In response, because of their land occupation as well as the challenge to tribal sovereignty this occupation represented,

they were seen by many Indians as uppity (just as white former slave owners saw their former slaves) and as agents of settler colonialism.[101] As such,
Indian freedpeople bore the brunt of Native peoples' anger. One Choctaw
freedman was killed by his former owner, and there were reports of other
murders under similar circumstances. Morris Sheppard, a Cherokee freedman, recalled that "right after de War de Cherokees that had been wid the
South kind of pestered the freedmen some."[102] These so-called "night riders"
prompted Indian freedpeople from all five nations to report incidences of
mob violence and whippings, multiple murders, and general disorder following the war.[103] These incidents of actual violence and the fear of violence
were substantiated by reports on the part of Chickasaws and Choctaws
who had publicly sided with the Union Army during the war, and who also
faced violence in the Reconstruction period.[104] Indians realized that their
former slaves' advocacy for themselves was resulting in increased American intervention on their behalf, and Native peoples resented their former
slaves' status as settlers on what they viewed as their land.

Reminiscent of conversations in the United States about African Americans, over the course of several decades the Choctaw and Chickasaw Nations debated the place of their former slaves in their postwar societies. In
October 1865, Chickasaw Governor Winchester Colbert suggested a plan
of apprenticeship and indenture for Chickasaw freedpeople as a way to extract Black labor.[105] This proposal was very similar to Black Codes in southern states and the way in which former Confederates saw their freed slaves
not as fellow members of society but still merely as labor sources to be exploited or discarded. In a joint address made three months after they had
signed their combined Treaty of 1866, Choctaw Chief Peter Pitchlynn and
Chickasaw Governor Colbert claimed that the citizens of the two nations
would decide "whether the negro shall remain as a voter and a landholder,
to the extent of forty acres." If their former slaves were allowed to remain
among them as citizens, Pitchlynn and Colbert claimed, "With the conces-
sions to them embraced by the first alternative, outnumbering them, as we
do, ten to one, can they do us any harm? While their services as laborers
will be of importance and value for years to come." On the other hand, if

their former slaves were moved outside of their nation but nearby, establishing a "separate colony," according to Pitchlynn and Colbert, this would be "sustained and fostered by the government, and the friends of the negro, now so numerous and powerful. Thousands of other negroes will flock there, so that it will probably assume formidable dimensions in a few years. More lands and other advantages may be required for them, and you can judge for yourselves what will be the result with reference to our welfare and interests. To say the least, they will be anything but desirable neighbors as a separate community."[106]

In a September 1879 address to the Chickasaw legislature (later transcribed for the *Cherokee Advocate*), Chickasaw governor B. C. Burney stated his intent to put the adoption of former slaves as citizens, or, as he put it, "the status of the Negro," to a popular referendum. However, the process did not go as he hoped. The Chickasaw people were not able to fully express their opinions on the matter because, in some of the counties, "[the governor's] right to order such an election was doubted, and the people were not allowed to give an expression of their opinion by ballot."[107] Because the vote was never taken, we cannot know for sure what the prevailing opinion on this matter was in the Chickasaw or Choctaw Nations. Nevertheless, the Choctaw legislature finally made a decision in 1883: they would uphold their agreement to adopt their former slaves.[108] But the Chickasaws did not follow their longtime brother tribe's example in adopting their freedpeople. The Chickasaws' decision against adopting their freedpeople, in fact, became so important to their views of their nation and what it stood for that the winning candidate for governor of the Chickasaw Nation in 1888, W. L. Byrd, made it part of his executive policy, stating that he "ever shall be opposed to the adoption of the negro and shall use every effort to cause the Congress of the United States to remove the negro from among us."[109] In his 1898 annual message, Governor D. H. Johnston devoted a significant amount of time to refuting Chickasaw freedpeople's claims that they were members of the tribe, and to furthering the hope that they would be removed from the nation.[110]

Once people of African descent were no longer free sources of labor, the Chickasaws and Choctaws and, indeed, most Indians would have preferred that they removed themselves from their nations; Native violence against Indian freedpeople was meant not only to signal their anger but also to spur Black flight. Such violence also demonstrates Black people's precarious settler status: although the Five Tribes looked the other way when it came to violence against Blacks, for the most part, they did not dare perpetrate these sorts of violent episodes against white settlers because they knew that the U.S. government would intercede and prosecute.

~

While the United States had set into motion the mechanisms that would allow Indian freedpeople to use the settler colonial process, American assistance did not detract from the prejudice and violence Black people faced from fellow white settlers, from prejudiced white governmental agents, or from Native peoples who saw them as enemies. Indian freedpeople both benefited and suffered from land allotment. They received land that allowed them to create communities and provided them a measure of stability, but at the same time land allotment would eventually lead to the dissolution of the tribal governments that granted them more freedom and equality than that available to African Americans in the post-1870s South. After the suppression of these tribal governments, Indian freedpeople would be at the mercy of the state of Oklahoma's Jim Crow legislation. For Indian freedpeople, as for Native peoples, using the settler colonial process was indeed a double-edged sword. Making claims to land in Indian Territory was an important part of Indian freedpeople's coming to terms with their forced removal and creating vibrant communities in a new place. But coercion by the U.S. government shaped both the Five Tribes' and enslaved people of African descent's migrations to Indian Territory, and it would continue to frame their lives and choices during Reconstruction and into the early twentieth century.

Though Oklahoma is known in African American history circles for its all-Black spaces, like the famed "Black Wall Street" of Tulsa's Greenwood District, the first Black inhabitants of Indian Territory were those who came as enslaved people with their Native owners. In arguing for their claim to Indian Territory land, these Indian freedpeople utilized the strategies of the first wave of Indian Territory settlers, the members of the Indian nations in which they'd lived. Aware that their plight drew empathy from a number of American politicians and tribal agents, Indian freedpeople positioned themselves as people more invested in the system of settler colonialism than those whose claims they wished to call into question. In this last phase of a prolonged Reconstruction—the implementation of the Dawes Act of 1887 in Indian Territory—we can hear freedpeople and their descendants articulate the difference that the opportunity to obtain land made to their movements and priorities. By broadening our focus from the campaign for rights to include land and migration, we can better understand how these Black and mixed-race people defined their own freedom.[111]

Indian freedpeople could claim ownership of western land through the settler colonial process because white Americans saw Native title to land as temporary and undeserved, and advocated for the usurpation of Indian occupancy. Indian freedpeople such as Josie were motivated by the fact that they could actually obtain ownership of the land that held significance to them; they could make communities of their own and claim space in Indian Territory, and this structured their movements in the Civil War era. But there were still two even larger groups of settlers yet to come, Black and white Americans, and they too would use the settler colonial process in an effort to claim for themselves land in Indian Territory. Their claims would solidify the arrival of permanent American intervention via statehood.

CHAPTER 3

Whose Racial Paradise?

S PEAKING TO THE Dawes Commission in 1898 regarding his enrollment as a Chickasaw freedman, Jackson Peters summed up his basic information and most intimate relationships like so: "I am 27 years old. My mother is Amy Russell, enrolled [as a Chickasaw freedwoman] at Stonewall [part of the Chickasaw Nation]. My wife Lucy, 28, is a United States citizen. I was married to her by Houston Stewart, a minister of the Gospel. I was married in the Creek Nation. We have children: Ruthie, 5; Olie, 3; and Clara, 1."[1] In these six sentences, Peters described a world where African Americans from the United States were commonplace marriage partners for Indian freedpeople and where people of African descent in Indian Territory nonchalantly traversed different Indian nations. This world of the late nineteenth- and early twentieth-century West was one of porous boundaries and intercommunity racial coalition, where Indian freedpeople and African Americans came together, for better and for worse, in their quests to claim land and belonging using the settler colonial process. While Robertsville is an example of a community built and populated primarily by Chickasaw and Choctaw freedpeople from a few families, other Indian freedpeople looked to make broader connections. Some of them founded towns alongside African Americans and made these all-Black spaces the cornerstones of their identity, while other Indian freedpeople strove for greater inclusion in their tribal nations and

saw Blacks from the South as a threat to their land claims and their relationships with Native peoples.

These alliances and antagonisms in Indian Territory occurred against
the backdrop of American politicians' withdrawal of support for Black
rights and protection in the United States. In the 1880s and 1890s, as Democrats engineered the rise of Jim Crow laws and white terrorist groups
arose throughout the country and in various territories, the system set up
in Indian Territory to advance the dispossession of Indian peoples, the
Dawes Act and allotment process, allowed for a continued, extended Reconstruction period for people of African descent. This situation drew
increasing numbers of African Americans from the United States to Indian Territory, and in this way they served as the next wave of settlers.
By portraying themselves as more civilized than Native peoples and Indian freedpeople due to their long-standing presence among whites, Black
Americans used the settler colonial process both in attempts to demonstrate their desire to be a part of the American citizenry and in their efforts
to garner governmental assistance in realizing their dreams of landownership and upward mobility.[2] Land claims in Indian Territory came to represent each settler group's ideal of national belonging and citizenship. For
African Americans migrating from the United States and Indian freedpeople already in Indian Territory, land held multiple meanings, whether
inclusion in the American body politic, an all-Black space free from white
and Native prejudice, or a place within the Five Tribes. For the Five Tribes,
it meant Native nations with few Black or white citizens and the continued
insistence on their sovereign right to determine their own citizenship and
landownership laws.

In an effort to give proper attention to the narratives of people of African descent and their western land settlement claims, I have divided the
story of westward migration in the late nineteenth and turn of the twentieth centuries into two chapters: this one, which focuses on the journeys of
African American settlers to Indian Territory and their connections with
Indian freedpeople, and the next, which examines white American settlement in Indian Territory as a process that occurred concurrently with

Black American settlement but which brought with it a different, more permanent kind of American governmental investment. Around the same time that African Americans from the United States tried their hand at making Indian Territory their racial paradise, whites did the same, using the same avenues.

The most influential U.S. governmental policies that encouraged both Black and white migration to Indian Territory and the greater West were the Homestead Act, the legislation that endorsed construction of the transcontinental railroad, and the opening of the Unassigned Lands (lands not occupied by any of the Five Tribes), which together facilitated sanctioned land runs, illegal squatting, and the eventual creation of the Oklahoma Territory. The Homestead Act of 1862 formalized the migration that was already occurring and provided additional motivation to settlers in parts of the West—excluding Indian Territory, at first: settlers could claim, at the most, 160 acres of free land after January 1, 1863.[3] The act's only requirement was that a claimant had to be a head of household, a citizen, twenty-one years of age or older or with past military service, and "never borne arms against the Government of the United States."[4] On April 22, 1889, when Congress authorized the opening of the Unassigned Lands in central Indian Territory, this made settlement in Indian Territory possible under the Homestead Act. As Black and white settlers flocked there in the late 1800s, the railroad followed, bringing people, resources, and industry, encouraging migration and increased American intervention. This culminated in the 1890 creation of Oklahoma Territory, a signal that the U.S. government would heavily support settlement in the region and establish a territorial government, which would be followed by Oklahoma statehood in 1907. While none of these policies and developments used language that discriminated by race, Black Americans were largely denied assistance in using these avenues to obtain and maintain land and wealth. On the other hand, with the full strength of the U.S. government on their side, white Americans soon became the largest landowners in the region and triumphed in the narrative of civilization that justified their colonization.

In 1979, the famed African American writer and artist Ralph Ellison wrote of African Americans in the southern United States: "as slaves . . . they knew that to escape across the Mason-Dixon Line northward was to move in the direction of a greater freedom. But freedom was also to be found in the West of the Old Indian Territory."[5] This poetic statement by a son of Oklahoma is representative of the cultural cachet Indian Territory held for people of African descent throughout North America. During and after enslavement in the United States, the West, and especially Indian Territory, represented freedom, possibility, and amelioration. Rumors that Indian nations would take in runaway slaves or that enslaved people in the Five Tribes were treated better than enslaved people owned by whites bred this mythology.[6] While the truth behind these beliefs was far more complex, the West proved to be an attractive destination for an increasing number of southern African Americans after emancipation.

This postwar exodus was largely the result of congressional Republicans' failure to successfully legislate the receipt of free land within the United States for African Americans. The bill that created the U.S. Freedmen's Bureau, an organization that would later provide freed African Americans help with finding employment, locating lost loved ones, and general acclimation to freedom, was originally designed to include a provision for land that built on an idea of Gullah Geechee women and men from the South Carolina islands, relayed to General William T. Sherman. In the final months of the Civil War, as he prepared for his last invasion of South Carolina, General Sherman noted the sentiments of African Americans in the region, who asked for nothing more than to be able to claim ownership of the land they had worked for generations and which their owners had deserted. In a wartime measure designed to respond to this desire, but more so to provide resources for the many African Americans who had long followed and assisted his army, Sherman wrote his Special Field Orders No. 15, which, in short, provided for forty acres of land for each Black family in "the islands from Charleston south, the abandoned rice-fields along the rivers for thirty miles back from the sea, and the country bordering the Saint John's River [Florida]."[7]

Congress's attempts to codify the accommodations within Sherman's order were unsuccessful. Various versions of the Freedmen's Bureau Bill included a nod to the issue of Black landownership, from the first version that permitted African Americans "to occupy, cultivate, and improve all land which had been abandoned and all real estate to which the United States might acquire title within the rebel states," to the second, more radical iteration of the bill, which stated that "from the confiscated and abandoned southern lands forty acres should be given to every male refugee or freedman as a rental for three years, thereafter eligible for purchase from the U.S. government."[8] However, after much negotiation and division within the Republican Party, it became clear that in order for the Freedmen's Bureau Bill to be passed, the land section of the act would have to be discarded. The issue was made moot when President Andrew Johnson decided that one of his first acts as president would be to return confiscated land to those slave owners who sought pardons.[9]

Only the most radical of the Republicans, such as Thaddeus Stevens and Charles Sumner, supported a measure that included land reparations, and these two did not give up after the failure of the Freedmen's Bureau Bill. In 1866, the same year in which the Department of the Interior made it part of its negotiations with the Five Tribes that Indian freedpeople receive land, Representative Stevens spoke to Congress in support of giving confiscated land to African Americans, saying that the bill he was introducing (H.R. 29) was "important to four millions of injured, oppressed, and helpless men, whose ancestors for two centuries have been held in bondage and compelled to earn the very property a small portion of which we propose to restore to them, and who are now destitute, helpless, and exposed to want and starvation under the deliberate cruelty under their former masters. . . . Nothing is so likely to make a man a good citizen as to make him a freeholder. Nothing will so multiply the productions of the South as to divide it into small farms."[10]

Stevens even set out a plan for how land could be divided to benefit as many Black families as possible.[11] In March 1867, Charles Sumner raised a resolution that asserted, "not less important than education is the homestead, which must be secured to the freedmen, so that at least every head of a family may have a piece of land."[12] When Senator William P. Fessenden argued that African Americans had access to the Homestead Law, and that any other privilege set aside for African Americans would be "more than we do for white men," Sumner responded, "white men have never been in slavery; there is no emancipation and no enfranchisement of white men to be consummated."[13] Sumner even suggested that perhaps the president should have required "that the person who was to receive a pardon should allot a certain portion of his lands to his freedmen."[14] With these remarks, Sumner established that the Homestead Act was not adequate for African Americans and that he believed they, as former slaves, deserved legislation that took into consideration their particular circumstances.

But for most whites, even those who supported emancipation and a degree of Black rights, the idea of separating white men from their private property, one of the most hallowed protections in the Constitution, was blasphemous. Unlike for Indian freedpeople, plans for African Americans in the United States to obtain land had to make it through Congress— through white men unwilling to cede white former slave owners' property, the cornerstone of American capitalism and democracy; through hesitant Republicans more moderate than their radical fellow party members; and through Democrats, many of whom believed Black people should still be enslaved. It is no wonder, then, that this proposal did not come to fruition in the United States, where the most valuable Indian land had already been transferred into white hands, and thus where there was no need to use Black possession as a lever through which to implement settler colonialism.

Instead, African Americans freed in the United States had to secure their own economic foundations and search for their own sense of belonging. Some traveled to Liberia, becoming involved in colonization efforts of their own, while others made their way to Kansas, Mexico, Canada, or California, among other places.[15] Driven from the South not just by a desire for land but also by violence, coercive labor contracts, and state and federal governments that refused to firmly intervene for their protection,

African Americans hoped to find respite from white intimidation and an opportunity for a new start in new places. Those African Americans who chose Indian Territory as their destination had the particular experience of sharing land with Native peoples and Indian freedpeople, groups with whom they saw common cause, but who had their own reasons to be wary of these interlopers. To navigate this world, African Americans from the United States seized on the process of settler colonialism in their attempts to access the same opportunities as Indian freedpeople and to make their own freedom.

Although whites and African Americans had emigrated from the United States to Indian Territory since the creation of the region as a Native outpost, their population numbers were largely insignificant until the late nineteenth century. Between 1890 and 1907, the Black population of Indian Territory (including both Indian freedpeople and African Americans) increased from 19,000 to over 80,000. The white population increased from 109,400 to 538,500 as a result of the Homestead Act and the opening of the Unassigned Lands. Throughout these other demographic changes, the Indian population remained stable at roughly 61,000.[16] Yet, not everyone benefited equally from this legislation that would so radically change the lives of the inhabitants of Indian Territory. The Homestead Act rule requiring citizenship (or naturalization) would seem to purposely limit African Americans' access, as they were not yet considered U.S. citizens.[17] In addition, though January 1, 1863, the date of effect for the Homestead Act, also marked the enactment of the Emancipation Proclamation, most African Americans were still enslaved at this time and thus did not have the ability to freely make their way to the West. The Homestead Act was also cost-prohibitive in a number of ways. Most people of African descent could not afford to fulfill all of the terms: to pay to file an initial land claim (termed a "preemption" claim), to live upon and "improve the land" (which required building a home), to plow the land and tend it for five consecutive years, and, finally, to pay to apply for a land patent. Even if an African American woman or man could pull together the funds and resources required for these stipulations, they were still at a disadvantage. As petitioners were required to pay per acre for their preemption claim, monied whites had the ability to amass large tracts of land, privileging them even in this supposed bid for equality in western land access.[18] These requirements also negatively affected poor whites. Thus, a number of white and Black Americans illegally squatted on lands, earning themselves the enmity of both Indians and Indian freedpeople.[19] Despite the financial burdens inherent in the process, by 1900, 80 million acres had been patented and 270 million acres granted through the act.[20]

Black migrants particularly required encouragement that the West was a viable space for economic and social success. Federal policies introduced the mechanisms that made possible the successful migrations that followed, but in large part this reassurance came in the form of Black newspaper editorials. The *St. Cloud Democrat* touted Minnesota as having lands "better adapted to successful agriculture in soil, climate and situation relatively to the great avenues of inland commerce, than any other western state," with a lake consisting of "rich mineral ranges on its shores" and "pine forests. . . [with] inexhaustible supplies of lumber."[21] The *Big Blue Union* in Marysville, KS, distilled the main points of this "important and beneficial act," stating that emigration to lands bordering the Pacific Railroad would be great and that the Homestead Act would "form a new era in western emigration."[22]

Black newspapers created a diasporic information network, with African American writers and editors reporting on slavery, emancipation, citizenship, and land allotment in Indian Territory. At times, their language was meant to evoke empathy with Indian freedpeople's situations; at other times, writers' rhetoric took on a tone of covetousness. In 1893, the *Freeman*, an African American newspaper in Indiana, published the letter of a J. A. Turner. The author, presumably an African American man, thought it necessary for the newspaper's readers to know about "this hidden fraction of the Afro-American race in the United States of America."[23] "Some of them," he wrote, are "very peculiarly situated, while others are enjoying so-called rights of their country and tribe."[24] Chickasaw freedpeople were those who were, in his words, "very peculiarly situated." Turner described the indeterminate status of the Chickasaw freedpeople as a lack of recognition by

either the "Big Chief" (the United States) or the "Little Chief" (the Chickasaw government).[25] Reflecting the belief that Native Americans treated
their slaves more honorably or benevolently than whites, Turner blamed
the "molestation" of the Chickasaw freedpeople on Chickasaw admixture
with "the white man."[26] After briefly detailing the fates of freedpeople in
the other Indian nations, Turner claimed the Chickasaw freedpeople were
worse off, because "they have no regular school system furnished them."[27]
That Turner's letter is titled "Information not Generally Known" demonstrates the *Freeman* editor's belief that African Americans in other parts
of the country were unaware of the experiences of their brethren in Indian
Territory, and that they needed to be spurred to empathy for this distinct
group that shared similarities with their own experience.

The passage of American political measures regarding land allotment
encouraged Black writers to publish editorials that extolled the land and
wealth available to Indian freedpeople and called for their own people's
participation in this process of securing Native land. As the twentieth century dawned, some editorial writers made plain their opinion that African
Americans had a right to claim these gains for themselves. With the headline "Millionaire Indian Slaves," the *Washington Bee* reported that Indian
freedpeople had received land as well as per capita payments due to treaty
stipulations, proclaiming that this made them "absolutely the wealthiest . . .
negroes in the United States with the exception of, perhaps, the Chickasaw
and Choctaw Freedmen."[28] Calling Indian freedpeople "inexperienced,"
the newspaper announced that they were already becoming involved in
"banking and trust companies, real estate companies," and the like.[29]

The *Missouri Republican* even went so far as to make false claims, reporting that "The Freedmen's Oklahoma Association . . . promises every
freedman who will go to Oklahoma 160 acres of land free. . . . The Freedmen's association bases its claim to entry on the lands of the Indian Territory on the treaties of 1866, made by the government with the Creeks and
Seminoles."[30]

Of course, the Treaty of 1866 applied only to the former slaves of members of the Five Tribes, but this did not stop African Americans from hop-

ing that, once in Indian Territory, they could share in the bounty of these treaty provisions. And even more than hoping, these writers and the Black settlers that heeded their call were actively willing to engage in settlement on lands they knew were set aside for Indians and Indian freedpeople. The *Washington Bee* claimed that Indian freedpeople desired to have their African American brethren from the United States join them in Oklahoma to organize colonies so they would be ready for new opportunities that would present themselves as "the Indian government dissolves itself and statehood comes into existence."[31] The column emphasized that "only honest and sincere people of enterprise . . . are wanted."[32] Once again utilizing a false claim to spur migration, this editorial also touted a desire for the American settler state to win out over Indian sovereignty so that African Americans could benefit. Black newspapers applauded the successes of Indian freedpeople and sought to tie their fates to freedpeople's by creating empathy with their struggles and encouraging Black migration to Indian Territory.

Beginning in the late nineteenth century, African American leaders supplemented their rhetorical overtures for increased migration, aimed at Black southerners, with political and social arguments regarding their qualifications for landownership, aimed at whites. In 1880, J. H. Williamson, a former slave, the longest-serving Black nineteenth-century state congressman (of North Carolina), and the founder of the *Banner*, a paper advocating for Black industrial education, testified in front of the Senate. As African Americans were leaving the South in droves because "in many of the Southern States the colored people are denied rights," Williamson made a case for African Americans' ability to civilize the West, arguing that whites should support the creation of an all-Black state there.[33] Williamson juxtaposed the "civilized" United States where Blacks were murdered "because of their political opinions," and "where the cry of relief from 'negro rule'" echoed, with the untamed West, where one might be "scalped by the wild Indian," maintaining that even life there would be preferable to the indignities African Americans suffered in the South with no recourse. Despite the presence of "wild Indians," Williamson felt that the West offered African Americans the opportunity to "carve out [their] future destiny under the shining sun of heaven."[34] What of the Indians already living in the West? Williamson felt African Americans would quickly show they were preferable to them as neighbors to the United States. He asserted, "The Indians are savage and will not work . . . [in contrast], we, the negro race, are a working people. Should we emigrate we would endeavor to clear the forests and drain the low lands, build houses, churches, school-houses, and advance in all other industries and work out our own destinies." While Williamson's brazen acknowledgment of white supremacy sets his words apart from the language used by the Five Tribes and most Indian freedpeople, make no mistake: his argument was couched in the approval of settler colonialism—a process that allowed for hardworking Black women and men to "clear" the lands of Native peoples and then prosper on them.

Williamson continued his argument by comparing the civilizing work African Americans could carry out in Indian Territory with that of "the first settlers at Jamestown and Plymouth Rock," mentioning that they had encountered difficulties like "disease, starvation, and death" but overcame it all. So, too, Williamson suggested, would African Americans, if given the resources.[35] He advocated for independence but also for the right to exercise American citizenship in a separate, Black space that would represent Black belonging and nationhood. Though Williamson did not mention Indian freedpeople, his request ran parallel to the thoughts of Secretary Harlan and other Republicans in the 1860s—that hardworking people of African descent could better civilize the West than could Native Americans. Indian freedpeople's supposed industriousness, along with white Americans' desire to access Indian land, allowed for special considerations. But Black Americans' efforts to obtain the financial, social, and political assistance and sanction that Indian freedpeople received, as they advocated for a Black colony or smaller-scale settlement, would come to naught.

A statement made by Frederick Douglass, well known for his advocacy of African Americans' and women's rights, highlights even progressive Black Americans' willingness to engage in the settler colonial process in order to participate in western settlement. In a speech to the American

Anti-Slavery Society in 1869, Douglass argued that "the negro is more like the white man than the Indian, in his tastes and tendencies, and disposition to accept civilization. The Indian . . . rejects our civilization. . . . It is not so with the negro. He loves you and remains with you, under all circumstances, in slavery and in freedom." Douglass used logic similar to that of white Republicans who advocated for Indian freedpeople's land-development skills above those of Indians, positing that people of African descent were more closely aligned with white America's march of progress than Native Americans. Douglass joined African Americans' goals and behavior with whites' by using the term "our civilization," even going so far as to use coercive enslavement as an example of African Americans' devotion to white Americans and their values![36]

In another, earlier, speech, "Land for the Landless: The Record of Parties on the Homestead Principle No. 20," Douglass explained his belief in the value of settler colonial principles, specifically:

> The proposed donation of the public lands to actual settlers—to the landless masses as free homesteads—the peopling of the national domain with an enterprising, intelligent, and hardy race of emigrants—transforming the savage wilderness into flourishing civilized communities, multiplying new States, and adding immensely to the wealth and productive industry of the Nation [would] extend the area of Freedom [and] would increase the political power of the North and West—the power of the people—would dangerously menace the perpetuity of the institution of slavery and the Democratic slaveholding aristocracy built upon it.[37]

Douglass, an educated man who was familiar with both Native peoples and Indian reformers, knew that this land was not "free" and that it had not always been "the national domain," that rather it had been taken from Indian hands; Douglass also knew that American emigration into the region would change and worsen circumstances for Native peoples

and impede tribal sovereignty.[38] Yet, he used the language of savagery and
civilization to juxtapose what the region was allegedly like in Indian hands
and what it might be like after the emigration of African Americans, who,
in his imagining, were more similar to whites than were Indians in their
ability to tame the land. While Douglass's two speeches were given four
years apart, they represented the sustained belief on the part of one of the
most famous Black radicals of his time that African Americans deserved
to share in the settler colonial spoils of the Native West.

The belief in the value of the settler colonial process extended to Black
leaders in the West, such as Edwin P. McCabe, whose advocacy for Black
resettlement culminated around the time of the creation of Oklahoma
Territory. McCabe had been the first Black county clerk in Graham County, Kansas, in 1880—a place he had arrived in in 1878, seeking the promise
of western paradise—and was elected as state auditor in November 1882.
Four years later, after Kansas Republicans chose another nominee for auditor, McCabe left Kansas to realize his dream of a Black state in Oklahoma
Territory, and in March 1890 he traveled to Washington, DC, to present to
President Benjamin Harrison the idea of making the Unassigned Lands an
all-Black state. While the president's reaction is unknown, unsurprisingly
many whites were not pleased.[39]

Nonetheless there were some whites who embraced the notion of an
all-Black colony in the West, as it combined their ideas of segregation and
colonization, allowing them to avoid the (imagined) difficulties of integrating former slaves into a post-emancipation society in the East.[40] As early
as the 1790s, white American thinkers, such as St. George Tucker, a lawyer and law professor; Anthony Benezet, the Huguenot abolitionist; and
politicians including the Virginia magistrate William Craighead and future
president James Madison, suggested the "Northwest" as a site of a potential
Black colony.[41] In the nineteenth century, these ideas took on greater speci-
ficity as Native land opened up in Indian Territory and full African American emancipation was nigh. A few months after the Civil War, Senator J. R.
Doolittle raised the issue anew. In September 1865, he wrote to President
Johnson, "What lies West of the Indian Territory could be . . . given to the

Indians. The remainder could be organized into a Freedman's Territory for the colored soldiers [and] for all other colored men heads of families . . . there could be ample room in this territory to receive the full benefits of the Homestead Systems, of which you are the author."[42]

However, the majority of white Americans were no more willing to financially support this idea in the nineteenth century than they were in the eighteenth century. In both periods, white Americans presenting the idea of Black colonization within North America recognized that people of African descent had faced, or would face, discrimination in the confines of the United States, and thus settlement elsewhere was preferable. But in shunting African Americans to another location, whites were simply declining to fix the problem in their own home, perpetuating the racism they claimed would not allow African Americans to live peacefully in the United States as free people.

Thus, for Black Americans, there were many reasons to want a separate territory: they desired freedom from harassment and racial violence and the ability to exercise the political, economic, and social rights they had finally won, while staying within the boundaries of North America and maintaining some sort of relationship with the nation that they had helped build.[43] The idea of an all-Black territory or state would never gain as much support as other colonization efforts, such as migration to Liberia or Sierra Leone, for the same reason African Americans embraced it—the West was simply too close, and large-scale Black migration there would interfere with white settlers' and politicians' plans to exploit Indian Territory. When the idea of an all-Black state failed, African Americans' multifaceted deployment of the settler colonial process and Black diasporic connection allowed them to create their own spaces of Black belonging within Indian Territory and Oklahoma Territory. Once Black Americans had been inspired to go West and had exhausted potential governmental resources to help them in this endeavor, they began settling in different places, using assorted methods, with varying degrees of success.

Though African Americans from the South did not receive the sort of bureaucratic advocacy from the U.S. government as did Indian freedpeople, they did have wealthy white benefactors and charismatic Black leaders who saw potential profit in western Black settlements. This financial and social support enabled and motivated African Americans to move onto Native land. With them, these Black Americans brought their ethics and principles, changing the face and culture of the West. Both Kansas and Indian Territory drew the attention of promoters of African American migration. In 1877, two Black Tennessee ministers by the names of William Smith and Thomas Harris originated the idea of an all-Black town in Kansas called Nicodemus. With the help of a white Kansas land speculator named W. R. Hill, they formed a colonization society in Lexington, Tennessee, to plan a departure to Kansas the next year.[44] Nicodemus would become the best-known Black settlement in Kansas, and other Kansan communities would primarily trade on their proximity to Indian Territory.

Intermarriage between African Americans from the United States and Indian freedpeople also facilitated Black settlement in Indian Territory. Among Chickasaw freedpeople alone, around 367 of these intermarriages occurred.[45] In this newly blended climate, the positive interactions between Indian freedpeople and African Americans from the United States resulted in the creation of so-called Black towns, often founded upon allotments owned by Indian freedpeople after the Dawes process and populated by a mixture of natives of Indian Territory and Blacks from the United States. Of the twenty-eight Black towns founded in present-day Oklahoma, twenty-four were located in Indian Territory on land allotted to former slaves of Indians, while only four were located in Oklahoma Territory in the aftermath of the land runs. The majority of the towns based in Indian Territory were located in the Creek Nation, the nation most inclusive of and friendly to people of African descent."[46]

The town of Boley is perhaps the best example of the complexity of the interactions between African Americans from the South and Indian freedpeople. Located within the Creek Nation, Boley began as the land allotment of six-year-old Abigail Barnett, a Creek freedgirl. Boley would become the largest predominantly Black town in North America at the turn of the century after a trio of white and Black investors began promoting it around 1901 as the site of a future railroad station. In Boley, Indian freed-people and African Americans mixed, and Lula Mixon remembered that "people were coming in so fast that there was no place for them to sleep." They lived in tents until they acquired the funds and resources to build homes.[47] With the successful construction of the railroad station came capital, resources, and increased migration to the town, and residents could soon patronize over 55 businesses as diverse as T.B. Armstrong Hardware Store, Mrs. J. H. Bagby Drugstore, Boley Printing Company, Mrs. Annie Cowan Millinery Shop, and Burnett Brothers Groceries and Drygoods.[48] The town had a newspaper, the *Boley Progress*, and several churches. Boley became a symbol of Black progress, particularly for its excellence in educating its townspeople, who eventually built two private high schools and one public high school. African Americans in the United States carefully surveyed Indian Territory, if not as a place of refuge for themselves then as a study in the type of opportunities for belonging and economic success seemingly available only in the West.

Boley experienced its prime after Oklahoma statehood before being largely decimated economically by the Dust Bowl and socially and politically by white racism. But it was Boley's founding *before* statehood, while its land was still a part of Indian Territory, that allowed its residents the ability to prosper at a later date. As part of an Indian freedperson's land, its founding was enabled only through the actions of American officials and as part of Indian freedpeople's involvement in the settler colonial process. Some Indian freedpeople saw African Americans' co-optation of this land as unacceptable. In several instances, Indian freedpeople, along with several Native American men, disrupted some of the nighttime church services in Boley and attempted to interfere in other matters, resulting in several people being killed or wounded.[49] Apparently, for some Indian freedpeople and Native Americans, African Americans from the United States were unwelcome intruders, just as much as whites, if not more so, and they resented African Americans' efforts to disturb their settler colonial claims.

Though Edwin McCabe was unsuccessful in gaining American political and financial backing for the colonization of an all-Black state in the

FIGURE 5. Members of the Boley Town Council. Oklahoma Historical Society Photograph Collection. Courtesy of the Oklahoma Historical Society.

West, McCabe was able to establish a town in Oklahoma Territory that he called Langston, after John Langston, a long-standing Black abolitionist and activist, and now a congressman from Virginia. In May 1890, McCabe, along with Charles Robbins, a white real estate speculator, officially purchased, surveyed, and platted the land that would make up the town.[50] While for many the creation of Oklahoma Territory signaled an end to the hope of a permanent, all-Black space, McCabe took it as an opportunity to establish a Black town, a smaller version of his vision of Black separatism and autonomy. Langston was composed almost entirely of southern expatriates, inspired at Black churches and community institutions by McCabe and his followers' tales of a western utopia set apart from Indian freedpeople and the benefit of their land allotments.[51] Newspapers also contributed to the promotion of the town. The *Langston City Herald* exclaimed, "Freedom! Peace, Happiness and Prosperity. Do you Want all these? Then Cast Your Lot With Us & Make Your Home in Langston City . . . and to open the race new avenues through which they may obtain more of the good things of life."[52] By April 1890, the *St. Louis Globe-Democrat* reported that large groups of immigrants from Arkansas and Memphis had left for Langston.[53]

Langston residents grew cane, cling peaches, wild plums, possum grapes, greens, and white corn. They built dugout houses, composed of logs and dirt roofs, and founded stores, churches, and schools.[54] In 1897, Langston became home to Langston University, one of the first Black universities in the West. While Langston was not perfect, Mildred Robertson's observation of her family's experiences sums up many African Americans' thoughts about settling in the West: "My people lived down at the bottom of Mississippi close to Louisiana. . . . Well, they had a little more freedom in Oklahoma. They didn't have nothing, but they had a little more freedom, cause those people [in Mississippi] worked the whole year round and bought their groceries at the store and when they gathered their cotton crop and paid this man off, they didn't have nothing much to live on."[55]

While most settlers in the Indian and Oklahoma territories did not achieve great wealth, their ability to live and work on their own terms was an important difference from what they had found in the South.[56]

Black towns cultivated an air of respectability and self-sufficiency, demonstrating that without white or Indian racism, people of African descent could thrive. Regardless of whether they were created only by African Americans from the United States or through African Americans' dealings and relationships with Indian freedpeople, Black towns succeeded in large part because of the treaty rights and activism of Indian freedpeople, whose interactions with the American government through the settler colonial process had yielded them land and a degree of rights within Indian nations.

But all was not completely well when it came to members of the Five Tribes and their former slaves. The Five Tribes already had varying degrees to which they were willing to include their former slaves in the social and political aspects of tribal nationhood. As Black migration to Indian Territory increased, the degree to which Indians were willing to share their land and nations with people of African descent changed as well, and this in turn affected Indian freedpeople's relationships with African Americans from the South, who they often blamed for the change in their treatment by Indians. Indian freedpeople reasoned that if the latter had not come, scaring the Indians with fears of being overwhelmed, they would still be living well (though white settlers were actually a larger issue). In truth, though, regardless of the presence of Black Americans, Indian freedpeople's place within the Five Tribes was never idyllic.

Although freedpeople in the Creek, Seminole, and Cherokee Nations (unlike those in the Chickasaw and Choctaw Nations) were able to participate in most of the rites of tribal citizenship, there were some distinct differences between their rights and those of Indians. As the Dawes Commission completed its enrollment process, it categorized applicants two ways: the former slaves of members of the Five Tribes were put onto the "Freedmen" Roll, which did not record Native ancestry, though many former slaves possessed such ancestry as a result of rape or loving relationships between free Blacks and tribal members.[57] Persons determined to be Indian by the Dawes commissioners were placed on the "Blood" Roll, which signified that they had some degree of Native ancestry.[58] Commissioners considered nearly any evidence of African-descended ancestry to be disqualify one for the "Blood" roll. The primary purpose behind the creation of these two separate rolls was to differentiate which land parcels applicants received, as Indians could claim larger allotments than freedpeople.[59] But the differences in freedpeople's treatment went beyond land allotment, because the same settler colonial process that had allowed, and even pushed Native Americans to adopt African chattel slavery allowed them to ignore the contributions Indian freedpeople had made to their societies.

In their 1866 treaty negotiations, the Five Tribes had agreed to sell portions of their land holdings to the United States, albeit for far below market price. However, even though they had also agreed to adopt their former slaves as citizens with accompanying rights, all but the Creeks insisted that their former slaves not have access to the per capita payments that would follow the sale of their lands.[60] In fact, the Choctaws' and Chickasaws' treaty specified that people of African descent would have "the rights, privileges, and immunities, including the right of suffrage, of citizens of said nations, except in the annuities, moneys, and public domain claimed by, or belonging to, said nations respectively."[61] For all four nations, this distinction inaugurated an immediate difference in the citizenship enjoyed by persons defined as "Black" and "Native" in Indian Territory. Cherokee freedpeople unsuccessfully petitioned the Cherokee and American governments for inclusion in land payments.[62] As the Cherokee Nation encountered new opportunities for profit, such as selling grazing rights on tribal land, the tribal government continued to vote to exclude freedpeople from these benefits, demonstrating their belief that their former slaves were not equal citizens.[63] But in October 1888, Cherokee freedpeople experienced a victory. The commissioner of Indian affairs, J. D. C. Atkins, had drafted a bill to allocate $75,000 for per capita payments of $20 each to freedpeople to compensate for their exclusion from previous distributions, and two years later Congress passed the bill.[64] Once again, the United States interfered in tribal affairs on behalf of Indian freedpeople, discounting tribal sovereignty but crucially bettering the welfare of people of African descent.

While Indian freedpeople certainly faced issues of discrimination and violence in Indian Territory, they still retained many of the political and social rights into the late nineteenth century that their counterparts in the American South had lost. Soon, though, Indian freedpeople found that the influx of African Americans from the South worked in tandem with the prejudices that many Indians already had, leading them to turn against *all* people of African descent—even their former slaves who had lived among them for generations. While the Chickasaws' rejection of their freedpeople went against their agreement with the United States, their decision makes some sense when viewed in the larger context of the changing demographics of Indian Territory. Black migration had increased to the extent that the Choctaws and Chickasaws no longer outnumbered their former slaves and their descendants. As the smallest of the Five Tribes, they began to worry about their power in the region.[65] In a letter to his friend Ben Watkins, Choctaw national treasurer Green McCurtain (who would later serve as tribal chief) gave voice to such worries. Though there is no copy of Mc-Curtain's letter, the June 1893 response by Watkins, an intermarried white citizen, is demonstrative of their (presumably) shared opinion of people of African descent in Indian Territory. Watkins wrote, "The Negroes of this Nation intermarry with Negroes of [the] states, and but a few years can intervene, before the negro, numerically will surpass the Choctaw, lessening year by year the future possessions of the Choctaw people—a few years more and the negro will come forth, educated and more difficult to manipulate than at present, and the finances will be depleted with the negro above the beneficiary—Prolific as rabbits and gregarious by Nature—will furnish at all times lucrative schools thereby securing the most profitable teachers—Now Green, you know these are, simply, truths."[66]

Watkins's expressions may have simply been part of an effort to convince the Choctaws that an American takeover via statehood was inevitable. But these thoughts still represented a fear, shared by many Indians, that people of African descent would soon overtake Indians numerically, and subsequently wrench political and social power from them.

Most everyday Indian citizens agreed with Watkins that Indian freedpeople and other Black people did not belong within their nations. In an 1885 congressional investigation, William Wilson, a 74-year-old Cherokee citizen, said that freedpeople should be moved out of the nation because "this land is Cherokee land." When reminded that the Cherokee Nation had agreed to adopt them in the Treaty of 1866, Wilson replied, "I didn't make any treaty with the United States. . . . It was dictated to us after the war and we accepted it." Where did Wilson think Cherokee freedpeople should go? "You [Americans] have millions of acres of land, why don't you send them [freedpeople] out and settle them on it?"[67] Wilson articulated his belief that though Cherokee freedpeople and their ancestors had lived in Indian Territory for decades, and for decades before that in the Southeast, they possessed no claim to Cherokee land or identity. Wilson's sentiments may have revolved around the idea that most freedpeople racially identified as Black and thus did not belong in an Indian nation. But there could also be political reasons behind his attitude. Though the Cherokees were not as demographically small as the Chickasaws or Choctaws, by the 1880s Cherokee freedpeople were said to make up a large portion of the voting bloc.[68] Perhaps it is not surprising, then, that some Cherokees would be anxious that they would be overwhelmed in their own nation, with important decisions being made by people they saw as racially and socially different from themselves. Apart from Cherokee freedpeople, Cherokee citizens also spoke out against the presence of African Americans from the United States. In 1894, the editor of the *Cherokee Advocate* incited his fellow tribesmen to resist both Black and white migration, telling them to "Be men, and fight off the barnacles that now infest our country in the shape of non-citizens, free Arkansas ni––ers, and traitors."[69]

Anti-Black sentiment like this encouraged Native peoples to ignore Indian freedpeople's shared histories with their nations and to inaccurately associate them with Black interlopers from the United States. Indian freedpeople fought this attitude by attempting to differentiate themselves. When Mary Grayson was interviewed in 1937 as part of the Works Progress Administration Slave Narrative project, she illustrated this dichotomy, saying, "I am what we colored people call a 'native.' That means I didn't come into the Indian country from somewhere in the Old South, after the War, like so many Negroes did, but I was born here in the Old Creek Nation and my master was a Creek Indian."[70] Mary felt that her experiences of enslavement were better than those of Black Americans, arguing that "I have had people who were slaves of white folks tell me that they had to work awfully hard and their masters were cruel to them, but all the Negroes I knew who belonged to Creeks always had plenty of clothes and lots to eat and we all lived in good log cabins we built." Mary clearly demarcated her history and circumstances from those of African Americans from the United States. Mary's assertion of her identity as a "native" rather than a newcomer (like other Blacks in the West) is reflective of a key component of the settler colonial process—strategic differentiation.

Aside from the desire to declare their history and provenance in Indian Territory as different from that of Blacks from the South, Indian freedpeople had another reason to differentiate themselves from African Americans from the United States: these new migrants sometimes deceptively played the role of Indian freedpeople to try to get a Dawes land allotment. Lewis E. Lucky, a Creek freedman, remembered that a Black family by the name of Smeeds had "got by the Dawes Commission and secured allotments. They were not entitled to them." And it was not just this one family that had succeeded in their deception. Lucky said that "many were aided in getting land by crooked lawyers. Some succeeded, but others were removed from the Creek rolls."[71]

Despite these tensions, Indian freedpeople and African Americans often managed to overcome their differences. Witness, for example, Henry Clay's change in opinion of Indian freedpeople: Clay, an African American who moved from Louisiana to the Creek Nation before the war, recalled in an interview in the 1930s that he "never did get along good with these Creek slaves out here and I always stayed around the white folks. In fact . . . I always got off the road when I seen Creek Negroes coming along. They would have red strings tied in their hats or something wild looking. . . . Them Creek Negroes was so funny to talk to anyways." But Clay obviously changed his mind, as he later married a Creek freedwoman and settled down to raise a family in the Creek country.[72]

~

In the post-1877 United States, African Americans contended with Jim Crow laws, vigilante and state-sanctioned violence, and loss of resources for the creation of community institutions, such as schools. This led those African Americans who wanted to stay within the boundaries of the current and future United States to look to the West for hope, particularly Indian Territory, where the U.S. government was actively deploying programs for Black landownership and capital through Dawes land allotments to Indian freedpeople. African Americans were in search of a place where they could inhabit the American archetype of landownership, and they were willing to infringe upon the land rights of Indians and Indian freedpeople in an effort to do so. The calls of Williamson, Douglass, Mc-

Cabe, and other Black leaders for an all-Black state or Black settlement in the West were the ultimate expression of African Americans' desire for citizenship as defined by engagement in the settler colonial process—to take over an Indian space and use it better than Indians and Indian freedpeople, in the model of white Americans.[73]

Yet, because they were forced to, the Black Americans who ventured West were willing to go without citizenship, creating lives for themselves in a space that had not yet been absorbed by the American nation-state. African Americans from the United States portrayed themselves as models of civilization, sculpted by their proximity to whites and able to bring productivity to Indian Territory. At the same time, African Americans came together with Indian freedpeople to create marriages and friendships that built towns and institutions that still live on today as symbols of Black achievement. Some of the former slaves of Chickasaws, Cherokees, Choctaws, Creeks, and Seminoles were interested in dissolving their ties to their former owners by becoming part of Black spaces—like Langston, a Black space outside of the confines of an Indian nation. But other Indian freedpeople were invested in maintaining their connections to the Five Tribes in concrete ways that went above and beyond merely living upon tribal land, with varying degrees of success.

While it is true that the West did not, and could not, live up to all the hopes and dreams of people of African descent—be they Indian freedpeople or African Americans—they would find that the space of Indian Territory held opportunities that would be closed to Black women and men for decades once a sustained white presence was made permanent through Oklahoma statehood.

CHAPTER 4

The Last Wave

I HAD THE PRIVILEGE of interviewing my great-aunt, Lillie Booker, neé Roberts, in 2011, when she was 101 years old—women and men in the Roberts family tend to live to quite the ripe old age. As do many older people when questioned about their lives, Lillie answered my questions dutifully, but she frequently dismissed the importance of her recollections, insisting that her experiences were insignificant. In these moments, Lillie's son, Herbert Jr., would often supplement her answers by providing additional information or by editorializing on the brief but rich nuggets of history Lillie dispensed. Toward the end of our interview, after Lillie had told me of growing up in Robertsville, of creating delicacies for wealthy families through her own catering business, and of integrating a white neighborhood as a mixed-race Black woman in twentieth-century Oklahoma City, she turned to the issue of race relations, mentioning that back in Ardmore, "The Blacks were mean. The whites didn't get too much over on them, [because the Blacks] would speak up for themselves." Herbert then elaborated that it was this characteristic that had led to a skirmish in Ardmore sometime after statehood which, in his opinion, defined the Roberts men as people who were "mean, had Winchesters and rifles, and didn't put up with things." They had fearlessly fought back when their family was confronted with racial violence, though it could have cost them their lives. Willie Roberts (my great-grandfather and Lillie's father) fought side-by-side with a close friend named Sid, who killed two white men during the melee. After Sid was lynched by white supremacists in retribution, Willie named his next-born son after him.[1] The turmoil in Ardmore, too small to be even a footnote in Oklahoma history, and the 1921 Tulsa Race Massacre which followed not long after, along with changes in the economic and political opportunities available to Black and Native peoples during this period, were signals that times in this corner of the West had changed drastically for the worse. The late nineteenth century brought with it increased American migration and territorial government followed by statehood, which allowed white Americans to introduce laws that segregated whites from African Americans and Native Americans, limited Black and Native political participation, and restricted tribal sovereignty.

The same settler colonial process that had brought the Five Tribes, Indian freedpeople, and African Americans to Indian Territory and allowed them to prosper by favorably comparing themselves to others in terms of civilization and Americanization facilitated the migration and supremacy of whites, the creators and ultimate beneficiaries of this process. White settlers' involvement and investment in settler colonialism is far more familiar than that of the Five Tribes or people of African descent: they used the American government (of which they were both the primary representatives and constituents) to sanction their settlement in Indian Territory, their theft of Indian and Black land, their corporatization of the region, and their violence against Native and Black peoples. Because the story of Oklahoma's white settlers has been told so many times, the perspective in this chapter is different—rather than documenting the wave of yet another group of settler colonialists, I will tell of how white settlers disrupted the lives of Black and Native peoples in the region, and how they, in turn, fought against this final wave of white settler colonization. Just like the Roberts family when in the throes of brutality, people of Native and African descent refused to go down without a fight.

Like African Americans, white Americans and white immigrants came to Indian Territory seeking a space that would enable them to exercise more social and economic autonomy. They came by railroad, by wagon, and by foot. Former Confederates constituted the majority of early white western settlers. Seeking freedom from social and economic hierarchies that relegated them to a place barely above African Americans, these men and women saw themselves as fugitives escaping from the reach of an elite class that did not value them as fellow whites.[2] Late nineteenth-century settlers also drew upon a mythology of an all-white West where they could be free from the biased government they felt unfairly upheld Black rights over theirs.[3] Yet southerners who had been firmly invested in a weak federal government, like Arkansan J.C. Gilbreath, found that they could accept federal intervention if it created space for their settlement and economic interests in the West. Gilbreath came from Fayetteville to Oklahoma City in 1892 and worked first for a government contractor, then driving cattle. Though he was unable to secure a claim due to his age, Gilbreath's father and brother both participated in the 1889 Land Run and filed claims for land.[4]

Other settlers, recent immigrants from such European countries as Poland, Ireland, Germany, Russia, and Italy, as well as Asian, Jewish, and Mexican immigrants, conceived of western settlement as the chance to make a place for themselves in the American body politic.[5] George Elexander Lambe was born in Ulster Province, Ireland, and came to the United States with his sister. After arriving in Illinois, Lambe went to Kansas in 1885. But in Kansas he found that the "land was thought to be no good" and "everybody was starving." Searching for a better opportunity, Lambe went by covered wagon to the Unassigned Lands, where he squatted until the Land Run.[6]

Though among themselves the inferiority of nonwhite peoples was already largely assumed, white settlers still used the settler colonial process to rationalize their incursions into Indian Territory, a region their government had promised not to penetrate. Into the late nineteenth and early twentieth centuries, U.S. government officials articulated their biased belief that the West would benefit from white American settlement. The secretary of the interior for several years in the 1880s, Henry M. Teller, captured the changing status of the Five Tribes from civilizers to those who must be civilized. In his annual report for 1884, Secretary Teller wrote, "It may well be questioned whether the Government has adopted a mistaken policy in regarding the Indian tribes as quasi-independent nations, and making treaties with them for the purchase of lands they claim to own. They have none of the elements of nationality; they are within the limits of the recognized authority of the United States, and must be subject to its control. Indeed, whatever may be the theory, the Government has always demanded the removal of Indians where their lands were required for agricultural purposes by advancing settlements."[7]

Teller challenged Indian tribes' status as sovereign nations and stated his belief that Indian removal in any place or time was acceptable to make way for "advancing settlements." In the same report, the secretary of the interior mused that "the time has passed when large and valuable tracts of land fit for agriculture can be held by Indians for either hunting or grazing to the exclusion of actual settlers." That the Five Tribes were no longer considered settlers of some sort in the mind of governmental agents and decision makers was an important and politically expedient transformation. Earlier in the nineteenth century, they had been portrayed as models of civilization for other tribes already present in and arriving to Indian Territory. Yet, at this juncture in the 1880s, Indian involvement in settler colonialism was no longer enough. While "actual" was likely used to separate individuals from corporations and speculators, the term equally works to symbolize the secretary's sentiment: now it was time for the "actual" settlers—individual white Americans—to civilize the West.

The American media had an important hand in advancing this line of thinking that white settlers were needed to truly civilize Indian Territory. Newspapers, particularly the *New York Times*, crafted an image of a dangerous Indigenous West—hence the still-familiar moniker "the wild West"—that needed to be tamed by whites. They proclaimed that Indian Territory was a lawless space where "murder and robbery is an every-day occurrence." Though the media covered all sorts of crimes, it thrived on murders of whites supposedly committed by Indians. In August 1873, the *Times* claimed that eight murders had recently occurred within a two-week period. Among these murders, the paper focused on that of a "German traveler" allegedly shot by two Choctaw men.[8] In 1883, the *Times* reported that the secretary of interior had been notified by an Indian agent at the Ute reservation that Utes had possibly murdered a white man. Upon closer inspection, though, the paper noted that it was possible that this had actually been merely white-on-white crime.[9]

The paper's rush to place blame on a Native suspect is indicative of the white desire to see Native Americans as criminal, inferior, and in need of American intervention. In fact, a *Times* columnist summed up general American sentiment when he wrote that, in Indian Territory, "the worst characters have pretty much their own way, as besides the small United States marshal's force, there is no restraining power. Native jurisdiction is a farce." Posing a rhetorical question, the writer then asked, "How much longer are these things to continue? The Native papers dare not mention these things."[10] Not only was the *Times* rejecting the idea that Native nations had competent governments and police forces, but the paper was also attempting to discredit the journalistic integrity of the territory's Indian newspapers. The settler colonial process involves erasing the existence of prior history, culture, and institutions, and American newspapers played an important role in Native American erasure. Even after the creation of Oklahoma Territory, the narrative stayed the same: the Kentucky paper, the *Daily Public Ledger*, described Indian Territory as an "unprecedented carnival of crime" where "bandits are virtually unmolested in their appalling depredations."[11] According to these columnists, American intervention was needed to reign in Indian misconduct and keep non-Indian settlers safe. Even as a *Times* correspondent admitted that "many of the stories of Indian outrages telegraphed throughout the country are either manufactured with a purpose or grossly exaggerated," stereotypes of Native peoples as lazy or hostile helped create an image of Indian Territory as an unlawful space. Americans then moved themselves in, playing the parts of civilizers and promoters of industry and progress."[12] While white views of Indian Territory were largely shaped by the narratives created and manipulated by American newspapers, the reality on the ground was different.

It was most often whites committing atrocities against Native Americans, Indian freedpeople, and African Americans rather than the other way around. The arc of violence toward people of color in Indian Territory peaked after statehood, when tribal governments had lost much of their power to pressure Americans into responding to them, but violence was always present. Though people of African descent in Indian Territory had a different political and economic trajectory due to land allotment and tribal jurisdiction, when it came to violence due either to race or to others' jealousy of what they owned, Indian Territory was home to the same periodic episodes of physical assault and murder that the North and South were. Indeed, throughout the United States, African Americans dealt with violence during and after Reconstruction.[13] But the violence people of African descent faced in the late 1800s was minor relative to that after statehood. Thirty-three of Oklahoma's forty lynching victims in the statehood era were Black. Comparatively, while Indian Territory and Oklahoma Territory remained, only seventeen of the 110 lynching victims were Black, demonstrating that smaller acts of violence were few and far in between.[14] Still, there were instances before statehood that made evident the intrusion of white supremacist terror into Indian Territory brought by postwar migration.

In 1901, the African Americans living in Centralia, a town within the Cherokee Nation, experienced racial violence when "a number of white men made an attack on the home of a negro named Whitmore . . . [firing] a volley [of gunfire] into the roof of his house and [compelling] his family to fly for safety." The likely reason this act received the attention of the *New York Times*, though, was not this initial attack on a Black man's life. Rather, the *Times* was concerned with the Black response to this act of terrorism. According to the paper, when a "mob" of African Americans "took possession of the town" and demanded they be protected in response to this violence, the white residents barricaded their homes and the police made an arrest, presumably of a Black man, for this unrest.[15] Even the rhetorical framing of lynch mobs and Black anger had now made its way to Indian Territory, erasing the sort of racial exceptionalism that had previously

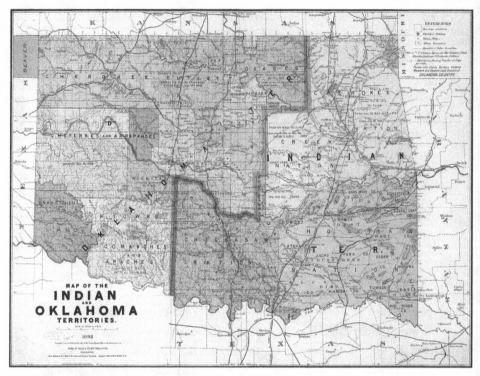

FIGURE 6. Map of the Indian and Oklahoma territories created in 1892. Library of Congress, Geography and Map Division (98687110).

characterized Black life, when Black unrest had been seen as a response to Indian malfeasance. Lynching was a way for white settlers not only to enforce their new claims to Indian Territory land, but also to demonstrate the triumph of white supremacy in this post-emancipation society.

White mob violence in Indian Territory also came for Indians. Perhaps the most famous such incident is known as "Seminole Burning," when, in 1897, white vigilantes burned alive two Seminole men accused of murdering a white woman, Mary Leard, and fatally injuring her child. The true murderer remained unknown at the time, but friends and relatives of the victims resorted to creating two lies to rally community support: first, that there were two perpetrators rather than one, and second, that

Leard had been raped after her killing. In response, a crowd amassed to intimidate, interrogate, and eventually brutally harm Indian men within the Seminole Nation, where Leard and her daughter had resided.[16] Unlike most incidences of torture or murder of Black people, an arrest followed the violence against these Seminole men—in total, the U.S. District Attorney charged 48 persons involved with "complicity," though ultimately only six served time for the crime.[17] While whites were able to use language of racial otherness to provoke anger and extralegal punishment for both African Americans and Native Americans, Native peoples had tribal sovereignty and a system in place to specifically prosecute interracial crimes like this, though it, too, was limited. Although tribes had jurisdiction over crimes committed by and against a tribal citizen and used lighthorsemen to make arrests and police their nations, jurisdictional issues arose when conflicts and crimes occurred between Indians of different tribal nations. In 1885, Congress passed the Major Crimes Act, which made major criminal acts committed by Indians on Indian land federal offenses.[18] After the 1890 creation of Oklahoma Territory and the passage of the Oklahoma Organic Act, law enforcement passed from U.S. military and Indian lighthorsemen to U.S. marshals.

The violent intrusion of white settler colonialism was not only physical—it also took economic and social forms. The railroads introduced large-scale corporate greed into Indian Territory, bringing Indian nations into contact with capitalist behemoths who refused to honor treaties and did not respect Indian property; the railroads also brought individual settlers who served as laborers, and entrepreneurs who strove to serve these laborers and the populations that sprung up around the products of their exertion.[19] Though laborers were often white, Black, Asian, and Mexican, the corporate powers that sanctioned their actions were run by whites and protected by a white American government. During construction, workers often stole Choctaws' animals or killed them through apathy—many were hit by passing trains because the train companies refused to build fences around their right of way. When the Creeks tried to enforce a law that prohibited cutting and selling timber by non-tribal citizens without a permit, railroad employees ignored their jurisdiction.[20] And even though railroad had to pay for the Indian land they built on through stock exchanges, per the Treaties of 1866, this initial purchase meant they then had the built-in ability to also purchase the six miles on either side of the railroad track. This quickly wore away at tribal land holdings.[21]

In some ways tribal governments welcomed, or at least capitalized on, the business brought by the railroads, implementing policies to regulate and tax the sale of construction materials such as timber and stone to the railroad companies.[22] Individual tribespeople often violated tribal law by leasing land to white noncitizens who would then pay (with cash or a portion of their crop) to live on and improve these spaces. Some entrepreneurial Indians even leased land to African American settlers. Joanna Draper and her family moved from Mississippi after emancipation and "leased a little farm from the Creek Nation for $15 an acre," but had to give up this arrangement when allotments were parceled out.[23] Mary Lindsay and her family also leased Creek land for $15 an acre.[24] While this system benefited individuals, it negatively affected tribal sovereignty, as these contracts allowed noncitizens to obtain as much free land as they desired, tax-free. Soon many of these white tenants attempted to exercise rights granted only to tribal citizens, such as hiring noncitizen laborers.[25] Aside from individual settlers undermining Native claims to Indian Territory land, the very existence of these corporations, their products, and their people within Indian nations meant that there was less land for Native peoples to occupy and own, and the social toll these foreign entities had on tribal governments and everyday Native life was significant.[26] Because tribal governments could not police non–tribal citizens, Native peoples often found themselves at the mercy of the American government's court system as well as an American military force sent to restrict white immigration.[27]

The process for dealing with intruders was, as described by U.S. Indian Agent JNO Q. Tufts, "When intruders are reported to this office by the authority of the nations, investigation is made, and if the party [is] found to be an intruder he is notified to remove beyond the limits of this agency at once. If he shall refuse or neglect to do so, the troops are requested to re-move him. If they find him, and remove him across the line to the States, in nine cases out of ten he will return in advance of the troops. They are again called to take the intruder to Fort Smith, to the United States court, where a judgement of $1,000 is entered against him."[28]

Clearly, this process was defective. The story of the Boomer movement best illustrates the limits of both the American courts and military to truly defend Native land and sovereignty. Led by southerner David L. Payne and then William L. Couch, the Boomers were white settlers who illegally settled in Indian Territory from the 1870s through the 1880s. These squat-ters were a constant source of theft and violence for the Native peoples whose lands they squatted on. In 1870, whites near the border of Kansas and Indian Territory assaulted Osage people in an effort to take possession of their land claims. However, American officials refused to arrest these men, for this was not "within official instructions, and would be attended with considerable risk to the officer assuming the responsibility."[29] Even white Americans tasked with the very duty to protect the rights and safety of Indian peoples were not willing to place their safety on the line to do so. In March 1872, the U.S. agent to the Osage reported that, "twenty miles south of the Kansas line, he found hundreds of settlers who informed him that all the good lands for fifteen miles down the river were claimed up; that most of the timber land and valleys are claimed." There were also many white intruders in the Cherokee Nation and "along the lines of the railroad in Indian Territory."[30]

According to the *New York Times*, the Boomers claimed (inaccurately) that the land they wanted to settle within the Unassigned Territories had been ceded (in the Treaties of 1866) and opened to them with the Home-stead Act of 1862, and thus they had "a right to settle and they are greatly wronged by military interferences."[31] The American military had been or-dered to Indian Territory to expel these intruders, but they kept return-ing, and they eventually enlisted the services of a lawyer to fight for their right to the lands they occupied.[32] The Boomers were well-armed with "all kinds of firearms" and "well supplied with horses and wagons," and the

American forces put up paltry resistance, failing to "capture [their] camp." In response to a threat to open fire on them, the Boomers said if they were "driven from the settlement, they will fire the grass, and thus burn all the ranches and destroy all the cattle ranges in the Indian Territory." The *Times* headline referred to the altercations between troops and the Boomers as a "war."[33] Tribal courts could not prosecute Boomers and the U.S. courts would often press charges only of "resisting troops," rather than the initial crime of illegal incursion onto Indian territory.[34]

Even the secretary of the interior lamented that more was not done to staunch the flow of white immigration to Indian Territory and stop corporations from taking advantage of Indian nations, writing in his 1884 report that railroad companies' failure to apply for patents and pay for associated costs [such as taxes] contributed "nothing to the fair support of the burden and revenue of the local [tribal] governments."[35] The *Times* agreed, referring to Boomers as "raiders," and calling for the "land grabbers" to obey the laws.[36] But this didn't mean the paper thought they should indefinitely remain unable to move onto the Unassigned Lands. Rather, the *Times* called for the Boomers to obey the American law only "until the vast areas held by them unlawfully have been opened to the settler." The *Times* was assuredly not against white settlement of Indian land. It was only that the Boomers were not willing to claim Indian land in the way the government had set out for them. They were not willing to follow the regulations set out by whites of a higher social and political status than they, and therefore they were upsetting the settler colonial process and unfairly infringing on the ability of other whites to claim Indian property. But because this process was ultimately designed to ensure that whites always won access to Indian land, the Boomers' repeated attempts wore down the American government's commitment to the regulations they had promised to Native peoples, and with the 1889 Land Run in the previous Unassigned Lands and the creation of Oklahoma Territory shortly after, whites triumphed in legalizing their illegal actions. At this point in the chronology of Indian Territory, Boomers and squatters were occupying land that was claimed by both Native peoples and Indian freedpeople, though freedpeople's claims were rarely mentioned in this context. On this larger stage, in the battle between Native nations and white American settlers, people of African descent were far from the primary focus, and their claims, which had previously been enough to offset a degree of Indians' ownership, were insignificant in the face of American support of white settlers. This is evident in their invisibility in most of these newspaper accounts and editorials.

With this act, the U.S. government sanctioned not just Native land loss but also the loss of many Native peoples' and Indian freedpeople's ability to live freely and provide for themselves—and in this regard the Five Tribes actually suffered the least. William Foster, a chief of the Sac and Fox, a tribe that had been removed from Kansas to Oklahoma, described his tribe's life as "easy" in Indian Territory. That is, until "the opening" of the Unassigned Lands. After this, he said,

> Indians began dying out fast. Plagues took many of them, and other sicknesses took others until there are few left of our tribe. Before the opening cattlemen had five or six big ranches on this reservation, and many cattle and horses were pastured here. They were forced to leave, however, to make room for the white settler. The cattle were driven west through Fort Dodge and beyond. The broad ranges were gone. The Indian's freedom was gone; the wild game and abundant fish were no more. Soon the Indians were again without land, or they were being taxed. Money became scarce, and the tribe began to feel the sensations of hunger and cold. Our customs are dying fast. It will not be long before out tribe will be no more. The older Indians foresaw this. They said this would be our last move, our last stopping place. We would scatter, intermarry with whites, and become poor.[37]

Foster provides a bleak treatise on the effects of the settler colonial process. The Five Tribes certainly suffered from the change in demographics, but less so than Plains peoples and other removed tribes, who did not have the protection brought by the Five Tribes' wealth and influence.

Though physical violence and illegal settlement characterized many of the interactions between whites and Native peoples in Indian Territory, even when whites engaged in relationships ostensibly in cooperation with Native peoples, social or economic violence often followed. While most white Americans believed that tribal sovereignty was null and void, making them the rightful inhabitants of the West, some whites were willing to work within the frameworks of Indian nations to benefit themselves. One way of doing this was to marry a tribal citizen, which, at different points in the Five Tribes' history, endowed upon the intermarried white person different degrees of rights to communal tribal land and political participation. The changes in these rights reflected the ever-evolving landscape of white intrusion and American–tribal relations.

Initially, from the 1700s to the early 1800s, intermarried white men had few rights of their own within the Five Tribes because they had no matrilineal clan, though they had the option of adoption, and their mixed-race progeny often rose to high positions of tribal leadership because of their mothers' connections.[38] But as the nineteenth century progressed, intermarried white men in the Cherokee Nation—the majority of intermarried spouses—gained the right to vote and to improve communally owned lands, though they still could not hold high office nor would they receive annuity funds, and they lost their citizenship if their Native partner died or remarried.[39] In 1834, several commissioners of Indian affairs warned both their white superiors and Native peoples that these whites were, in their opinion, the greatest danger Native peoples faced. They spoke of whites who used Indian nations to hide from American justice for crimes committed, or, inversely, who committed crimes within Indian nations and then escaped by moving back into the United States. They also mentioned white traders, claiming, "The passage of the trappers through the Indian villages is marked by a long train of woes entailed by debauchery and disease upon illicit connexion."[40]

Apparently some Cherokees agreed that intermarried whites exercised outsize influence, since by 1840 several council members sought to completely prohibit any marriage between whites and Native women. This law did not pass, but through the 1840s and 1850s the Cherokees continued to revise their regulations regarding intermarriage. In 1843, the National Council decided that whites wishing to marry into the nation must apply for a license and renounce their allegiance to any other government; in 1846, the council ruled that widowed whites could remain citizens as long as they did not subsequently marry a white person. The 1855 intermarriage act added the additional rigorous requirement that white prospective marriage partners must obtain oaths and testimonials of their worthiness from members of the tribe and pay a large sum.[41]

While these nuptials may have been motivated by true love and affection, many of them were inspired by far more practical desires: to cull land and other resources from Indian citizens. Intermarried whites actively expanded their landholdings in the Cooweescoowee district of the Cherokee Nation by making improvements and claiming land. Through the late 1800s, they joined noncitizen ranch hands, tenants overstaying their leases, and other laborers (both white and Black Americans) who desired to exploit the Cherokee Nation and other Indian nations to some degree.[42] Tribal officials reacted to this issue. In their Treaty of 1866, the Choctaws and Chickasaws ensured that they included a provision: "Every white person who, having married a Choctaw or Chickasaw, resides in the said Choctaw or Chickasaw nation, or who has been adopted by the legislative authorities is to be deemed a member of said nation, and shall be subject to the laws . . . and prosecution and trials before their tribunals, and to punishment according to their laws in all respects as though he was a native Choctaw or Chickasaw."[43]

While this protected the rights of whites within the nation, it also was a safeguard put into place by these two nations, establishing that they could punish intermarried whites with their laws, in their courts. The Chickasaws also wrote laws into their constitution that taxed noncitizens living in their nation, required them to apply for a permit, and, after 1898, did not allow marriage between a citizen of the United States and a Chickasaw citizen until the American citizen applied to the probate judge of the court of his residence for a license, proved to the judge that his "character and habits" were satisfactory, and then received from the judge a license to marry under the laws of the Chickasaw Nation. For this license the American citizen would pay $600, the primary balance of which would "be placed in the National Treasury."[44]

Despite these requirements, by 1900 there were around 200,000 recorded whites living legally as spouses or land lessees in the Five Tribes— and many more squatting illegally.[45] As the Dawes Commission went about their task of enrollment, they noted that generally "Indian Territory has been overrun by white people," creating an environment where "crime is rampant, the timber, the coal, and the land are monopolized by a few to the detriment of the many, [and] large towns have been built up by the whites."[46] The commissioners also specifically mentioned that there were "many cases" where intermarried whites had abandoned their spouse or experienced the death of their spouse but then surfaced in an attempt to enroll for a land allotment.[47] The commission included examples of this fraud, such as that of F. R. Robinson, who, in 1896, applied to the Dawes Commission to be enrolled as an intermarried citizen. In 1873, Robinson had married a woman of Choctaw and Chickasaw ancestry and had five children with her. But after his wife died, Robinson married again, this time to a white woman, with whom he still lived. The Dawes Commission accepted his enrollment, since Robinson had once been married to an Indian woman, but the Choctaw Nation appealed, arguing that Robinson "has not shown by his evidence that he has not forfeited his rights as such citizen by abandonment or remarriage."[48]

All of the Five Tribes, but particularly the Chickasaw and Choctaw Nations, launched many such legal appeals. The disagreements between the Indian nations and the Dawes Commission over whether a white person's divorce from their Native spouse terminated their citizenship rights spawned the term "court claimants" or "court people" to refer to these white enrollees, because when they won the right to place their names on the Dawes rolls it was through the will of the U.S. courts, rather than Indian nations.[49] In one of his addresses to the Chickasaw Legislature, Governor D. H. Johnston spoke of this issue ruefully: "These 'Court people' do not look like Indians. They do not act like Indians, and have none of the features or attributes of Indians. They are white people from the hillsides of the surrounding states, and would be so declared by any intelligent jury of citizens from any state in the Union. When the law of 1896 was passed they speculated as to the possibilities of acquiring allotments of land. They heeded the beacon. They determined to take the chances, adopted the means here described, and these judgements resulted."[50]

Choctaw Chief Gilbert W. Dukes would give similar remarks the next year in front of the Choctaw legislature. Though the Chickasaws and Choctaws had successfully appealed many of these rulings, saving, in the words of Johnston, "millions" of dollars, they had still taken a substantial hit in the legitimacy of their rolls, and therefore had been forced to distribute annuities and land allotments to those not rightfully owed them.[51]

As we have discussed, on a much smaller scale, Indian freedpeople similarly dealt with a contingent of calculating spouses looking to avail themselves of their resources. While most of these partners were Black, one of my family stories may suggest that there were some whites willing to cross the color line. A white settler named Calvin Jackson shaped our family's maternal line. Wandering into town around 1871, Calvin impregnated Lydia Jackson, who would give birth to Josie Jackson. Learning that their allotments possessed no extraordinary wealth, Calvin soon left, leaving Lydia a divorcée and Josie a fatherless child. Statehood would exacerbate the issues of intermarriage and fraud in the Five Tribes, as well as those of resource exploitation and allocation.

While allotment and statehood would forever change the circumstances of all the peoples present in the West, the transformation of Indian Territory (along with a portion of land formerly claimed by Texas and Arkansas) into the state of Oklahoma did not occur overnight or without active resistance from Native peoples. White politicians and businessmen had long used the argument that Native peoples deserved citizenship (as a reward for civilized behavior) or needed citizenship (to become civilized) as a way to establish territorial governments and states that absorbed and taxed Native peoples destroyed, or at least weakened, tribal sovereignty.[52] After the issuance of the Emancipation Proclamation, and during Reconstruction as Republicans announced their intentions to pass legislation that would allow for Black equality, arguments for Native American citizenship took on a new dimension. For instance, one *Times* writer advocated for allotment and white settlement on "leftover lands." He framed his motivations as altruistic, because he alleged that "the loyal members of these nations [in Indian Territory] are fully as capable of using the ballot as are the majority of the white men of Arkansas and Missouri." In this writer's mind, white migration and settlement made clear the path to eventual statehood and inclusion of Native peoples as part of the American body politic. After all, he continued, "it is certainly more in accord with the spirit of our institutions, that so far and fast as practicable, those who are part of our population should be elevated to and accorded the privileges of American nationality."[53] Now that the sentiment of the times was on the side of increasing inclusion of people of African descent, Native Americans were swept into the resurgence of a discussion about their potential for citizenship that had not been seen since the advent of the "civilization" policy in the 1700s.[54] Unfortunately, these supposed "privileges of American nationality" came at the cost of the privileges of Native autonomy and tribal sovereignty. As early as the 1840s, the U.S. Congress considered a bill that would unite all of Indian Territory under one territorial government. This attempt brought tribes together to fight it, which they did successfully. Peter Pitchlynn persuasively convinced Congress that "dissolving the national boundaries of Indian Territory's tribes would violate every one of their removal treaties and would, therefore, undermine the legality of those agreements."[55] Later, the Five Tribes would not be so fortunate.

After the war, as American immigration to Indian Territory increased, so did discussions about the possibility of statehood. The 1887 Dawes Act and the 1889 Land Run built on the Treaties of 1866 in signaling that not only was Indian land to be allotted, and not only was settlement going to be opened to whites, but Indian Territory was going to be absorbed into the United States and Indian nations must get on board. While the Dawes Act specified that Indian peoples whose land was allotted would then become citizens of the United States, the Five Tribes were exempt from this act due to their powerful lobbies. Instead, the United States tried to get these nations to voluntarily vote to take part in allotment.[56] Various factions within these tribes either actively protested involvement in this process or set out to prove to their fellow tribespeople that it would be beneficial to them; some who started out protesting eventually conceded in the face of unending, enormous pressure from the American government.

Protest took different forms: while some Native women and men vowed to never take part in the allotment process on account of each individual Indian nation's tribal sovereignty, others protested through a pan-Indian lens by reinvigorating an earlier idea for an all-Native territory or state where Indians would determine land settlement and citizenship.[57] The makings of this alliance between the Five Tribes and some Plains peoples go back to the post-Removal period, when Indian Territory nations met together to try to end raids and mistrust.[58] While this was largely unsuccessful, this history formed the foundation of intertribal political efforts in the late nineteenth century. The Treaties of 1866 had required that the tribes in Indian Territory meet in a council to discuss eventual consolidation into a territorial government. Instead, Native leaders used this as a venue at which to plan their opposition to it.[59] In 1870, the Cherokee, Creek, Seminole, Ottawa, Eastern Shawnee, Quapaw, Seneca, Wyandot, Osage, Peoria, Sac and Fox, and Absentee Shawnee Nations held a conference in Okmulgee (Creek Nation), where they first seriously raised the idea of forming a united government. Delegates created a model for a constitution, a court system, and a form of government. But when it came time for the Indian nations to ratify the constitution, not all of the tribes present would agree to do so. From the 1870s to the 1890s the council continued to meet but could not agree on a constitution, though most representatives agreed that they did not want the Dawes Commission to have the authority to determine allotment and tribal citizenship.[60]

For smaller tribes like the Choctaws and Chickasaws, the idea of a unified Indian government was unpalatable because they felt their interests would be less served. Going into the twentieth century, the two nations refused to believe they would truly be written out of tribal sovereignty, and they tried to argue that their removal treaties along with the Treaty of 1866 guaranteed them perpetual autonomy even through allotment.[61] In fact, the Chickasaws and Choctaws had been the first of the Five Tribes to agree to have their lands surveyed and allotted directly after signing their Treaty of 1866, believing that individual landownership was the key to maintaining tribal sovereignty. Choctaw Chief Peter Pitchlynn and Chickasaw Governor Winchester Colbert declared that "if we had held our land in this manner before the war, we would have been now under no necessity to have parted with an acre of them."[62] This may have been mere wishful thinking on the part of these tribal leaders, but it demonstrates that some in the Five Tribes had still not yet grasped that no degree of involvement in the settler colonial process was going to save their nations from enduring hardship and impairment. The final attempt by Native nations to turn Indian Territory into an all-Indian nation occurred at the Sequoyah Convention in 1905. Reflecting the divisions between Indian peoples regarding this decision, Chickasaw Governor D. H. Johnston did not attend—another Chickasaw tribal leader appeared in his stead. Even with the rare agreement between all of the Five Tribes, the U.S. Congress refused to even consider the proposal. However, representatives from the Five Tribes were present at the Constitutional Convention for Oklahoma state and influenced decisions made about statutes and symbols.[63] American newspapers delighted in proclaiming that the convention celebrated influential Indian leaders of the past, even displaying portraits of a select few.[64]

The Dawes Act was the legislation that formally introduced the reality of allotment of Native lands in North America. But it was the 1898 Curtis Act that followed up on the promise made in the Treaties of 1866 by ensuring that this process of allotment and absorption would be carried out in Indian Territory, thereby nullifying tribal courts and legislation and extending American citizenship to all Native peoples in the region. Despite concepts put forth for an all-Black state or an all-Indian state, the settler colonial process ultimately won. In 1907, the union of the Oklahoma and Indian Territories was marked with a performance: a mixed-race Cherokee

FIGURE 7. Great Seal of the state
of Oklahoma.

woman (representing Indian Territory) and the white chairman of Oklahoma Territory's statehood committee (representing, of course, Oklahoma Territory) enacted a marriage ceremony to represent the inextricable bond with which these two regions, artificially carved out of Native peoples' land by the United States, became the 46th state to enter the American union.[65]

Though unwilling to see them as the permanent, rightful owners of the land or even as equal partners in diplomacy, white settlers were eager to use Native peoples as representations of this new state. This sort of representation is a part of the settler colonial process—as the actual prior residents diminish in number and in influence, they become important symbols of the settler colonial state's past. The Oklahoma state seal is a veritable smorgasbord of symbolism starting with the very method by which it came to be: the idea for the seal was taken from that proposed by representatives of the Five Tribes at the Sequoyah Convention. Literally and metaphorically, this new state was created from that which was taken from the Native peoples of Indian Territory.

On the seal, the Five Tribes make up a five-pointed star (representing one of the stars that symbolize each individual American state on the American flag), with each point of the star encapsulating each Indian nation's seal. In the middle of the star, inside a wreath, a Native man wearing the headdress of a Plains Indian shakes the hand of a white man in front of a figure of blind Justice, symbolizing equality for the two races. Perhaps most telling of all, above Justice's head are the Latin words "Labor Omnia Vincit," which translate to "labor conquers all things." Reflecting white settlers' belief that hard work, rather than support of the settler colonial process, led to their success, the adage is an interesting juxtaposition to the state's modern-day colloquial name, "the Sooner State," which honors those who refused to abide by legal and moral rules requiring them to wait to stake their claim to land during the 1889 Land Run.

With statehood came many profound changes for people of Native and African descent. But one thing that stayed the same—or actually worsened—was white economic exploitation. By 1895 speculators had located the major petroleum and natural-gas fields within several of the Five Tribes but largely failed to realize their vast potential; this would take several more years. White settlers would exploit these resources through the use of a new tool: guardianship.[66] Land allotment carried with it distinctions between different "classes" of people. Indian freedpeople received less land than those deemed Indians, but even among Indians there was an important difference imposed after allotment was processed: one's supposed racial identity determined the actions they could take with regard to their land. After many arguments, hearings, testimonies, and letters between politicians, tribal citizens, reformers, and speculators, white American legislators decided that those Indians deemed "full-blooded" were barred from the ability to "alienate, sell, dispose of, or encumber in any manner" the entirety of their allotment for 25 years after the passage of the 1906 Five Tribes Act (until 1931). During this period, their allotments were also not taxed.[67] This was a way to paternalistically protect them from swindlers and force them to learn the ways of yeoman agriculture.[68] Mixed-race persons of white and Indian descent and freedpeople did not have the same extent of protection: women and men of mixed white and Indian descent and freedpeople had their allotments portioned into a forty-acre "homestead" and a "surplus." The homestead portion had the same restrictions as those for "full-bloods" for 21 years, whereas the surplus could be sold and taxed after only five years. These policies enacted allegedly to protect Indian women, men, and freedpeople often hurt them, because the policies meant that for varying periods of time they could not sell or mortgage parts of their allotments to raise capital and so were cash-poor and could not improve their land. Thus, many of them ended up simply leasing their land to cattle grazers.[69] The land-speculation lobby succeeded in getting any restrictions on freedpeople's ability to sell, lease, and pay taxes on their allotments completely removed by 1908.[70]

Schemes to defraud Native members of the Five Tribes, particularly those who could not read, write, or speak fluent English, began with the very process of selecting allotments. "Grafters," as historian Angie Debo calls them, would ensure that these Indians received plum surplus allotments—as these could be sold the soonest—by financing their transport to and from the allotment office and coaching them on which allotment locations were preferable based on the sorts of natural resources available there or whether the grafter already held a possessory title or lease to this land. The Indian woman or man would then be left with no allotment or with an arrangement where they would receive a pittance doled out to them monthly or yearly. Another plot involved lumber dealers who would help Choctaws select allotments and then purchase the abundant timber on their land for "a grossly inadequate consideration," leaving the allottee with land that now had little value.[71]

Indians and freedpeople on whose land significant resources were found had guardians appointed to them by the federal court to assist in executing business related to their allotments.[72] If oil or other natural resources were found on these owners' land, their guardians could pick and choose among companies that wanted to extract it and keep much of the profit for themselves, making sure to give the landowners only the bare minimum. White civilians as well as lawyers, civil servants, and government-mandated caretakers hurried to take advantage of these Black and Native women, men, and children who were often illiterate or did not speak or write fluent English. As such, they were prime victims for clever crooks who had the backing of a settler colonialist government in deceiving these people into signing away their valuable land and mineral rights.[73]

A number of resource-rich land allotments had been given to Indian freedpeople, as they often appeared infertile and undesirable or were in locations where freedpeople had long settled.[74] But when oil became a huge industry, white speculators devised ways to part these Black women and men from their land or their mineral rights.[75] Adam Doyle was an Indian freedman around 90 years of age when it was discovered that his land allotment held underneath it a large and profitable amount of oil. Though Doyle was assigned a guardian because he was "insane" and therefore "incompetent to make a deed or a contract," his guardian was either inept or crooked, as under his care Doyle apparently made a disastrous agreement after being approached by a number of businessmen. Though his guardian lodged a suit to recover his lands on the grounds of his incompetency, the court allowed Doyle's initial agreement, which provided him barely any compensation, to stand on the grounds that "he is a man of unsound mind, but capable of some understanding." This was a clear equivocation, meant to honor only, as the paper referred to them, the "soulless white individuals and corporations which secured his lands under deeds and contracts which he as an insane man signed."[76]

Other Black and Native peoples were left with nothing after individual white Americans or the economic systems inaugurated by Oklahoma statehood finished with them. Morris Sheppard said that he "lost [his] land trying to live honest and pay [his] debts."[77] Mary Nevins, a Cherokee freedwoman, had been taken to Texas during the war and returned after emancipation. She suffered the loss of most of her family members to cholera and then ended up losing her land as well, saying, "We had an allotment but it's all gone now. I had forty acres surplus in the oil belt but it's all gone now." For Nevins and many other Indian freedpeople, life was different after statehood. Nevins had previously had "no trouble making a livin, but now [she had] nothing. . . . Used to be plenty of game and tall prairie grass but there ain't nothin now . . . there ain't nothin now."[78] Fannie Rentie Chapman had a similar story but provided more details of her travails. Chapman's parents came from Alabama to Indian Territory as the slaves of a Creek woman, along the way witnessing the deaths of tens of Black and Native women and men in a steamboat sinking. Chapman drew her allotment "three miles north of Boynton" and lived there until 1933, when she was "finally swindled out of the property by loan companies, individuals, and people in whom I had misplaced confidence." Chapman's use of the word "finally" gives the sense that this loss was the result of a protracted legal battle or perhaps repeated attempts by these companies to deceive her into signing away her land. She also may have fallen into debt, unable to pay her property taxes. Chapman's life in Indian Territory had changed for the worse after white settlement had become permanent. In remembering her childhood days in the Creek Nation, Chapman said, "I have seen great herds of deer grazing in the dells near the timber. . . . I have seen the prairie chickens, so common they would come into the yard with our ten chickens. . . . In those days all the little streams were clear, clean of filth and uncontaminated, and inhabited by every variety of fresh water fish in abundance, which proved no problem for the native to supply himself."[79]

Chapman and Nevins describe twentieth-century Oklahoma, then, as the absence of these things—a wealth of food and wild animals, cleanliness and a lack of contamination, and even ownership. Before statehood and the sustained white presence in Indian Territory of the post-1880s, the land that Indian freedpeople obtained through the Treaties of 1866 and the Dawes Act substantially changed their lives. Through a study in which she focused only on Cherokee freedpeople, economist Melinda Miller found that they were five times more likely than Blacks in the South to own a farm in 1880, which was a measure not just of their income but also their ability to accumulate general wealth. This economic autonomy and success allowed for their children to obtain upward mobility, leading the children of Cherokee freedpeople to have "higher levels of human capital accumulation than Black children in both the South and the territories. They are more likely to attend school, attend for a greater number of months, and have higher literacy."[80] In addition to the economic foundation basic landownership provided, some Indian freedpeople found that their allotments were rich with minerals or agricultural abundance. These resources gave them a foundation upon which to accrue long-term wealth and funds to send their children to school. Education gave these children literacy and the opportunity to access better jobs. This cycle then had more likelihood of continuing into the next generation. Freedpeople's presence in Indian nations played an important part in their ability to access education, as all but the Chickasaw freedpeople had some provided for them by the Indian nations in which they lived (in addition to those they provided for themselves, often in conjunction with a religious organization), and this education likely facilitated their higher rate of political literacy into the late nineteenth century. The land the U.S. government had taken from Native peoples to give to Indian freedpeople in their mission to minimize Indian land holdings made more than an economic difference: it created an upwardly mobile social class of Black and mixed-race women and men in Oklahoma. These freedpeople then built and invested in towns like Boley, Oklahoma City, and Tulsa.

White settlement affected Indian freedpeople's and African Americans' landownership in a different way, as well—one that demonstrates the insidious nature of the settler colonial process. Because white farmers refused to include them in farming cooperatives, African American farmers did not homestead alone. To support one another, they settled near each other's farms. But this had negative long-term effects: their farms were smaller and more intensely farmed than white-owned farms. They were often "located in clusters on marginal lands," that then suffered from ills like erosion. Soon, their farming completely depleted their soil and they could no longer support themselves from the fruits of their land. This left them with little money to invest in mechanized farming—which allowed white farmers to become more prosperous—and often led Black farmers to hire themselves out to white farmers as sharecroppers.[81] Land could not always protect people of African descent from the racism and exclusion brought by the new settlers, and the American government was not willing to mitigate these effects.

Across North America, corporations, court-appointed guardians, and lawyers used the cover of the law to defraud and fleece Black and Native peoples and tribal governments of land and money.[82] Taxation was another way to separate women and men from their land. Allotments through the Dawes Act were originally untaxable, but after the restriction on selling was lifted, the restriction on taxation followed, so many people lost their land because they were unable to pay taxes or because they did not understand that they now had to pay taxes. Their land would then be put up for sale in the local newspaper for anyone who could pay the taxes on it.[83] The confluence of forces that emerged in the late nineteenth- and early twentieth-century Indian Territory—American settlement, corporate requisition, and an insistence on individualism, even as it fed growing economic inequality—changed the lives of Native and Black peoples in many ways.

Tribal governments no longer had the ability to intervene on their citizens' behalf because their courts had been taken away and their sovereignty disabled. In addition to the Dawes and Curtis Acts, another important piece of legislation in the transformation of Indian Territory into Oklahoma was the Five Tribes Act of 1906. This act transferred oversight of tribal schools from tribal governments to the secretary of the interior, allowed the entrance of numerous American corporations (such as light and power companies) into the region, and gave the American government the ability to select the tribal leader of Indian nations in the region (in certain circumstances) and control most tribal financial matters.[84] With tribal governments no longer able to play as active a part in Native peoples' economic, political, and social lives, the Oklahoma state legislature immediately set out to disembowel the unique properties of this formerly Native-controlled space—foremost, the autonomy for Native people and a select group of Black people. American laws of segregation and racialized policing replaced tribal rights for Indian freedpeople and limited some Native peoples' political participation.

The very first article of the state constitution provided for separate schools for Black and white children, stating that despite language regarding provisions for schools "open to all the children of the State," in fact, "this should not be construed to prevent the establishment and maintenance of separate schools for white and colored children."[85] Most schools in Indian Territory had been segregated (children of African descent were sent to one school that received fewer resources, while white and Native children were sent to another), so this language allowed for the continuation of this practice. This particular way of separating children continued after statehood because, in a state so defined by its Native presence, whiteness had a unique property: it could encapsulate Indianness, if it so chose. The constitution specified that for the purposes of education, colored "shall be construed to mean children of African descent. The term 'white children' shall include all other children."[86] In practice, this meant that in most other contexts—political rights, access to public and private spaces—Native peoples, as well as Asian, Mexican, mixed Native and white, and other non-Black peoples, were included in this definition of white. On the other hand, Oklahoma did not account for people of mixed Black heritage—they were all subsumed within this category of "colored," making Oklahoma the first state to legally define a "one-drop rule." It was not until 1924 that Virginia, often touted as a pioneer in this regard, would draft its own "one-drop rule."[87] So was Oklahoma seeing the arrival of the American post-Reconstruction racial order? Or was it helping to create it, demonstrating that the West sometimes led the way in producing racial demarcation and hierarchy?

Although Oklahoma's original constitution followed the Fifteenth Amendment's guarantee of suffrage for all men regardless of race, three years later an amendment that became known as the "Grandfather Clause" attempted to restrict this aspect of citizenship. The language of the clause: "No person shall be registered as an elector of this State or be allowed to vote in any election herein, unless he be able to read and write any section of the constitution of the State of Oklahoma; but no person who was, on January 1, 1866, or at any time prior thereto, entitled to vote under any form of government, or who at that time resided in some foreign nation, and no lineal descendant of such person, shall be denied the right to register and vote because of his inability to so read and write sections of such constitution."[88]

The clause, then, required that a voter be literate (reading and writing), but it could also be interpreted in a way that allowed voting officials to disallow anyone who had not memorized the entire state constitution—allowing them to "read and write any section" of the document. In this way, the constitution discriminated against Black people, as many people of African descent in this period were illiterate. Many illiterate whites were rescued by the fact that their parents or earlier ancestors were likely able to vote before 1866, and if they were not, they were likely living in a foreign nation. These two clauses specifically allowed political participation for whites who had long been in the United States, as well as recent immigrants classified as white, while purposely excluding people of African descent whose ancestors would have either been enslaved before 1866 or likely illiterate. Clearly, this was a racialized piece of legislation. This clause was struck down by the U.S. Supreme Court in *Guinn v. United States* in 1915, but following this loss the state imposed rigorous registration processes with waiting periods for Black voters that still often kept them from being able to vote.[89]

With statehood, the United States abandoned the gains they had engineered for Indian freedpeople (just as they had done with African Americans in the United States), resulting in many of these gains being taken back by the settler colonial state. The *Topeka Plaindealer*, a Black newspaper, made apparent the change that had occurred. In 1910, it declared the Creek Nation, of all the Five Tribes, to possess the "densest Negro population."[90] The paper reported that the large Black population in Muskogee had enabled an African American, Archie Johnson, to represent the county on the Republican State Committee after statehood. However, the paper went on, the introduction of the Grandfather Clause in 1911 eliminated this African American representative and curbed Black political participation in general.[91] Thus, the *Topeka Plaindealer* made clear that Creek freedpeople, who previously had represented a unique example of economic, social, and political success that continued past the traditional timeline of U.S. Reconstruction, now faced straits similar to African Americans in the American South.

African Americans' and Indian freedpeople's issues also extended to
their social lives. Through segregation, Indian freedpeople in the Cherokee, Creek, Seminole, and Choctaw Nations lost the rights tribal governments had granted them, and so the extended period of Reconstruction
that Indian freedpeople had navigated as they sought kinship, land, and
belonging in Indian Territory now ended. This experiment in Reconstruction was put into place by the U.S. government and it was ended by
the U.S. government. The very first law introduced in the state legislature
(Senate Bill 1) detailed the creation of separate facilities for drinking (water fountains), waiting (waiting rooms), and traveling (railroad cars). In
the 1890s, Bert Luster, a Black immigrant from Watson County, Tennessee, had come to Oklahoma Territory and become "a prosperous farmer,"
winning a blue ribbon at a cotton contest in Guthrie, Oklahoma. Through
"being a good Democrat," Luster was well-liked and got a job as "a clerk
on the Agriculture Board at the State Capitol."[92] While Luster's continued political participation may have been allowed, since he voted for the
Democratic party, for the majority of people of African descent—Indian
freedpeople and Black American migrants alike—segregation meant a
significant change in quality of life. The last wave of immigrants to this
western space cared deeply about creating and enforcing the racial hierarchy of the settler colonial state that had previously been relatively lax in
Indian Territory.

While the Oklahoma Territory legislature gave each county the option
to segregate (an offer that nearly all of them accepted), this change did not
affect Indian freedpeople in the Cherokee, Creek, Seminole, and Choctaw Nations, who still fell under the jurisdiction of their respective Indian
nations.[93] It was only with statehood that they felt a true difference, for
the worse, in their lives. On the other hand, Chickasaw freedpeople were
the only Indian freedpeople whose rights were not diminished from the
change in jurisdiction that followed statehood. As residents of the Chickasaw Nation, they had possessed no rights, but as official American citizens
living in the state of Oklahoma, they had the presence of national constitu-

tional legislation that gave them equality and enfranchisement, in theory, and the hope that these would once again be realized. Such hope for similar legislation from the Chickasaw Nation had long petered out. Because Chickasaw freedpeople had the least to lose, they gained the most from statehood—though, certainly, an existence lived underneath the thumb of Jim Crow was not the American intervention Chickasaw freedpeople had hoped for.

The records of William H. Murray, a close friend of the Chickasaw Nation and the white husband of a Chickasaw woman, may elucidate the feelings of Native peoples, or at least their white allies, about some of these new restrictions put upon Black people in Oklahoma. After a Harvard student wrote in 1915 to Murray inquiring about the circumstances surrounding the installment of the Grandfather Clause, he wrote back that it was due to "the large Negro population in the state" which was a result of "certain Republican politicians" inducing them to come to the region, promising them "franchise, office, and everything else" there. According to Murray, part of the problem that prompted this clause was that these African Americans "were not scattered over the state." Rather, they settled in "certain congested centers, where they elected the school boards for whites as well as themselves, [and] township and county officers." Murray was very clear that the Grandfather Clause was necessary to "eliminate [African Americans] so as to prevent their control of local affairs." In other parts of his reply, Murray denounced Black property ownership and stated his belief—shared by many Democrats of the time (and, indeed, a significant number of Republicans)—that the Black vote was "controlled by prominent white men for whom they are working" or "bought outright," all the while liberally peppering his letter with derogatory slurs.[94] During his lifetime, Murray served as a lawyer to the Chickasaw tribe, as the president to the Constitutional Convention, as an Oklahoma state representative (as a Democrat), and as governor of Oklahoma from 1931 to 1935.[95] While he was not Chickasaw, the fact that Murray worked closely with many influential tribal leaders as he campaigned for political office on racist platforms would seem to demonstrate the extent of continued anti-Black racism present in Indian nations.

What Murray does not note is that some Indians were politically disenfranchised in a similar way by statehood and discriminatory legislation like the Grandfather Clause. As the clause focused on literacy, it caught in its web many Indian men who could not read or write English fluently— and, of course, their forebears had not been able to vote (or interested in voting) prior to 1866. In addition, while the state constitution specified that other languages could be taught in schools, other venues, like election polling stations, did not cater to non–English speakers.

While the segregation and political oppression introduced through statehood were real issues for Black and Native people, these changes did not immediately and necessarily manifest in an uptick in physical violence. In many spaces, Black, white, Native, and Chinese people learned to coexist. Mrs. John Hawkins remembered an Oklahoma where Black, Native, Chinese, and white people had cultural spheres that were open to others. Her parents were Black immigrants from Texas, and in the 1890s Hawkins attended Fourth of July celebrations and stomp dances held by Chickasaws, observed white square dances, and patronized Chinese laundromats.[96] John Luther Branchcomb (a white man) had never met an Indian before he moved from Illinois to Indian Territory. But once there, he was surprised to find that after being "deceived" by a number of people, his first real friend was George Houston, an Indian man. According to Branchcomb, Houston had shown himself to be "a true friend through every trial and a near friend in times of sickness and death." It is doubtful that this friendship completely changed Branchcomb's thinking about Indians, as he referred to Houston as an Indian with "something good about him," perhaps implying that this is what other Indians lacked, but the interactions white, Black, and Native people had in this multiracial space sometimes allowed them to cross racial lines in an egalitarian way that was not often the case in the segregated South.[97]

Residents of the Black town of Boley, Oklahoma, reportedly had "cordial" relationships with whites in neighboring towns; they traded with each other and stayed in each other's hotels overnight. White residents even utilized Boley's railroad station to have their goods shipped to them, exhibiting feelings of trust between the two groups.[98] The town of Tatums, Oklahoma formed from a core group of mixed-race families, and was different from most of the other Oklahoma Black towns in that it was not built near a railroad station, nor was it touted as a utopian destination. Located in Carter County within the Chickasaw Nation, Tatums included log cabins made of mud and shingled roofs, various craftsmen, a subscription school, a Baptist church, and a significant amount of oil beneath its surface. Like the residents of Boley, those of Tatums also found that their relationships with white settlers were largely complementary before the 1920s. Their self-segregation removed the propensity for everyday interracial hostility that might lead to violence.[99] Cora Gillam, in fact, believed that Oklahoma was not encumbered by the racialized violence that many Blacks in the South dealt with. Gillam said that "the Ku Kluxers never bothered us in the least. I think they worked mostly out in [the South]. We used to hear terrible tales of how they whipped and killed, both white and black, for no reason at all. Everybody was afraid of them, and scared to go out after dark."[100] Gillam's correlation of violence only with the KKK and only in the South is indicative perhaps of Black Oklahomans' desire to differentiate themselves from the experiences of African Americans.[101] But this did not completely stave off racial violence from the outside world nor did it stop the tide of time from overtaking and changing the relationships between residents of Oklahoma. Outbursts of violence occurred in Berwyn, Oklahoma in 1895, and on December 24, 1907, whites in Henryetta used the alleged murder of a white man by two Black men (one who carried out the crime and another who supposedly hired him to do so) as an excuse to take "guns, rocks, anything and everything" and use them to "run the negros out of town. From that day on there hasn't been a negro stay in town [over] night."[102] With that, white citizens in the new state began creating sundown towns that restricted Black women and men's movements.

Although the KKK was active in the West and served as a living, breathing representation of the exportation of white southern racism to

Indian Territory, Oklahoma escaped the Red Summer of 1919 (a year that saw lynchings and mass destructions of Black property by whites in places like Chicago, Atlanta, Omaha, and Montgomery) without a large incident of racial violence.[103] But as the twentieth century went on, Oklahoma became a hotbed of white racial resentment, primarily revolving around Black and Indian economic gains through natural resources found on their land allotments. In 1921, the overlapping claims made to Oklahoma land by whites, Indians, and people of African descent were a powder keg that exploded in a brutal episode of mass racial terrorism in Tulsa. First an Osage hunting ground and then a Creek town, pre–Civil War Tulsa's production of petroleum had been a source of annoyance for Native settlers, seeping into water holes and farmlands. But once the technology for the exploitation of the resource was created, Tulsa became a place where oil speculators bought large pieces of land from Creek citizens, and the population grew exponentially, from a town of less than 1,000 to a city of 35,000 after the First World War.[104] Businesses owned by whites, people of African descent, and Native Americans supplied oil workers with mining supplies, laborers, and scientists.[105] A portion of Tulsa defined by its all-Black-owned businesses, called the Greenwood District, became known colloquially as "Black Wall Street" because of the financial success of the rooming houses, movie theater, grocery stores, auto repair shop, and dentists' offices that lined its avenues. It was these very accomplishments that had long provoked the envy of whites in the community. These white settlers retaliated using the pretext of an African American man's purported assault of a white woman—a common excuse for violence—to massacre over a hundred Black women and men.

On May 30, 1921, an African American teenager named Dick Rowland had an interaction of some kind with a white teenage elevator operator, leading the operator to scream. Although it is doubtful that the elevator operator, Sarah Page, was sexually assaulted, this was the story that quickly spread across Tulsa, making its way into the next day's afternoon newspaper.[106] On May 31, whites reacted, rousing friends and family members to violence under the cover of avenging white femininity; Black Tulsans hurried to protect their property and the now-jailed Dick Rowland. This rush to the jail was seen as an "attack" by whites, and, really, as an unacceptable assertion by African Americans of their rights. In return, Tulsa whites razed a thousand different Black homes and businesses, all the while murdering women, men, and children indiscriminately; they shot off their guns excitedly, whooping as if at a carnival or another venue of entertainment. As Black people ran about, fleeing fires, shootings, and beatings by civilians, policemen, and national guardsmen alike, they stumbled onto atrocious acts of violence. B. C. Franklin described observing a woman running down the street in a hail of bullets searching for her lost toddler; she survived to tell the tale. A group of three Black men were not so lucky; as they tried to cross the street, all three were cut down by over a dozen bullets. Said B.C. of the oldest victim, "He dropped [a trunk he was holding] and shrieked and fell sprawling upon the hard paved street. Blood gushed from every wound and ran down the street. I turned my head from the scene." B.C. and other witnesses also saw buildings catching fire from the top, betraying the use of airplanes to rain down fiery ruin from above, showing the power and influence possessed by whites involved in this organized terrorism.[107] B.C. barely escaped with his life. By June 1, the white mob had destroyed millions of dollars in property, the majority of which would never be fully recovered, and killed an estimated 100 to 300 African Americans.[108] Many survivors were left homeless, and the city and various insurance companies denied their property claims, leaving them with no restitution.[109]

In the aftermath, postcards depicting the carnage circulated in the white community, celebrating the desolation wrought by white supremacy and settler colonialism.[110] Biased accounts of the violence emerged almost immediately. The June 5 edition of the *New York Times* featured an article about the African Blood Brotherhood, a Tulsa organization dedicated to Black empowerment and self-defense. Perhaps purposely choosing an organization known for their assertive stance in response to white violence, the *Times* asked why the group "did not encourage its members to resort to the courts to correct any grievances." Executive head of the brotherhood

FIGURE 8. Aftermath, hunting through the rubble. Ella Mahler Collection. Courtesy of the Oklahoma Historical Society.

Cyril V. Briggs responded, "The negro has long lost faith in the 'justice of the white man toward the negro.'"[111] The June 2 edition of the *Prescott Daily News* (Prescott, AR) reported that 85 were dead after a race riot in "the negro quarter." While the article mentioned that "many negroes had been burned to death in their homes" and that "negro refugees [had] fled into the country surrounding Tulsa [after] being attacked by armed posses of whites," the paper still blamed the "riot" on the "200 armed negroes [who] stormed the court house to release Dick Rowland"; the story's subtitle read, "Troops Restore Quiet After Lurid Race Clashes—Black Agitators Are Blamed for Disastrous Riots." The paper failed to clarify that *it* was, in fact, the entity blaming African Americans.[112] Ever resilient, Black Tulsa residents rebuilt, though the city attempted to stifle them by imposing new laws that required buildings to be taller and made of fireproof materials. After lawyers including B.C. Franklin succeeded in getting this law struck

FIGURE 9. Iron bed frames rising out of the rubble of burned-out buildings. Ella Mahler Collection. Courtesy of the Oklahoma Historical Society.

down, nearly eight hundred new structures were erected, and in 1925 the district's rebirth was christened when it hosted the annual National Negro Business League conference.[113] But the capital required to rebuild after incidences of property destruction and the emotional and social trauma passed down from incidences of racial terror are two major causes, often forgotten by the mainstream media, of the stunted economic development of so many Black communities. The money, lives, and opportunities that were lost can never be regained, and this is one way in which the settler colonial state impairs nonwhite peoples, making them unable to compete with white settlers on an even playing field.

This 1921 event became known as the Tulsa Race Riot. The word "riot," used to describe many historical incidents like that in Tulsa, suggests that Blacks and whites were equally involved in the destruction and belies the fact that this was a very deliberate targeting of black success—thus, I follow recent historians and Tulsa residents in referring to it as a massacre rather than a riot. The Tulsa Race Massacre served as the destruction of not only (literal) Black wealth but also the Oklahoma Black memory of self-sufficiency, economic success, and racial coalition. The massacre was not taught in Oklahoma schools, nor was the awe-inspiring reality of Black Wall Street. This was not the first nor the last act of racial violence by whites against Black women and men living in the former space of Indian Territory. But as the largest destruction of Black wealth in the region (and, according to economic historians, in the country) and the deadliest in American history, the Tulsa Race Massacre represents the end of the largest representation of what Blacks were able to build economically and socially within Native spaces and under tribal jurisdiction within their extended Reconstruction.[114] Indian freedpeople's allotments, hard won as a result of a lifetime of enslavement but also through participation in the settler colonial process, provided them with economic autonomy and, for some, incredible wealth through natural resources. Angry that landownership stymied some of the effects of Jim Crow, whites decimated the businesses, homes, and dreams of Black people in the Greenwood District of Tulsa.

Though it may be a cliché, it truly was through blood, sweat, and tears that the Roberts family carved out a homestead for themselves after emancipation. This space was a rare piece of land owned by a Black family who would maintain possession of it over generations and to this day. It allowed a community to provide itself with food and an infrastructure for institutions, such as a church and a cemetery. It serves as a reminder of Black self-determination, as do the many Black towns sprinkled throughout Oklahoma. But the hard work, economic success, and communal effort that had brought these places to life through the settler colonial process from the late nineteenth to early twentieth centuries was largely undone by the final triumph of settler colonialism: white settlement. The Tulsa Race Massacre and the smaller events of racial tension and violence that preceded it, like that in Ardmore, stand as symbols of the end of the opportunities Native Americans had through tribal sovereignty, and which Indian freedpeople and African Americans found in the land allotments afforded by Native dispossession. During this massacre, angry white Americans rose up against Black success and demanded the ultimate wages of settler colonialism: inequality for all but themselves.

When Lillie Booker and her son, Herbert Booker, recalled the overall lack of racial confrontations between Black and white townspeople in Robertsville and broader Ardmore, they emphasized Black people's defense of their homes and families. According to Herbert: "They wasn't like you see in the movies. . . . They didn't put up with no crap. . . . That's when Blacks didn't back down." On a number of occasions, Lillie's father, Willie Roberts, defended his family from white attacks using a gun or his fist, which in itself could have been cause for his own lynching. Yet, no harm ever came to Willie or his family. Why? What made Robertsville different? Perhaps it was its location in a space that had previously known more freedoms and rights for people of African descent; perhaps it was simply the mere luck that often characterized Black women and men's near escapes from interracial violence. Whatever *it* was, it was an outlier in Oklahoma by the time of the 1900s, as symbolized by the death of Willie's friend, Sid, and the horrific event that occurred in Tulsa.

The Tulsa Race Massacre was the result of more than just the two decades or so of racial tension that had transpired in the state of Oklahoma. It was the result of waves of migration, of movements of people looking to prove that they belonged in a space and deserved ownership of a plot of land more than another group. While the massacre primarily affected Black Americans and Indian freedpeople, the more expansive symbolism behind the massacre affected Native peoples as well, because the violence reinforced and upheld the white supremacist foundations of settler colonialism.

～

Indian Territory was bequeathed its name by white American politicians and reformers, and this name was then used by Native, Black, and white settlers. It was subsequently referred to as the dual territories of

Oklahoma and Indian Territory, and then, finally and still to this day, the state of Oklahoma.[115] This land, like much of North America and, indeed, much of the world, had transferred hands for millennia. If land transfer is so common, why focus on Indian Territory? Indian Territory is an exaggerated and easily delineated example of the settler colonial process in North America because it encapsulates the two primary means of carrying out settler colonialism—Indigenous land theft and the use of coercive labor (in this case, Black slavery) to cultivate this land—while also serving as a space in which various waves of migrants (Native peoples, people of African descent, and whites) were able to inhabit the process of the settler to build or rebuild, creating success and opportunity for themselves through the basis of American governmental intervention.[116]

It was American intervention that made these long-existent land transfers different. When the U.S. government facilitated land transfer from Plains Native hands into Five Tribes hands, and then from Five Tribes hands to the possession of Indian freedpeople, African Americans, and whites, the United States did not perform an act of selfless beneficence. Rather, it carried out this process for the sake of western "progress," for the sake of wresting land from uncivilized Indigenous peoples to give to relatively civilized Indigenous peoples, people of African descent, and then to white settlers who they saw as more productive and hardworking, and who represented American expansion and empire. In Indian Territory, this transfer of possession occurred within the short span of a few decades and thus provides an extraordinary example for an exploration of the politics of claiming land.

The United States created white, Black, and Indian settlers through Removal and the land allotment promised in the Treaties of 1866 and the Dawes Act. In this way, my revised Reconstruction timeline reflects a transformative time period for Indian freedpeople and African Americans from the United States, freed from emancipation and offered the chance to own their own land. These same decades also encapsulated a significant step in colonial settlement by whites and Blacks who saw the space of Indian Territory alternately as a blank slate on which to project archetypal racial and gender roles and as an ancestral home that might admit them as tribal citizens. Poor whites and non-Black people of color joined in this project, using the actualities and imaginings of westward movement to frame their own views of land and belonging. Societal norms, a need for protection, and a desire to fit into a white supremacist culture organized by racial hierarchy drove nonwhites to participate in the settler colonial process in an attempt to win an unwinnable game. The Five Tribes, Indian freedpeople, and African Americans briefly benefited from using the settler colonial process—it allowed them to claim ownership of space and legitimacy of identity. But ultimately, the process, which prizes above all white supremacy and white landownership, worked against them.

In pitting Native Americans, people of African descent, and whites against one another, the settler colonial process as exerted through language, government initiatives, and individual settlers in the latter half of the nineteenth century worked to subdue nonwhites, minimize their economic, social, and political gains, and relegate them to second-class citizenship. At the same time, Black and Native people drew upon narratives of themselves created in the earlier part of the nineteenth century to feed their sense of self. They also delineated their individual and national identities and carved out physical and metaphorical spaces for themselves in a new homeland. So, Indian Territory functioned as a dreamscape of hope and inclusion for different groups of people, who then weaponized it against others. While all three groups—Native peoples, Indian freedpeople, and African Americans—then occupied Oklahoma together after the Civil War, by the 1890s the societal framework of the region had been irrevocably transformed from a space of hope to one of exploitation and white supremacy. By the late twentieth century, the Black towns started by African Americans and Indian freedpeople were on the decline. Many Black and Native peoples had had their land stolen and were now impoverished and without property of their own.

The United States' failure to ensure that African Americans had a stable economic foundation through landownership after emancipation led to their migration to Indian Territory and constant search for a space of possibility—and also to the realization of land possession for Indian freedpeople, which in turn fed Black and white American migration. The struggle over landownership in Indian Territory, now Oklahoma, concluded with whites largely taking control of valuable, resource-rich land, and many Blacks and Indians being saddled with barren parcels or no land at all. Indian leaders, African Americans, and Indian freedpeople invested their hopes in the promises of the American state, despite searing histories of oppression by U.S. citizens, and ultimately the United States protected only white settlers.

Epilogue

A FTER A LONG day of interviewing my cousin Travis Roberts and driving around to various sites important to our family history, Travis and I sat down to rest in his home. I asked him what had compelled him to spend decades of his life cobbling together a list of our ancestors dating back six generations and a sprawling record of Roberts descendants—quite a feat for a family with a history of enslavement and an overwhelming number of siblings and cousins.[1] As Travis was wont to do, he responded with an analogy. He said,

> If I was up in the air somewhere in an airplane, and someone dropped me out, and I hit the ground, [and] I wanted to call [you] and tell [you] to come get me, [you] would ask me where I am, and I've got to give [you] some direction. I have to tell you I'm north of Ardmore, south of Ardmore, east of Ardmore. . . . If I say I don't know where I am, you can't find me. That's the way our young people are. Our young people didn't come from any place, so how can they get where they're going? They don't *know* where they're going. So, give them a base of where they came from, then they can point a direction to where they want to go. And that's the reason you need that history. So that you will know where you are going, *from* somewhere.[2]

Travis grew up with a grandfather born a slave, with stories of racial animosity that remained raw, in an Oklahoma that was still very much a vestige of the Jim Crow laws enacted after the transformation of Indian space into an American state. For a man like Travis, remembering his history—and by this he meant his family's history and the land it was tied to—held a certain importance. For him, it was important to remember that, though white settlers may have successfully claimed the practical benefits of space and influence in Oklahoma, through the oral histories that he imparted Travis could recall the progressions of settlement that came before them, which had shaped Indian Territory; he could recall the fruit trees and farm animals that permeated the space of Blackness within the Chickasaw Nation that was Robertsville.

I grew up in California, the grandchild of Black immigrants to the West Coast who sought jobs and opportunity. Unlike my cousins in Oklahoma, I learned very little about our provenance in Indian Territory and, before that, Mississippi. The story keepers before Travis were dead and gone before I had any interest in knowing where I came from. My father possessed only tidbits—some true and some false—about our unique origin story. I started digging too late to record all of the histories of the Roberts family from the mouths of most of those who experienced it. And so, it was important to me to tell this story as best as I could without these resources. I have done so using many different actors, but primarily my family and other Chickasaw freedwomen and freedmen, using their stories as a framing device when possible, because so often theirs have been mere sentences in the chronicles of people of African descent in the United States and even within Indian nations. Interviews I conducted as an undergraduate novice oral historian have allowed me to give a voice to some of my kin—those willing to relive their own past and to memorialize the pasts of others.

Even so, this book is about far more than just the Roberts family or even Chickasaw freedpeople. This book is about the meaning of freedom, about hopes—both dashed and realized—and about identity. The history of the American West is at the same time pervasive and esoteric. The images of the region—the (white) cowboy, the Plains Indian, the self-sufficient pioneer family—are known in places far outside of the United States, from Germany to Vietnam. Yet, the diverse peoples and narratives that make up "the West" remain obscured in many ways. When Indians are thought of only as symbols of a passing era, running from inevitable American progress, this obscures the acculturation of the Five Tribes and their complicity in much of the culture and ideologies of the United States, including slavery, institutionalized racism, and individual prejudice; when people of African descent are confined to the South in our narratives of American history, this obscures the realities of Indian freedpeople's enslavement, emancipation, resilience, and community building with other Black people in the West, creating places like Black Wall Street.

How does changing the way we think about Black and Native history change our narrative of broader American history, specifically Reconstruction and the late nineteenth and early twentieth centuries? Using the space of Indian Territory to examine changing land claims allows us to see how Black, Native, and white women and men used land as an important signifier and representation of their identities—identities that often functioned in ways that put others down in order to lift themselves up. In Indian Territory, Removal and Reconstruction were times of mass upheaval and violence, but also of hope. Hope allowed the Five Tribes to believe they could rebuild themselves and allowed them to portray themselves as similar to the colonizers who had forced their migration. Hope allowed Indian freedpeople to express their freedom by petitioning the U.S. government and their respective Indian nations for rights and land, and, when this failed, allowed them to use Indian agents' beliefs that they were more civilized than their former captors to their advantage. Hope brought Black and white Americans to Indian Territory in anticipation of forging new lives and opportunities for themselves, and in the process allowed them to denigrate the Indians and Indian freedpeople already living there. Indian Territory makes it possible to study how these groups, which we do not usually associate with this particular *side* of settler colonialism, weaponized hope, freedom, and identity for use against others. Only the

American settler state truly benefited in the long run from these brief up-
sets of the status quo.

Though all Indigenous peoples across North America suffered the
same settler colonial project that would eventually envelop most of the
continent, only the Five Tribes experienced emancipation and land dis-
bursement to former slaves enforced by an external government—an external government that had encouraged their adoption of chattel slavery in
the first place as a marker of assimilation.[3] This amazing story of people of
African descent actually receiving land from their oppressors seems at first
to represent a lost story of realized reparations and a degree of restorative
justice. But looking at this through the lens of western expansion, Reconstruction in Indian Territory appears more like settler colonialism.

Settler colonialism shaped the western Reconstruction period, oblig-
ing us to recognize that Indian freedpeople and African Americans from
the United States engaged in an exercise of freedom that revolved around
landownership and rhetorical claims to western space, rather than necessarily, or solely, around access to political rights. When the African American presence in the West has been acknowledged at all, it has most often
been lauded as the rare scenario in which people of African descent had
the space and freedom to take charge of their own destinies with little state
constraint or white violence (at least until the late nineteenth century).[4]
But without the inclusion of the stories and land claims of Native peoples,
these become simply more incomplete, nationalistic (Black nationalist or
American) tales that eschew responsibility for Native American dispossession and serve the settler colonial goal of erasing Indigenous land claims
and visibility.

There are details upon details of the allotment process, of Native, Black,
and mixed-race life within the Five Tribes before and after Removal, and
of the intricacies of statehood that I have not covered. They have been covered amazingly in works that have preceded this book or remain to be covered in a future work. This book is not meant to be the definitive work on
Indian Territory. Rather, I have sought to provide a compelling narrative
in the hope of providing the reader with a desire to wrestle with questions

like: How do we recognize a more nuanced Reconstruction that enfolds varying definitions of Black freedom *and* Black involvement in settler colonialism? How do we define Indigeneity while allowing for migration and overlapping land claims? How do we grapple with the broad history of settler colonialism in North America?

Our family's ties to land loomed large in the stories Travis told me about Indian Territory. Though it was known, and retold, that as slaves of Chickasaw and Choctaw Indians my family had come from Mississippi, we considered Oklahoma to be our ancestral homeland; it was where the Roberts family's stories about the exhilaration of freedom, the hopeful yet unstable nature of Reconstruction, and communal resilience during Jim Crow and horrors like the Tulsa Race Massacre resided. In telling the stories that I've threaded throughout this book, I have tried to let the land guide me. This is because, like Travis, I believe that it is only by knowing where we came from—in this case through the inclusion of all these narratives, those of Native Americans, African Americans, Indian freedpeople, and white settlers—that we can truly know where we are going.

Notes

INTRODUCTION

1. Eli Roberts, Works Progress Administration Microfilm, Oklahoma Historical Society, Oklahoma City, OK. This excerpt has been altered to correct its spelling and grammar. In an essay in *Western Historical Quarterly*, I said that Eli *himself* arrived in Indian Territory in the mid-1800s. I now believe the correct interpretation of his words is that his family arrived here at that time, and that his descriptions of Indian Territory encompass both their first glimpses of the region and his own at a later date. Dawes record testimony and other data about the people who owned my family show that they would have arrived in the 1830s–1840s, rather than the date listed on the fieldworker's form. As the Works Progress Administration narratives were recorded by people, they are fallible; yet, the information they contain is so important for the purposes of historians and descendants. Alaina E. Roberts, "A Hammer and a Mirror: Tribal Disenrollment and Scholarly Responsibility," *Western Historical Quarterly* 49, no. 1 (2017): 91–96.

2. Michael F. Doran, "Population Statistics of Nineteenth Century Indian Territory," *Chronicles of Oklahoma* 53, no. 4 (1978): 501. For information on the Five Tribes' cotton production, see Gilbert C. Fite, "Development of the Cotton Industry by the Five Civilized Tribes in Indian Territory," *Journal of Southern History* 15, no. 3 (1949): 342–353.

3. Historian Gregory Smithers agrees that the Cherokee Nation's leaders brought proslavery sentiment with them to Indian Territory (and that some non-slave-owning Cherokees brought antislavery sentiment with *them*). Gregory D. Smithers, *The Cherokee Diaspora: An Indigenous History of Migration, Resettlement, and Identity* (New Haven, CT: Yale University Press, 2015), 127.

4. While I have given the most basic definition of settler colonialism, the two definitions scholars most often cite as either foundational or oppositional to their own analysis of the concept are those created by the anthropologist Patrick Wolfe and the historian Lorenzo Veracini. Wolfe, considered by many to be the father of our modern-day discussions about settler colonialism, used the model of Australian history to define settler colonialism as a structure. This structure uses the idea of "empty land" to erase the Indigenous presence (and history and culture) on Australian land and to justify settlement

and violence toward Indigenous peoples. The structure operates through a "logic of elimination," wherein the colonial government forces Indigenous peoples to rely on it for recognition and then uses procedures of recognition that ultimately limit the population of people deemed Indigenous. Patrick Wolfe, *Settler Colonialism and the Transformation of Anthropology: The Politics and Poetics of an Ethnographic Event* (New York: Continuum Press, 1999). Nearly ten years after Wolfe's first articulation of his definition of settler colonialism, Lorenzo Veracini defined the concept as a formation, often without an end. Unlike Wolfe, though, Veracini parsed the identity of settlers, arguing that "not all migrants are settlers," for "settlers come to stay," and they are "founders of political orders who carry with them a distinct sovereign capacity." In addition, for Veracini, the difference between colonialism and settler colonialism is that "settlers want Indigenous people to vanish"—another distinction between settlers and nonsettlers. Lorenzo Veracini, *Settler Colonialism: A Theoretical Overview* (New York: Palgrave Macmillan, 2010). Historians of Native North America, such as Nancy Shoemaker and Daniel Richter, have used specific historical episodes to define settler colonialism. Richter demonstrated that even within one empire, different leaders used different tactics in the process of settlement: William Penn's 1681 letter to "the King of the Indians" bargaining for peace and land was not necessarily settlement by force as in other locations. Penn's letter is also one of many pieces of evidence that settlers' articulation of *terra nullius* (uninhabited ground) might work in theory but not in practice, for colonists who did not negotiate with Native peoples quickly ran into issues of war or lack of resources. Further, even among European powers, claims to land were often contested. Daniel K. Richter, *Trade, Land, and Power: The Struggle for Eastern North America* (Philadelphia: University of Pennsylvania Press, 2013), 143–144. In *A Strange Likeness: Becoming Red and White in Eighteenth-Century North America*, Nancy Shoemaker similarly argued that Europeans recognized that Native peoples claimed territorial sovereignty over their land and that they must negotiate with them, to some extent, in order to inhabit it. Shoemaker also described landscapes as spaces that people could write "their presence on," which, in turn, "established and nurtured national identities." Nancy Shoemaker, *A Strange Likeness: Becoming Red and White in Eighteenth-Century North America* (New York: Oxford University Press, 2006), 14–15.

5. My definition of settler colonialism is specific to the time and space of Indian Territory in the nineteenth and early twentieth centuries. I draw from the foundational definitions of Wolfe and Veracini in that I agree that settler colonialism is ongoing and I agree that settler colonialism brings with it the necessitation of the erasure of Indigenous peoples. It is really the terms of the erasure of Indigenous peoples and the importance of layered claims that make my definition different. For Indian Territory, erasure was predominantly about what Nancy Shoemaker describes as writing one's presence on a particular landscape. The Five Tribes, Indian freedpeople, African Americans, and whites were not (necessarily) concerned with killing off the people who inhabited Indian Territory before them. Rather, they were interested in nullifying the claims of these people by portraying them as not just uncivilized and inferior to them but also further away from

the model of "civilization"—American whiteness—which ultimately served the settler
colonial state's goal of establishing and maintaining white supremacy. If the people who
resided in Indian Territory before them were considered "uncivilized" because they did
not practice agriculture in the Euro-American model or because they did not pursue
capitalistic endeavors in the Euro-American model, the Native, Black, or white settler
could claim a version of *terra nullius* that then allowed them to disregard land claims and
establish a new narrative that rewrote history, erased humanity, and established them as
the true indigenous inhabitants of the region. Because of the rapidity of the changes in
claims in Indian Territory, we are able to see more clearly how the settler colonial process
worked for and within different groups of settlers. The rhetoric facet of my definition of
the settler colonial process is essentially Mary Louise Pratt's idea of an "autoethnographic
text." Pratt proposed that an "other" could represent themselves to a conquering state in
a manner that involved "a selective collaboration with and appropriation of idioms of the
metropolis or conqueror." Mary Louise Pratt, "Arts of the Contact Zone," *Profession* 1 (1991):
35. Jonas Bens uses Pratt's concept to argue that the lawsuit *Cherokee Nation v. Georgia*
was the beginning of the creation of the category of "Indigenous," and thus this category
has always been defined by a relationship to a colonial/postcolonial state. My model of
settler colonialism builds on this by contending that the Five Tribes, Indian freedpeople,
and African American and white settlers were aware that the state granted indigenous
status, or at least recognized the right of a group of people to settle (or not), and thus
advocated for the settler colonial state's approval through the settler colonial process.
Jonas Bens, "When the Cherokee Became Indigenous: Cherokee Nation v. Georgia and Its
Paradoxical Legalities," *Ethnohistory* 65, no. 2 (2018): 247–267. Eve Tuck, K. Wayne Young,
Jodi Byrd, and Tiffany Lethabo King among others have taken on the question of whether
we should follow Patrick Wolfe's model of a strict Native/Settler binary. In the July 2019
issue of *William and Mary Quarterly*, a number of scholars wrestled with this same binary
and how we might reimagine settler colonialism as carried out by nonwhite actors with
complicated backgrounds. My positioning of settler colonialism as a process allows for the
governmental structure to be any power that my settlers appeal to, and for the petitioner
of the governmental structure to be potentially anyone, as represented within my narrative.
As many of the aforementioned scholars have brought out, most people of African descent
in the Americas in the eighteenth and nineteenth centuries were brought here forcibly,
not as voluntary participants in a settler project. Further, they faced racism that did not
allow them to necessarily choose where they lived and what destinies they followed. The
same might be said for the Five Tribes—they came to Indian Territory against their will.
However, the Five Tribes chose to use specific language and actions that they knew would
appeal to the American state's ideas of civilization to gain protection and better treatment
(relative to western Indians). Through the narratives they told about their national history,
they chose to perpetuate the idea that they found a "wilderness" when they arrived in
Indian Territory, and that they proceeded to tame it. This fed into the settler colonial state's
goals. Similarly, Indian freedpeople and African Americans perpetuated ideas about Indian

savagery and lack of knowledge about agriculture and capitalism as they attempted to wrangle governmental support and protection for their western settlement from the United States. This was active participation in a process of dispossession for individual and group gain. Shoemaker, *A Strange Likeness*, 14–15; Eve Tuck and K. Wayne Young, "Decolonization Is Not a Metaphor," *Decolonization: Indigeneity, Education & Society* 1, no. 1 (2012): 1–40; Jodi Byrd, *The Transit of Empire: Indigenous Critiques of Colonialism* (Minneapolis: University of Minnesota Press, 2011); Tiffany Lethabo King, *The Black Shoals: Offshore Formations of Black and Native Studies* (Durham, NC: Duke University Press, 2019); *William and Mary Quarterly* 76, no. 3 (2019).

6. Some of the earliest historians to use the term "freedpeople" in reference to Black people in Indian Territory, and to thus inspire me to do so, include Claudio Saunt, "The Paradox of Freedom: Tribal Sovereignty and Emancipation During the Reconstruction of Indian Territory," *Journal of Southern History* 70, no. 1 (Feb 2004): 63–94; Celia E. Naylor, *African Cherokees in Indian Territory: From Chattel to Citizens* (Chapel Hill: University of North Carolina Press, 2008); Barbara Krauthamer, *Black Slaves, Indian Masters: Slavery, Emancipation, and Citizenship in the Native American South* (Chapel Hill: University of North Carolina Press, 2013).

7. Colin Calloway, *First Peoples: A Documentary Survey of American Indian History* (New York: MacMillan Learning, 2015), 276–277; Theda Perdue, *Cherokee Women: Gender and Culture Change, 1700–1835* (Lincoln: University of Nebraska Press, 1998), 8–9; Krauthamer, *Black Slaves, Indian Masters*, 32–33.

8. For further information on the struggles for reparations for slavery around the world, see Ana Lucia Araujo, *Reparations for Slavery and the Slave Trade: A Transnational and Comparative History* (New York: Bloomsbury, 2017).

9. Some of the scholars who use the concept of belonging in the same vein (to denote the importance of kinship and "communitarian ethic," as historian Julie Reed terms it) include Mikaëla M. Adams, *Who Belongs: Race, Resources, and Tribal Citizenship in the Native South* (New York: Oxford University Press, 2016); Linda Williams Reese, *Trail Sisters: Freedwomen in Indian Territory, 1850–1890* (Lubbock: Texas Tech University Press, 2013); Julie Reed, *Serving the Nation: Sovereignty and Social Welfare, 1800–1907* (Norman: University of Oklahoma Press, 2016); Tiya Miles, *Ties That Bind: The Story of an Afro-Cherokee Family in Slavery and Freedom* (Berkeley: University of California Press, 2015); Tiya Miles, *Dawn of Detroit: A Chronicle of Slavery and Freedom in the City of Straits* (New York: New Press, 2017); Malinda Maynor Lowery, *Lumbee Indians in the Jim Crow South* (Chapel Hill: University of North Carolina Press, 2010); Stephanie Camp, *Closer to Freedom: Enslaved Women and Everyday Resistance in the Plantation South* (Chapel Hill: University of North Carolina Press, 2004); Circe Sturm, *Blood Politics: Race, Culture, and Identity in the Cherokee Nation* (Berkeley: University of California Press, 2002); Naylor, *African Cherokees in Indian Territory*; bell hooks, *Belonging: A Culture of Place* (New York: Routledge, 2008).

10. Scholarship on emancipation and Reconstruction has largely focused on the

political aspects of African Americans' actions during these eras. Eric Foner's renowned book *Reconstruction: America's Unfinished Revolution* devoted the majority of its space to the grassroots political campaigns of southern African Americans, and Steven Hahn's *A Nation Under Our Feet* followed suit in arguing that African Americans during and immediately after the Civil War prioritized seeking and defining their rights through political means. Of course, Hahn stipulates that his focus is on Black politics, but my point is that his and Foner's books have become touchstones of Reconstruction scholarship, and thus this focus on politics lives on. These two works, in addition to Stephen Kantrowitz's *More than Freedom*, have shaped the field and oriented the importance historians place on the Black pursuit of policy change. Eric Foner, *Reconstruction: America's Unfinished Revolution, 1863–1877* (New York: HarperCollins, 1988); Steven Hahn, *A Nation Under Our Feet: Black Political Struggles in the Rural South from Slavery to the Great Migration* (Cambridge, MA: Belknap Press of Harvard University Press, 2003); Stephen Kantrowitz, *More than Freedom: Fighting for Black Citizenship in a White Republic, 1829–1889* (New York: Penguin, 2012). While the political lives of Black women and men are important, I seek to add to the work of scholars such as Dylan Penningroth, Heather Williams, Tera Hunter, and Leslie Schwalm who have written monographs that allow us to glimpse the importance of family and community in the postwar period. Dylan Penningroth, *The Claims of Kinfolk: African American Property and Community in the Nineteenth-Century South* (Chapel Hill: University of North Carolina Press, 2004); Heather Williams, *Help Me to Find My People: The African American Search for Family Lost in Slavery* (Chapel Hill: University of North Carolina Press, 2012); Tera Hunter, *Bound in Wedlock: Slave and Free Black Marriage in the Nineteenth Century* (Cambridge, MA: Harvard University Press, 2017); Leslie Schwalm, *A Hard Fight for We: Women's Transition from Slavery to Freedom in South Carolina* (Urbana: University of Illinois Press, 1997).

11. It is not a complete comparison to say that, unlike African Americans in the United States, Chickasaw freedpeople chose land over political rights, because Chickasaw freedpeople had direct access to landownership through governmental processes, whereas African Americans in the United States did not. Perhaps if African Americans had also had this option, they would have made the same choice. However, since they did not, and their options for acquiring land within the United States were minimal, African Americans focused on politics as a way to obtain equality, which they hoped (among other aims) would allow them to eventually purchase their own land and obtain economic autonomy. In a way, though, African Americans who chose to journey to Indian Territory *did* make this choice between political rights and land—they ventured outside the boundaries of the United States to a space where they had no citizenship in an effort to obtain land. Walter Johnson's "On Agency" is a great framework with which to imagine alternative actions made by freedpeople, actions that might seem surprising to us but that accurately reflected their desires and needs. Walter Johnson, "On Agency," *Journal of Social History* 37, no. 1 (2003): 113–124.

12. David Chang's *The Color of the Land* provides an enlightening examination of the

importance of land, specifically Creek land in Oklahoma, to people of white, Indigenous, and Black ancestry. However, I seek to connect land and spatial geography to Reconstruction scholarship in a way that Chang does not. David A. Chang, *The Color of the Land: Race, Nation, and the Politics of Landownership in Oklahoma, 1832–1929* (Chapel Hill: University of North Carolina Press, 2010). Black-Indian scholarship has, in my opinion, been the historical field that has consistently taken into account the importance of land and nation (outside of the United States but within North America) in the Civil War and Reconstruction eras. I build on this scholarship to make broader claims about Reconstruction historiography and Black-Indian community and identity. Daniel F. Littlefield Jr., Tiya Miles, Celia Naylor, Fay Yarbrough, Barbara Krauthamer, and Claudio Saunt have covered these topics, and their monographs allow me to use their sources and arguments to create an overarching narrative that utilizes the framework of Black-led Reconstruction. Littlefield Jr., *The Chickasaw Freedmen: A People Without a Country* (Westport, CT: Greenwood Press, 1980); Miles, *Ties That Bind*; Naylor, *African Cherokees in Indian Territory*; Williams Reese, *Trail Sisters*; Yarbrough, *Race and the Cherokee Nation: Sovereignty in the Nineteenth Century* (Philadelphia: University of Pennsylvania Press, 2008); Krauthamer, *Black Slaves, Indian Masters*; Saunt, *Black, White, and Indian: Race and the Unmaking of an American Family* (New York: Oxford University Press, 2005); Saunt, "The Paradox of Freedom," 63. Indigenous studies scholar Kevin Bruyneel has called for further exploration of the connection between the Reconstruction-era calls for Black landownership in the West and settler colonialism. Kevin Bruyneel, "Creolizing Collective Memory: Refusing the Settler Memory of the Reconstruction Era," *Journal of French and Francophone Philosophy* 25, no. 2 (2017): 236–44.

13. Joshua Paddison also ties together the development of Black and Indian citizenship, but the circumstances of California Indians were different from those of the Five Tribes, as tribes in California were, for the most part, not protected by the autonomous political sovereignty brought by recognition of nationhood. Joshua Paddison, *American Heathens: Religion, Race, and Reconstruction in California* (Berkeley: University of California Press, 2012).

14. The Dunning school, of course, characterized Reconstruction as the former, an unfair penalization of the South. William Archibald Dunning, *Reconstruction, Political and Economic, 1865–1877* (New York: Harper & Brothers, 1907).

15. Greg Downs has created a different timeline altogether. He argued that the Civil War did not end until 1871, with the seating of a Georgia senator; thus, his timeline of federal backing for Black emancipation and enfranchisement is slightly different. I subscribe to his thesis that only wartime powers allowed for the occupation of the South and the governmental backing of legislation such as the Fourteenth and Fifteenth Amendments. Gregory P. Downs, *After Appomattox: Military Occupation and the Ends of War* (Cambridge, MA: Harvard University Press, 2015). Heather Cox Richardson and Greg Downs (in his first book) broaden the Reconstruction timeline by arguing that Americans' reliance on the federal government during and after the Civil War created ties of social,

political, and economic dependence and a reliance on an expansive government (and an array of governmental actors) that extended beyond the end of the conflict. Heather Cox Richardson, *West from Appomattox: The Reconstruction of America After the Civil War* (New Haven, CT: Yale University Press, 2007); Gregory P. Downs, *Declarations of Dependence: The Long Reconstruction of Popular Politics in the South, 1861–1908* (Chapel Hill: University of North Carolina Press, 2011).

16. In some ways, this book is an expansion of Elliott West's and Richard White's ideas of a "Greater Reconstruction," wherein the United States simultaneously selectively incorporated and othered Native peoples, African Americans, white immigrants, and Chinese and Latino women and men, among others in the North, South, and West, and where the Mexican American War and other American wars expand the "traditional" periodization of the era. White (and West, slightly less so) focus on the traditional postwar western context of the Plains Wars and the Far West, while I seek to use the histories of the Five Tribes to call attention to the transnational relevance of a Greater Reconstruction in the Southern prairie plains and its effects on not just Native individuals but also tribal governments that were "reconstructed" spatially, racially, economically, and politically. Our story of a Greater Reconstruction looks different if we consider it from the perspective of tribal governments that, like the United States, were also looking to reconsider the place of people of African descent in their nations. Elliott West, "Reconstruction in the West," *Journal of the Civil War Era* 7, no. 1 (March 2017): 14; Elliott West, "Reconstructing Race," *Western Historical Quarterly* 34, no. 1 (Spring 2003): 6–26; Richard White, *The Republic for Which It Stands: The United States During Reconstruction and the Gilded Age, 1865–1896* (New York: Oxford University Press, 2017). I use the model of the anthologies *Empire and Liberty: The Civil War and the West* and *Civil War Wests: Testing the Limits of the United States* and monographs such as Ari Kelman's *A Misplaced Massacre: Struggling over the Memory of Sand Creek* and Karl Jacoby's *Shadows at Dawn: A Borderlands Massacre and the Violence of History*, which have positioned Indigenous peoples and the West as important settings and participants of the Civil War era. These books show that the violence, ideologies, and aftermath of the war were not limited to the South. Also, Stacey Smith notably refashioned the use of the term "Reconstruction" in order to show its application to the West. Virginia Scharff, ed., *Empire and Liberty: The Civil War and the West* (Berkeley: University of California Press, 2015); Adam Arenson and Andrew R. Graybill, eds., *Civil War Wests: Testing the Limits of the United States* (Berkeley: University of California Press, 2015); Ari Kelman, *A Misplaced Massacre: Struggling over the Memory of Sand Creek* (Cambridge, MA: Harvard University Press, 2015); Karl Jacoby, *Shadows at Dawn: A Borderlands Massacre and the Violence of History* (New York: Penguin Books, 2009); Stacey Smith, *Freedom's Frontier: California and the Struggle over Unfree Labor, Emancipation, and Reconstruction* (Chapel Hill: University of North Carolina Press, 2013).

17. I, of course, recognize that Black and white abolitionists forced a beginning to this conversation long before the Civil War era. See Manisha Sinha, *The Slave's Cause: A History of Abolition* (New Haven, CT: Yale University Press, 2016).

18. In doing so, they mediated the United States' westward movement and forced Americans to see them as autonomous sovereignties with legislative organization, societal ideals, and political agendas. Here, I use the model of historian Rachel St. John, who questions the U.S. government's authority in the western theater in the nineteenth century. Rachel St. John, *Line in the Sand: A History of the Western U.S.–Mexico Border* (Princeton, NJ: Princeton University Press, 2011).

19. As another example of the complexities of western Reconstruction, D. Michael Bottoms argued that citizenship actually narrowed in California during and after Reconstruction as a consequence of white fear of nonwhite dominance. D. Michael Bottoms, *An Aristocracy of Color: Race and Reconstruction in California and the West, 1850–1890* (Norman: University of Oklahoma Press, 2013).

20. Some Indigenous peoples were already citizens of the United States or would become citizens before the members of the Five Tribes, due to different laws regarding reservations and removal. For instance, Indigenous peoples who had stayed behind in the South and Southeast while the rest of their tribes removed to Indian Territory no longer had an official tribal status and often assimilated into nearby communities. Yet these people retained community and tribal identity despite their distance from their nations' political boundaries. See Clara Sue Kidwell, *Choctaws and Missionaries in Mississippi, 1818–1918* (Norman: University of Oklahoma Press, 1997).

21. See Martha S. Jones, *Birthright Citizens: A History of Race and Riots in Antebellum America* (New York: Cambridge University Press, 2018); Kate Masur, *An Example for All the Land: Emancipation and the Struggle over Equality in Washington, D.C.* (Chapel Hill: University of North Carolina Press, 2010); Christian G. Samito, *Becoming American Under Fire: Irish Americans, African Americans, and the Politics of Citizenship During the Civil War Era* (Ithaca, NY: Cornell University Press, 2009); Christian G. Samito, ed., *Changes in Law and Society During the Civil War and Reconstruction: A Legal History Documentary Reader* (Carbondale: Southern Illinois University Press, 2009); Laura Edwards, *A Legal History of the Civil War and Reconstruction: A Nation of Rights* (New York: Cambridge University Press, 2015); Paul Quigley, "Civil War Conscription and the International Boundaries of Citizenship," *Journal of the Civil War Era* 4, no. 3 (2014): 373–397; Paul Quigley, "State, Nation, and Citizen in the Confederate Crucible of War," in *State and Citizen: British America and the Early United States*, eds. Peter Onuf and Peter Thompson (Charlottesville: University of Virginia Press, 2012), 242–270.

22. Previous treaties had provided annuity payments to families put onto rolls, but this was not a permanent status per se. Reconstruction and the Dawes Act created the idea of permanent identification as a tribal citizen (or not) for a person and their descendants, and also the idea of a plot of land individually owned indefinitely (ostensibly).

23. While several nations in Indian Territory eventually introduced postwar Black Codes that limited Black autonomy and economic progress, I argue that these were not as inhibiting as those instated in the United States (nor were they observed as often). Further, the fact that most Indian freedpeople retained their land insulated them from some of the

economic limitations placed upon African Americans in the United States, despite the fact that many Indian freedpeople who actually derived great wealth from their land allotments occasionally experienced land theft. I acknowledge that in some parts of the South, African Americans were able to vote as late as the 1890s and successfully fought discrimination battles to maintain access to this right. However, this was not through systemic federal or state support, as existed for Indian freedpeople. Hahn, *A Nation Under Our Feet*.

24. In the vein of the work of Greg Downs, Heather Cox Richardson, and D. Michael Bottoms, I demonstrate that African Americans called on the state—both tribal governments and the U.S. government—to help them access their newly won rights and economic opportunity in Indian Territory. Downs, *Declarations of Dependence*; Cox Richardson, *West from Appomattox*; Bottoms, *An Aristocracy of Color*.

25. James S. Hirsch, *Riot and Remembrance: The Tulsa Race War and Its Legacy* (Boston: Houghton Mifflin Company, 2002); Randy Krehbiel and Karlos K. Hill, *Tulsa 1921: Reporting a Massacre* (Norman: University of Oklahoma Press, 2019); DeNeen L. Brown, "Tulsa Plans to Dig for Suspected Mass Graves from a 1921 Race Massacre," *Washington Post*, December 16, 2019, https://www.washingtonpost.com/history/2020/02/03/tulsa-mass-graves-excavation/.

26. I want to acknowledge the presence and influence of Chinese immigrants and Mexican people in the West, though they are largely not included in this narrative for reasons of space and clarity. For more on Chinese and Mexican history in the West, see Beth Lew-Williams, *The Chinese Must Go: Violence, Exclusion, and the Making of the Alien in America* (Cambridge, MA: Harvard University Press, 2018); Pekka Hamalainen, *The Comanche Empire* (New Haven, CT: Yale University Press, 2009); David J. Weber, *Myth and the History of the Hispanic Southwest: Essays* (Albuquerque: University of New Mexico Press, 1988).

27. Some groups of non-Black people of color (NBPOC) have also begun to formally acknowledge their involvement in settler colonialism despite the prejudice and economic inequality they faced historically and continue to face to this day. For a recent example (as of this writing), see the statement made by the Chinese Canadian National Council Toronto Chapter. Chinese Canadian National Council Toronto Chapter, "Statement of Solidarity with the Wet'suwet'en People," https://ccnctoronto.ca/2020/02/15/statement-of-solidarity-with-the-wetsuweten-people/, accessed February 18, 2020.

CHAPTER 1

1. Eli Roberts, Works Progress Administration microfilm.

2. This chapter borrows from the framework developed by historian Kathleen DuVal. DuVal argued that in their earlier interactions with the Osage tribe in Arkansas, members of the Cherokee Nation used language of "civilization" in an effort to create a "Native ground," where they could exercise dominating power and influence and be seen by other Indians as the "natives" of the region and by white Americans as a "vanguard of civilization." While the Cherokees were able to define and negotiate their own definitions of

so-called civilization, they were just as negatively impacted by the eventual mass white migration to the region as were the tribes they looked down upon. This is similar to the progression of settlement that I detail in this book. Kathleen DuVal, "Debating Identity, Sovereignty, and Civilization: The Arkansas Valley after the Louisiana Purchase," *Journal of the Early Republic* 26, no. 1 (2006): 26; Kathleen DuVal, *The Native Ground: Indians and Colonists in the Heart of the Continent* (Philadelphia: University of Pennsylvania Press, 2007). John P. Bowes situated non–Five Tribes eastern Indians as "pioneers" who settled in the West and worked to rebuild their societies before mass white American migration. Bowes did not claim that these Native peoples were part of a settler colonial process. John P. Bowes, *Exiles and Pioneers: Eastern Indians in the Trans-Mississippi West* (New York: Cambridge University Press, 2007).

3. The Indian peoples I reference in this chapter as "western tribes" are both tribes who have long lived in the area that became Indian Territory and others who were removed there before, or around the same time as, the Five Tribes. These tribes, such as the Osage, were more western than the Five Tribes, but I acknowledge that these groups are called different names by different scholars, including "Plains people," "prairie people," "southern Plains people," and "prairie plains people." I use all of these different terms at least once throughout this chapter for variety's sake.

4. In her book *Living in the Land of Death*, Donna L. Akers, an enrolled member of the Choctaw Nation (and professor of history), described how "the Kiowas' most sacred places became Choctaw without Kiowa consent." Donna L. Akers, *Living in the Land of Death: The Choctaw Nation, 1830-1860* (Lansing: Michigan State University Press, 2004), xiii.

5. In her contribution to the *William and Mary Quarterly* special edition on settler colonialism, Jennifer M. Spear chronicles a similar movement of a group of people from Indigenous to settler to colonized. Jennifer M. Spear, "Beyond the Native/Settler Divide in Early California," *William and Mary Quarterly* 76, no. 3 (2019): 427–434.

6. Bowes, *Exiles and Pioneers*, 17–18, 20.

7. Theda Perdue and Michael D. Green, *The Cherokee Removal: A Brief History with Documents*, 2nd ed. (Boston: Bedford/St. Martin's, 2005); Smithers, *The Cherokee Diaspora*.

8. Perdue and Green, *The Cherokee Removal*; Smithers, *The Cherokee Diaspora*.

9. Cornelia C. Chandler, Indian Pioneer Papers, Western History Collections, University of Oklahoma, Norman, OK, 154.

10. Sarah A. Harlin, Indian Pioneer Papers, 73.

11. Lucy Dunson, Indian Pioneer Papers, 334.

12. Ibid.

13. Some members of the Cherokee Nation moved West (first to Arkansas and then to Indian Territory) before this tribe-wide process began, from around the 1820s, and these people were known as the "Old Settlers." Brad Bays, "A Historical Geography of Town Building in the Cherokee Nation, 1866-1906" (dissertation, University of Nebraska, Lincoln, 1996), 37, https://digitalcommons.unl.edu/dissertations/AAI9715954/.

14. Amy C. Schutt, *Peoples of the River Valleys: The Odyssey of the Delaware Indians* (Philadelphia: University of Pennsylvania Press, 2007).

15. Mishuana Goeman, "From Place to Territories and Back Again: Centering Storied Land in the Discussion of Indigenous Nation-Building," *International Journal of Critical Indigenous Studies* 1, no. 1 (2008). See also Rose Stremlau, *Sustaining the Cherokee Family: Kinship and the Allotment of an Indigenous Nation* (Chapel Hill: University of North Carolina Press, 2011); Kent Carter, *The Dawes Commission: And the Allotment of the Five Civilized Tribes, 1893-1914* (Ancestry Publishing, 1999); Frederick E. Hoxie, *A Final Promise: The Campaign to Assimilate the Indians, 1880-1920* (Lincoln: University of Nebraska Press, 2001); Keith H. Basso, *Wisdom Sits in Places: Landscape and Language Among the Western Apache* (Albuquerque: University of New Mexico Press, 1996). These scholars assert the prominence of land to Indigenous identity formation and political sovereignty, demonstrating how white Americans' recognizance of the centrality of land to Indian societies meant they were aware that separating Native peoples from their lands of origin through various treaty agreements and ultimately the Dawes and Curtis Acts would drastically change Native family group and kinship composition and ideas of personal wealth.

16. Grant Foreman, *Advancing the Frontier, 1830-1860* (Norman: University of Oklahoma Press, 1933), 97–98, 147. The Osage had moved to a smaller part of their homeland, and their ability to access their former homes was greatly reduced due to others' new residence.

17. David La Vere, *Contrary Neighbors: Southern Plains and Removed Indians in Indian Territory* (Norman: University of Oklahoma Press, 2000), 9–13.

18. 1834. Regulating the Indian Department, Annual report of the commissioner of Indian affairs, for the years 1826–1839, 94.

19. United States, *American State Papers: Indian Affairs*, vol. 2 (Washington, DC: Gales & Seaton, 1832), 544.

20. Not every single member of the Five Tribes was receptive to Euro-American culture and norms. But societal laws show the values of those in power and those with the standing to influence a nation's trajectory, and the Five Tribes' laws are evidence that protection of property, including Black women and men, was increasingly important.

21. I agree with historian David La Vere's argument that the Five Tribes and the southern prairie Plains tribes were fundamentally different and that this would have led to issues between them in any circumstance. However, the Five Tribes' added desire to be seen as advanced and civilized led to the increased animosity that the archival documents bear out. La Vere, *Contrary Neighbors*, 7.

22. United States, *American State Papers: Indian Affairs*, vol. 2, 502.

23. Peter P. Pitchlynn to John Pitchlynn, Peter Pitchlynn, diary, November 27, 1828, typescript of original document, box 5, folder 2, Peter Perkins Pitchlynn Collection, Western History Collections, University of Oklahoma Libraries, Norman, OK, https://digital.libraries.ou.edu/cdm/singleitem/collection/pitchlynn/id/759/rec/1.

24. The western Indians also fought among themselves, and other removed tribes,

such as the Wichitas, faced raids from them. La Vere, *Contrary Neighbors*, 39. For more on the Cherokees' relationship with the Osage and Quapaw, see Kathleen DuVal, *The Native Ground*.

25. Slide 176, Letters Received by the Office of Indian Affairs M234, Roll 142, Chickasaw Agency, The National Archives, National Archives and Records Service, General Services Administration; M. Stokes to Lewis Cass, October 27, 1831, U.S. Senate, 23rd Cong., 1st sess., S. Doc. 512, Congressional Serial Set 246:623–624.

26. Edward Nail, Indian Pioneer Papers, 24.

27. Peter Pitchlynn used similar language in his private diaries and correspondence (for example, he referred to prairie Plains people as "wild, true Indians"), thus revealing that for him, at least, this was likely a true reflection of personal beliefs. Pitchlynn's beliefs may have changed later on in life, but he retained a sense that the Five Tribes were intrinsically different from western Indians. Peter Pitchlynn diary entry, November 27, 1828, typescript of original document, box 5, folder 2, https://digital.libraries.ou.edu/cdm/singleitem/collection/pitchlynn/id/759/rec/1.

28. Report on Indian Affairs, 1830, 29; Annual report of the commissioner of Indian affairs, transmitted with the message of the president at the opening of the 2nd session of the 25th Congress, 1837–1838, United States, Office of Indian Affairs, Annual report of the commissioner of Indian affairs, for the years 1826–1839, 22.

29. Cherokee Delegation to the Senate and the House of Representatives, February 28, 1840.

30. 1834. Regulating the Indian Department, 91, 93–94. Grant Foreman argued that it was primarily the Chickasaws' pleas that led to the erection and maintenance of Fort Washita. Foreman, *Advancing the Frontier*, 102.

31. 1834. Regulating the Indian Department, 19.

32. Instructions to A.P. Choteau, Special Agent to the Comanches and Others, Annual report of the commissioner of Indian affairs, transmitted with the message of the president at the opening of the 2nd session of the 25th Congress, 1837–1838, Annual report of the commissioner of Indian affairs, for the years 1826–1839, 37–38.

33. Report on Indian Affairs, 1828, Annual report of the commissioner of Indian Affairs, 1826–1839, 22.

34. Joshua M. Gorman, *Building a Nation: Chickasaw Museums and the Construction of History and Heritage* (Tuscaloosa: University of Alabama Press, 2011), 50.

35. "History and Culture," *Visit Cherokee Nation*, https://www.visitcherokeenation.com/history/Pages/a-proud-heritage.aspx, accessed 2019.

36. Instructions to A. P. Choteau, Special Agent to the Comanches and Others, Annual report of the commissioner of Indian affairs, transmitted with the message of the president at the opening of the 2nd session of the 25th Congress, 1837–1838, United States, Office of Indian Affairs, Annual report of the commissioner of Indian affairs, for the years 1826–1839, 37–38.

37. American soldiers did sometimes remove people by force from the Five Tribes' land, such as in the case of the Delaware and Shawnee in 1843. Foreman, *Advancing*

the Frontier, 102. The United States had promised to provide the Creeks with weapons in 1826, but the weapons did not arrive until several years after the Creeks had reached Indian Territory, limiting their ability to protect themselves. Foreman, *Advancing the Frontier*, 107.

38. Documents relating to the negotiation of an unratified treaty of July 1, 1831, between the Western Creek, Cherokee, and Osage Indians, Annual Report of the commissioner of Indian Affairs, for the years 1826–1839, Office of Indian Affairs, 1–13.

39. 1834. Regulating the Indian Department, Annual report of the commissioner of Indian affairs, for the years 1826–1839, 101; Foreman, *Advancing the Frontier*, 195–216.

40. In June 1865, representatives of the Cherokee, Chickasaw, Choctaw, Creek, Seminole, Osage, Caddo, and Comanche Nations met in Chahta Ta-ma-ha, coming together to "maintain the integrity of the Indian Territory, as the imminent and future home of our Race, to preserve and perpetuate the national rights and franchises of the several nations, to cultivate peace, harmony, and fellowship among ourselves, and to elevate, enlighten, and Christianize our race." They wanted to eliminate violence among Indians, cooperate to renew friendly relations with the U.S. government, and act as proxies for government negotiations if necessary. This council was meant to repair hostilities brought about by the Civil War, but also to organize the Indian peoples of Indian Territory against white encroachment and land allotment. Section X-Chickasaw Indians-Laws-Chickasaw Legislature, 1857, Resolutions of the Grand Council passed at Chahta Ta-ma-ha, June 16, 1865, no. 29, Book "A," Manuscripts/ Vertical Files, Oklahoma Historical Society, Oklahoma City, OK, 5; *Alliance Courier* 5, no. 60, February 19, 1894. The U.S government felt the Five Tribes had a positive influence on the other tribes. 1834. Regulating the Indian Department, annual report of the commissioner of Indian affairs, for the years 1826–1839, 86.

41. Smithers, *The Cherokee Diaspora*, 12–19; "Chiksa' and Chahta: First Leaders of the Chickasaw and Choctaw," *Chickasaw.TV*, https://www.chickasaw.tv/profiles/chikashsha- and-chata-profile, accessed 2019; "History," *The Chickasaw Nation*, https://www.chickasaw. net/Our-Nation/History.aspx, accessed 2019.

42. "History and Culture," *Visit Cherokee Nation*, https://www.visitcherokeenation. com/history/Pages/a-proud-heritage.aspx, accessed 2019.

43. Clara Sue Kidwell, *The Choctaws in Oklahoma: From Tribe to Nation, 1855–1970* (Norman: University of Oklahoma Press, 2007), 9.

44. Ibid., 9–10.

45. Christopher D. Haveman, *Rivers of Sand: Creek Indian Emigration, Relocation, and Ethnic Cleansing in the American South* (Lincoln: University of Nebraska Press, 2016), 152–153.

46. "Into the West," *Seminole Nation Museum*, https://www.seminolenationmuseum. org/history/seminole-nation/into-the-west/, accessed 2019.

47. Captive-taking was most often used to replace a dead loved one by situating a new person (the captive) in their former family position. The captive would then take on this deceased person's sexual and/or labor-related capacities. Through various avenues, such

as "sexual relationships, adoption, hard work, military service, or escape, captives could enhance their status or even assume new identities." Christina Snyder, *Slavery in Indian Country* (Cambridge, MA: Harvard University Press, 2010), 6, 46.

48. Alan Gallay, *Indian Slavery in Colonial America* (Lincoln: University of Nebraska Press, 2009), 1–2.

49. Snyder, *Slavery in Indian Country*, 68.

50. An important factor in the decline of the Indian slave trade was the Yamasee War. After colonists in Carolina began defaulting on some of their trade agreements and enslaving even members of their ally tribes, the Yamasee Nation began to question its own alliance with Carolina. Along with the Lower Creeks and the Savannahs, the Yamasees declared war on Carolina, killing 400 colonists (approximately 7 percent of the white population). The Upper Creeks, Choctaws, Cherokees, and Catawbas killed most of their resident traders, but did not participate in the battles. The Carolinian colonists put together a force of Black slaves, militia men, and volunteers from Virginia, North Carolina, and friendly Indian nations, which defeated the Yamasees and their allies. While the Yamasees lost, they succeeded in forcing European colonists to reconsider the risks inherent in the system of Indian enslavement. If Indians became angry at the terms of enslavement or allied Indians were accidentally enslaved, they might once again retaliate militarily. In addition, enslaved Indians often successfully escaped from their owners, as they were familiar with the geography and could elude slave catchers and return to their homelands. Snyder, *Slavery in Indian Country*, 76–77.

51. Theda Perdue, *Slavery and the Evolution of Cherokee Society, 1540–1866* (Nashville: University of Tennessee Press, 1987); Theda Perdue, *Cherokee Women*, 8–9; Krauthamer, *Black Slaves, Indian Masters*, 32–33.

52. Arrell M. Gibson, *The Chickasaws* (Norman: University of Oklahoma Press, 1971), 122.

53. John Inscoe, "Georgia in 1860," *New Georgia Encyclopedia*, https://www.georgiaencyclopedia.org/articles/history-archaeology/georgia-1860, accessed 2019.

54. Kevin Daniel Motes, "The Nation Must Change: Socio-cultural Acclimation and Instantiations of Ethnic Identity in the Choctaw Nation, 1830–1907" (dissertation, University of California, Riverside, 2008).

55. Doran, "Population Statistics of Nineteenth Century Indian Territory," 501; Perdue, *Slavery and the Evolution of Cherokee Society*, 50–56.

56. Troy Duane Smith, "Slavery, Race, and Nation in Indian Territory, 1830–1866" (dissertation, University of Illinois at Urbana-Champaign, 2011).

57. The Choctaws had a similar law. Krauthamer, *Black Slaves, Indian Masters*, 83.

58. This was a law passed by both the Choctaws and the Cherokees. Kidwell, *The Choctaws in Oklahoma*, 33; Naylor, *African Cherokees in Indian Territory*, 30.

59. Naylor, *African Cherokees in Indian Territory*, 27–29. I must note that all of the Five Tribes had different cultures with regard to slavery and acculturation. For instance the Creeks, particularly the Upper Creeks, had a very informal view of slavery for a time,

so slave laws were rarely enforced and Black enslaved people were still able to assemble household goods, carpentry tools, spinning wheels, and the like, as well as cultivate their own corn, rice, and peaches. Gary Zellar, *African Creeks: Estelvste and the Creek Nation* (Norman: University of Oklahoma Press, 2007), 22.

60. Williams Reese, *Trail Sisters*, 28.

61. These four nations forbade miscegenation to different degrees. Naylor, *African Cherokees in Indian Territory*, 27–29; Wendy St. Jean, *Remaining Chickasaw in Indian Territory, 1830s–1907* (Tuscaloosa: University of Alabama Press, 2011), 45–46; *Constitution, Laws, and Treaties of the Chickasaws* (Tishomingo City, Chickasaw Nation: E. J. Foster, 1860), 96; Miles, *Ties That Bind*, 123–131; Zellar, *African Creeks*, 21.

62. AMD 6, microfilm collection, Oklahoma Historical Society.

63. The Cherokees and Creeks had laws against Blacks' use of communally owned land to build houses or barns. Interestingly, free, mixed-race Afro-Cherokees could own property and up until the early 1830s could petition to become tribal citizens. Miles, *Ties That Bind*, 127; the Choctaws and Chickasaws had laws against tribal citizens hiring free Black people. Krauthamer, *Black Slaves, Indian Masters*, 71. Wonderful books have been written solely on the subject of the interactions between Native people within the Five Tribes and their slaves. Therefore, I do not wish to thoroughly outline these relationships and the laws that surrounded them, as that is not my goal for this chapter nor for this book. For more, please see Daniel F. Littlefield Jr. (*The Chickasaw Freedmen*; *The Cherokee Freedmen*; *Africans and Seminoles* [Westport, CT: Greenwood Press, 1977]), Tiya Miles (*Ties That Bind*), Celia Naylor (*African Cherokees*), Fay Yarbrough (*Race and the Cherokee Nation*), and Barbara Krauthamer (*Black Slaves, Indian Masters*), as these authors all discuss the evolution of tribal membership norms. In 1824, the Cherokee General Council passed an act banishing free Blacks from the Cherokee Nation and also outlawing Black-Cherokee marriages. The Cherokees did have a form of acknowledging mixed-race Afro-Cherokees, but this was dependent upon tribal vote, and support for this waxed and waned. Tiya Miles argued that by the 1830s, after Removal, this had permanently changed. These practices were similar to the anti–free Black laws across the United States in the same period. Miles, *Ties That Bind*, 127.

64. Joe Williams, October 14, 1898, Applications for Enrollment of the Commission to the Five Civilized Tribes, 1898–1914, Application 438, RG 75, M1301, National Archives and Records Administration, 13; Memorial of the Freedmen of the Chickasaw Nation, Letters Received Relating to Choctaw and Other Freedmen, 1878–1884, RG 75, NARA. I am not necessarily correlating phenotype with racial identity or racial heritage here. I am simply relaying any possible "evidence" of Cohee's mixed-race ancestry and trying to get at how and why he was viewed as part of the Chickasaw Indian community.

65. Daniel F. Littlefield Jr. and Mary Ann Littlefield, "The Beams Family: Free Blacks in Indian Territory," *Journal of Negro History* 61, no. 1 (1976): 16–35.

66. Littlefield and Littlefield, "The Beams Family," 18–19.

67. Miles, *Ties That Bind*, 127.

68. "Moses Lonian" in Patrick Minges, ed., *Black Indian Slave Narratives* (Winston-Salem, NC: John F. Blair, 2004), 60.

69. "Mary Grayson" in Patrick Minges, ed., *Black Indian Slave Narratives*, 102.

70. Some historians, such as Daniel Littlefield, argue that by the time of the Civil War the Seminoles had begun to mimic the ways of the other Five Tribes and in moving to Indian Territory had acculturated to the white Euro-American ways that they had previously fought. Historian Kevin Mulroy disagrees and argues that Seminole slavery stayed the same and that the nation's acceptance of their freedpeople as citizens after the war supports his argument. Kevin Mulroy, *The Seminole Freedmen: A History* (Norman: University of Oklahoma Press, 2007), xxvii–xxix; Littlefield Jr., *Africans and Seminoles*.

71. Mulroy, *The Seminole Freedmen*, xxviii.

72. Naylor, *African Cherokees*, 135.

73. While some argue that the Keetoowah society was a recent development at the start of the war, Celia Naylor quotes James W. Duncan, a member of the society, who said that at the time of the war the society had already been functioning for years. Naylor, *African Cherokees*, 135.

74. Kidwell, *The Choctaws in Oklahoma*, 33.

75. The United States' division over slavery can largely be categorized into two primary perspectives: Proslavery supporters wanted to extend slavery into all of the territories in which the United States had begun to expand (namely, the West), while Black and white abolitionists wanted to either stop the spread of slavery or, for the more radical among them, end slavery in the United States once and for all.

76. Eric Foner and Lisa McGirr, ed., *American History Now* (Philadelphia: Temple University Press, 2011), 79–80.

77. Abolitionists' belief that Indian slave ownership was more beneficent than that of white slave owners was crucial to this argument. Though the sources I've used here cover only the Removal period, they show that there was very likely a similar confluence of reformers focused on both emancipation and/or Black rights and white encroachment into the West. Lydia Marie Child (and Helen Hunt Jackson less so) were both abolitionists who also agitated against American western expansionism, but the bulk of their activism occurred in the late 1880s. Natalie Joy, "The Indian's Cause: Abolitionists and Native American Rights," *Journal of the Civil War Era* 8, no. 2 (2018): 215–242; Alisse Portnoy, *Their Right to Speak: Women's Activism in the Indian and Slave Debates* (Cambridge, MA: Harvard University Press, 2005); John Matthew Teutsch, "'We Wish to Plead Our Own Case': Rhetorical Links Between Native Americans and African Americans During the 1820s and 1830s" (dissertation, University of Louisiana, Lafayette, 2014).

78. Ralph Ellison, *Going to the Territory* (New York: Vintage International, 1979), 120–144; "Introduction," in *African Americans on the Western Frontier*, ed. Monroe Lee Billington and Roger D. Hardaway (Niwot: University Press of Colorado, 2001). Of course, as I establish in this chapter, slavery already existed in the West, within the Five Tribes, among other places. Tiya Miles has shown that chattel slavery existed in the Midwest as

well. Miles, *The Dawn of Detroit*; Heather Cox Richardson, *The Reconstruction of America After the Civil War* (New Haven, CT: Yale University Press, 2008). For more on the political machinations behind the territorial angst around slavery and land, see Michael A. Morrison, *Slavery in the American West: The Eclipse of Manifest Destiny and the Coming of the Civil War* (Chapel Hill: University of North Carolina Press, 1997). John P. Bowes examines how non–Five Tribes eastern Indians (the Shawnee, Delaware, Wyandot, and Potawatomi) in the West (specifically eastern Kansas) were affected by and part of American expansion, the Civil War, and dialogues about slavery. Bowes, *Exiles and Pioneers*.

79. The Choctaws' previous treaties had established that once they had ceded portions of land from their Southeastern homelands they would be able to stay in Indian Territory permanently.

80. Clarissa W. Confer, *The Cherokee Nation in the Civil War* (Norman: University of Oklahoma Press, 2007), 47.

81. Cyrus Harris, "Message of Gov. Harris, of the Chickasaw Nation, to the Legislature," *Nashville Union and American*, June 11, 1861, via Chronicling America, Library of Congress, http://chroniclingamerica.loc.gov.proxyiub.uits.iu.edu/lccn/sn85038518/1861-06-11/ed-1/seq-1/.

82. Annie Heloise Abel, *The Indian as Slaveholder and Secessionist* (Cleveland: Arthur H. Clark Company, 1919), 97–99.

83. This land was not officially recognized by American officials as belonging to Plains Indian tribes. Abel, *The American Indian as Slaveholder and Secessionist*, 76–104; Kidwell, *The Choctaws in Oklahoma*, 19. The Leased District was land (the land beyond the 98th meridian) originally granted to the Choctaws for their settlement in Indian Territory as part of Removal negotiations. It was later leased to the U.S. government by the Choctaws for the settlement of Wichita Indians and other related Indian nations as part of the Treaty of 1855.

84. Harris, "Message of Gov. Harris, of the Chickasaw Nation, to the Legislature."

85. Abel, *The American Indian as Slaveholder and Secessionist*, 91–92, 161–162.

86. "Treaty with the Cherokee, 1835," *National Museum of the American Indian*, https://americanindian.si.edu/static/nationtonation/pdf/Treaty-of-New-Echota-1835.pdf, accessed 2019. In 2019, the Cherokee Nation of Oklahoma took its first steps in attempting to have a tribal representative seated in Congress.

87. "From the Cherokee Nation: Proclamation of the Chief, John Ross," *Evening Star*, June 28, 1861, via Chronicling America, Library of Congress, https://chroniclingamerica.loc.gov/lccn/sn83045462/1861-06-28/ed-1/seq-1/.

88. "Ross, John (1790–1866)," *Oklahoma Historical Society*, https://www.okhistory.org/publications/enc/entry.php?entry=RO031.

89. Census of the Southern Refugee Indians in Kansas and the Cherokee Nation, 1863, Letters Received by the Office of Indian Affairs, M234, Roll 835, NARA. The Chickasaws had the third lowest refugee population during the war. At least two of the other nations mentioned in the document, including the Kickapoos and the Wyandot, had

smaller refugee numbers. However, these nations were also significantly smaller than the Chickasaws. Thus, it would require a more complicated mathematical equation to evaluate how these nations' refugee numbers actually compared relative to their total populations.

90. Report of the commissioner of Indian affairs, Annual report of the commissioner of Indian affairs for the year 1862, United States Office of Indian Affairs, 27.

91. "Mary Grayson" in *Black Indian Slave Narratives*, 105, 107.

92. Ibid., 107.

93. Gibson, *The Chickasaws*, 238.

94. Abel, *The American Indian as Slaveholder and Secessionist*, 161–162; Grant Foreman, *The Five Civilized Tribes* (Norman: University of Oklahoma Press, 1934), 130, 158–161; Southern superintendency, annual report of the commissioner of Indian affairs, for the year 1859, United States Office of Indian Affairs, 188.

95. *Arkansas Gazette*, October 8, 1835, Letters Received by the Office of Indian Affairs, Choctaw Agency, 1824–1876, microcopy 234, roll 170, frame 763, NARA.

96. John Stuart to Herring, 28 January 1836, frames 761–762, Infantry Capt, Ft. Coffee in Letters Received by the Office of Indian Affairs, Choctaw Agency, 1824–1876, Microcopy 234, roll 170, frame 763, NARA.

97. In 1862 about forty loyal Chickasaws arrived at Fort Arbuckle in an effort to join Union military forces. Southern superintendency, annual report of the commissioner of Indian affairs, for the year 1862, United States Office of Indian Affairs, 141.

98. Christopher Perello, "Warpath: Indian Territory in the American Civil War," *Strategy & Tactics* 291 (2015): 6–19.

99. Ibid.

100. William Blue, 1904, Applications for Enrollment of the Commission to the Five Civilized Tribes, Application 1463, 2; Isaac Kemp, 1904, Applications for Enrollment of the Commission to the Five Civilized Tribes, Application 34, 3; Henry Shannon, 1898, Applications for Enrollment of the Commission to the Five Civilized Tribes, Application 500, 14.

101. Annie Heloise Abel, *The American Indian as Participant in the Civil War* (Cleveland, OH: Arthur H. Clark Company, 1919), 223–224.

102. Thomas Spence, *The settler's guide in the United States and British North American provinces adapted to benefit the settlers in the various states and territories, being a synoptical review of the soil, climate, cereal, and other productions, with the minerals, manufactures, etc., etc., of each state separately; carefully arranged and compiled from manufacturing reports, state documents, and stand-alone works now extant, as well as personal observation and notes* (New York: Davis & Kent, Publishers, 1862), 234.

103. Report of the commissioner of Indian affairs, Annual report of the commissioner of Indian affairs for the year 1862, United States Office of Indian Affairs, 25.

104. Southern superintendency, Annual report of the commissioner of Indian affairs, for the year 1862, United States Office of Indian Affairs, 167.

105. Ibid.

106. Elliott West, *The Last Indian War: The Nez Perce Story* (New York: Oxford

University Press, 2009). As Elliott West argued, Indigenous peoples in the far West soon saw that their only recourse was war, as they had little bargaining power. Steven Hahn, "Slave Emancipation, Indian Peoples, and the Projects of a New American Nation-State," *Journal of the Civil War Era* 3, no. 3 (2013): 307–330. Steven Hahn connected the Civil War to the destruction of Native sovereignty in the far West and Native peoples' military reactions to this. He also described the dual emancipation of Black enslaved people and the "destruction of Indian sovereignty" in the West as part of the "Wars of Rebellion," which created an imperial nation-state in North America for the first time.

107. Southern superintendency, Annual report of the commissioner of Indian affairs, for the year 1862, United States Office of Indian Affairs, 167.

108. Anne S. Rubin, *A Shattered Nation: The Rise and Fall of the Confederacy, 1861–1868* (Chapel Hill: University of North Carolina Press, 2005), 143, 152.

109. James M. McPherson, *Battle Cry of Freedom: The Civil War Era* (New York: Oxford University Press, 1988), 849.

110. Once again, *most* Indians were not yet citizens, though some were—mainly those who had been absorbed in locations left behind by the majority of their tribes during Removal, and also many smaller tribes in the Northeast.

111. Cox Richardson, *West from Appomattox*, 4–5. Heather Cox Richardson's argument that the image of the West served an important function in the reconciliation of the North and the South during Reconstruction is important to my point here. I supplement her argument with the contention that the Black and Native people actually living in the West (Native Americans and African Americans) played an even more important part in the way settlement was carried out.

112. LeRoy H. Fischer, ed., *The Civil War in Indian Territory* (Los Angeles: Lorrin L. Morrison, 1974), 134.

113. Littlefield, *The Chickasaw Freedmen*, 21.

114. "Treaty with the Choctaw and Chickasaw, 1866," in *Indian Affairs Laws and Treaties*, vol. 2, comp. and ed. Charles J. Kappler (Washington, DC: GPO, 1904), 918–931, available online at Oklahoma State University Digital Collections, https://dc.library.okstate.edu/digital/collection/kapplers/id/26759, accessed May 5, 2016;

Kidwell, *The Choctaws in Oklahoma*, 19. The Treaty of 1855 between the United States and the Choctaw Nation had already provided a precursor for railroads through the nation as well as for the settlement of Wichita Indians and related nations.

115. "Treaty with the Choctaw and Chickasaw, 1866."

CHAPTER 2

A portion of this chapter was previously published as "A Different Forty Acres: Land, Kin, and Migration in the Late Nineteenth-Century West," *Journal of the Civil War Era* 10, no. 2 (2020): 212–232, copyright © 2020 by the University of North Carolina Press, used by permission of the publisher, https://www.uncpress.org.

1. "Ned Thompson" in *Black Indian Slave Narratives*, 135–136.

2. David Nichols, "All That Is Solid Melts into Money: Indian Removal and the Commodification of the Chickasaw Homeland" (paper presentation, British Association of Nineteenth-Century Historians Meeting, Madingley Hall, Cambridge University, October 10, 2015), 6.

3. The Dawes Act affected tribes across North America, but for the Five Tribes this piece of legislation was more or less portended in the Treaties of 1866.

4. The Dawes Act was formally named the General Allotment Act or the Dawes Severalty Act of 1887. The Dawes Act began the process of nationwide allotment, but this process did not affect the Five Tribes because they did not live on reservations, instead holding their land in fee simple. To remedy this, on June 28, 1898, Congress issued "An Act for the Protection of the People of the Indian Territory, and Other Purposes," or the Curtis Act, which terminated tribal title to all lands of the Five Tribes without their consent, and this placed questions regarding citizenship, property, and rights under the jurisdiction of the federal courts. Nonetheless, the origin of this process was the Dawes Act. Hoxie, *A Final Promise*, xviii.

5. Hoxie, *A Final Promise*, xviii. Also see C. Joseph Genetin-Pilawa, *Crooked Paths to Allotment: The Fight over Federal Indian Policy After the Civil War* (Chapel Hill: University of North Carolina Press, 2012), 89; William E. Unrau, *Mixed-Bloods and Tribal Dissolution: Charles Curtis and the Quest for Indian Identity* (Lawrence: University Press of Kansas, 1989).

6. Many Indians and freedpeople sought to claim land they already lived on and had improved.

7. Applications for Enrollment of the Commission to the Five Civilized Tribes.

8. When Civil War and Reconstruction scholarship has focused on African Americans' connections to land, it has most often fixated on its absence, namely, on the momentous loss for Black economic and social processes wrought by African Americans' inability to access land. Often this takes the form of the forty acres that General Sherman set aside in the Sea Islands for the Gullah Geechee people during the Civil War (an idea originated by Gullah Geechee people) or of a more generalized lamentation about Republicans' inability to grant African Americans free or low-fee purchases of land as a type of reparation. See Schwalm, *A Hard Fight for We*, 5–6, 151–152, 154–160; Akiko Ochiai, "The Port Royal Experiment Revisited: Northern Visions of Reconstruction and the Land Question," *New England Quarterly* 74, no. 1 (2001): 94–117; LaWanda Cox, "The Promise of Land for the Freedmen," *Mississippi Valley Historical Review* 45, no. 3 (1958): 413–440; Sydney Nathans, *A Mind to Stay: White Plantation, Black Homeland* (Cambridge, MA: Harvard University Press, 2017); Edward Magdol, *A Right to the Land: Essays on the Freedmen's Community* (Westport, CT: Greenwood Press, 1977); Karen Cook Bell, *Claiming Freedom: Race, Kinship, and Land in Nineteenth-Century Georgia* (Columbia: University of South Carolina Press, 2018).

9. Leslie Schwalm, Steven Hahn, and Anthony E. Kaye have argued that land and place were extremely important to African Americans, using Black people's own arguments that land redistribution might serve as remuneration for their labor. Schwalm, *A Hard Fight for*

We; Hahn, *A Nation Under Our Feet*; Anthony E. Kaye, *Joining Places: Slave Neighborhoods in the Old South* (Chapel Hill: University of North Carolina Press, 2009).

10. Naturally, African Americans in the United States found fulfillment in land and community as well. Once again, see Schwalm, *A Hard Fight for We*; Hahn, *A Nation Under Our Feet*; Kaye, *Joining Places*; Hunter, *Bound in Wedlock*.

11. Here I refer to failed *systematic* efforts to distribute land to African Americans in the United States. Some individual Black families throughout the country managed to buy and hold on to land for generations. *Forty Acres and a Mule: The Freedmen's Bureau and Black Land Ownership* examines the primary reasons most Black people were never able to obtain land but also delineates the strategies through which a few families did manage to do so. Claude F. Oubre, *Forty Acres and a Mule: The Freedmen's Bureau and Black Land Ownership* (Baton Rouge: Louisiana State University Press, 1978). *Beyond Forty Acres and a Mule: African American Landowning Families Since Reconstruction*; *A Mind to Stay: White Plantation, Black Homeland*; *Standing Their Ground: Small Farmers in North Carolina Since the Civil War*, and *The Black Towns* showcase Black families in the South and West from the early twentieth century to the modern day who managed to overcome individual and structural racism to purchase their own land parcels. All four of these books seek to show that the Black experience post–Civil War was not solely one of desolate sharecropping, though it still stands that this was the overwhelming experience of Black people in the United States. Debra A. Reid and Evan P. Bennett, eds., *Beyond Forty Acres and a Mule: African American Landowning Families Since Reconstruction* (Gainesville: University Press of Florida, 2012); Sydney Nathans, *A Mind to Stay: White Plantation, Black Homeland* (Cambridge, MA: Harvard University Press, 2017); Adrienne Monteith Petty, *Standing Their Ground: Small Farmers in North Carolina Since the Civil War* (New York: Oxford University Press, 2013); Norman L. Crockett, *The Black Towns* (Lawrence: Regents Press of Kansas, 1979). Also see Michael Lanza, *Agrarianism and Reconstruction Politics: The Southern Homestead Act* (Baton Rouge: Louisiana State University Press, 1990); Joel Williamson, *After Slavery: The Negro in South Carolina During Reconstruction, 1861–1877* (Chapel Hill: University of North Carolina Press, 1965).

12. There were also unique circumstances among Chickasaws and Choctaws that affected the way they treated their former slaves and the way they reacted to the latter's desire to live among them. While all of the Five Tribes agreed to adopt their former slaves as citizens in their Treaties of 1866, the Choctaws and Chickasaws alone were given a choice to actually carry this out, and money was on the line. In the treaty, they agreed to lease a portion of their lands (referred to as the "Leased District") to other tribes to live on as more Indian nations removed to Indian Territory. The United States stipulated, however, that they would get the monies for this land—which they had already been promised prior to the Civil War—only if they adopted their former slaves as citizens. If they chose not to do so, their former slaves would be removed from their nations and they would not receive their payment for the lands—rather, the United States would keep it. The historical records do not show why this option existed for Choctaws and Chickasaws alone, but, given the

history of these two nations and their actions and prejudice toward their former slaves, perhaps the United States saw a chance to again abuse Native Americans, because they believed the Choctaws' and Chickasaws' prejudice would win out and prevent them from adopting their freedpeople. Before the war the Choctaws and Chickasaws were to be paid $800,000 for these same lands. After the war, this was lowered to $300,000 and tied to this provision for freedpeople's citizenship. Donald A. Grinde Jr. and Quintard Taylor, "Red vs Black: Conflict and Accommodation in the Post Civil War Indian Territory 1865–1907," *American Indian Quarterly* 8, no. 3 (1984): 213.

13. Though Chickasaw freedpeople initially thought they would eventually gain citizenship in the Chickasaw Nation, as Choctaw freedpeople did, by the late 1870s they knew this was increasingly unlikely. Yet, many still made the same choice as Josie.

14. I have not included Seminole freedpeople here because the way in which they carried out the Dawes "system" was entirely different from that of the Choctaws, Cherokees, Chickasaws, and even Creeks. Most Seminoles appear to have boycotted the process by refusing to enroll, and the thoroughness of this boycott—many Dawes cards are blank and there are few real Dawes testimonies—suggests the Seminole tribal governmental approved of this boycott.

15. Joe Williams, 1904, Applications for Enrollment of the Commission to the Five Civilized Tribes, Application 438, 12.

16. Ibid., 4. A note on Dawes packets citations: The process of a freedperson's enrollment required testimony and information corroboration from many sources. Therefore, the name used in the citation is not necessarily always the person speaking or referenced in the testimony, as witnesses recounted events that implicated other persons of their own volition or at the behest of a commissioner or questioner.

17. "Kiziah Love," in *Black Indian Slave Narratives*, 182.

18. Choctaw freedpeople would later be adopted as tribal citizens, but their experiences right after the Civil War more mirrored those of Chickasaw freedpeople than any of the Black members of the other Five Tribes.

19. Naylor, *African Cherokees in Indian Territory*, 166.

20. Katja May, *African Americans and Native Americans in the Creek and Cherokee Nations, 1830s to 1920s: Collision and Collusion* (New York: Garland Publishing, 1996), 96–97.

21. Grinde and Taylor, "Red vs Black," 213.

22. Jennifer Morgan, "'Some Could Suckle over Their Shoulder': Male Travelers, Female Bodies, and the Gendering of Racial Ideology, 1500–1770," *William and Mary Quarterly* 54, no. 1 (1997): 167–192.

23. United States Congress, *Congressional Globe: Containing the Debates and Proceedings of the First Session of the Thirty-Ninth Congress*, 95, via University of North Texas Digital Library, https://digital.library.unt.edu/.

24. Report on Indian Affairs, 1830, Annual Report of the Commissioner of Indian Affairs, for the Years 1826–1839, 34.

25. Johnson Brigham, *James Harlan* (Iowa City: State Historical Society of Iowa, 1913), 165–166, 189.

26. Ibid., 211.

27. Ibid., 165–166, 189.

28. Ibid., 141–142.

29. Ibid., 143.

30. Ibid., 145.

31. Ibid., 165–166. In 1865, before the war's end, the Senate debated a bill (Bill 459) introduced by Senator James Harlan of Iowa. The Harlan Bill called for reorganizing Indian Territory along the lines of other federal territories, dissolving tribal jurisdictions, and allowing settlement by whites. Cherokee Chief John Ross argued strongly against the proposal. The bill did not become law, but by the end of the war Harlan was secretary of the interior. Clearly, Harlan was thinking about separating Native peoples from their land and tribal sovereignty at the same time that he originated the terms of land allotment to Indian freedpeople. Moulton, Ross Papers II, 630 quoted in Joyce Ann Kievit, "Trail of Tears to Veil of Tears: The Impact of Removal on Reconstruction" (dissertation, University of Houston, 2002), 138–141.

32. The precursor to the Fourteenth and Fifteenth Amendments, the Civil Rights Act of 1866, was ratified in April 1866, around the same time that the Treaties of 1866 were being negotiated.

33. The Supreme Court had ruled in *Worcester v. Georgia* (1832) that Indian nations were "domestic dependent nations" with the ability to create their own laws and regulate their own citizens.

34. "Treaty with the Choctaw and Chickasaw, 1866," 329; Kidwell, *The Choctaws in Oklahoma*, 19. Again, the Treaty of 1855 between the United States and the Choctaw Nation had already provided a precedent for allowing railroads through the nation as well as for the settlement of Wichita Indians and related nations.

35. Thaddeus Stevens, "Remarks on Choctaw Defense, March 2, 1867, in Congress," in *The Selected Papers of Thaddeus Stevens, Volume 2: April 1865–August 1868*, ed. Beverly Wilson Palmer (Pittsburgh, PA: University of Pittsburgh Press, 1998). In March 1867, while in Congress, Congressman Stevens did remark on the Choctaws' (and Chickasaws') legal fight to be paid the annuities owed them by the U.S. government for the cession of their lands. Stevens believed they should be paid and speculated that they had joined the Confederacy for the same reason that many Southerners had—because they were slave-holders. He also incorrectly stated that the Choctaws had "abolished slavery, even before it was abolished elsewhere"—perhaps confusing the Choctaws with the Cherokees. It seems that if he were to remark on African Americans being given land in Indian Territory, this would have been the instance at which he would have done so. Perhaps, then, this matter was confined to the specific congressional committee that handled the matters in Indian Territory (and across Native America).

36. United States Congress, *Congressional Globe: Containing the Debates and*

Proceedings of the Second Session of the Thirty-Ninth Congress; Together With an Appendix, Comprising the Laws Passed at that Session; A Supplement, Embracing the Proceedings in the Trial of Andrew Johnson, 1814, via University of North Texas Digital Library, http://digital. library.unt.edu/ark:/67531/metadc30918/. Doolittle had just compiled a report on the state of Native America and thus was likely the person with the most knowledge on the subject in the Senate at the time. Harry Kelsey, "The Doolittle Report of 1867: Its Preparation and Shortcomings," *Arizona and the West* 17, no. 2 (1975): 107–120.

37. United States Congress, *Congressional Globe*, 1814.

38. Ibid. Doolittle began advocating for Black homesteads outside of North America as early as 1862. "Speech of Hon. J.R. Doolittle of Wisconsin on Homesteads for white men in the temperate zone—homesteads for black men in the tropics—white immigration to and Black emigration from the United States—a continental policy, embracing all climes and races, bringing freedom and homes to all; delivered in the Senate of the United States, April 11, 1862" (Washington, DC: Printed at the *Congressional Globe* office, 1862), 11–12. For more on this, see Chapter 3.

39. Annual report of the commissioner of Indian affairs, for the year 1863, United States Office of Indian Affairs, 35.

40. Ibid.

41. 54th Cong., 1st sess., *Senate Document* 182, 111.

42. John Sanborn to Hon. James Harlan, Secretary of the Interior, January 1, 1866, M234, Roll 837, NARA.

43. This does not mean that Indian freedpeople were free from white paternalism. In earlier communications Secretary Harlan emphasized that Sanborn follow a similar system to Freedmen's Bureau agents in the United States, encouraging him to "impress upon [Indian freedpeople] the fact that they will not be supported or encouraged to idle habits but must labor for their own support and to this end you will encourage them in making contracts with such persons as may be willing to hire them as laborers either for wages in money or receiving a share of the crops to be raised." Secretary Harlan to Genl. John Sanborn, November 20, 1865, M234, Roll 837, NARA.

44. Report on Indian Affairs, 1830, Annual Report of the Commissioner of Indian Affairs, for the Years 1826–1839, 34.

45. Blain Holman, Indian Pioneer Papers.

46. Senate Bill 2033, February 9, 1892, Letters Received, 5579-92; Congressional Record, 52nd Cong., 1st sess. (February 3, 1892), 789; 54th Cong., 1st sess., Senate Document 12, 11-21; Loren N. Brown, "The Dawes Commission," *Chronicles of Oklahoma* 9 (1931): 71–105.

47. "Freedmen in the Indian Territory," *New York Times*, April 25, 1870.

48. Greg Downs discusses how African Americans in the United States similarly learned to lobby for themselves and, as Downs puts it, claim *both* self-determination and dependence. Downs, *Declarations of Dependence*, 45–46. Justin LeRoy touches on the complex relations between the United States, the Five Tribes, and Indian freedpeople in

his "Black History in Occupied Territory: On the Entanglements of Slavery and Settler Colonialism," *Theory & Event* 19, no. 4 (2016).

49. Memorial of a Committee on Behalf of the Colored People of the Choctaw and Chickasaw Tribes of Indians, Lee Harkins Collection Manuscripts, Oklahoma Historical Society.

50. John Sanborn to Hon. James Harlan, Secretary of the Interior, January 1, 1866, M234, Roll 837, NARA.

51. R. H. McDuffie to the Dawes Commission, December 21, 1899, Dawes Commission Roll 53, NARA.

52. William Love to the Dawes Commission, December 20, 1899, Dawes Commission Roll 53, NARA.

53. Frances Grayson to the Dawes Commission, January 9, 1900, Dawes Commission Roll 53, NARA.

54. "Eliza Whitmore" in *Black Indian Slave Narratives*, 39.

55. Travis D. Roberts (family member) in discussion with author, September 2, 2013.

56. "Charley Moore Brown" in *Black Indian Slave Narratives*, 198–200.

57. "Nellie Johnson" in *Black Indian Slave Narratives*, 133–134.

58. In various records, the surname "Stephenson" is alternately spelled "Stevenson."

59. Lillie Roberts and Herbert Booker (family members), in discussion with author, August 12, 2013; Travis D. Roberts (family member), in discussion with author, September 2, 2013.

60. Travis D. Roberts (family member) in discussion with author, September 2, 2013.

61. Roberts family, Roberts family ledger, accessed September 2, 2013.

62. Travis D. Roberts (family member) in discussion with author, September 2, 2013.

63. Ibid. There are no existing figures on the number of weekly attendees at the church's peak, but the church holds around seventy people, and according to Travis D. Roberts, the church was often at capacity in the early twentieth century.

64. Black slaves sometimes spoke more English than their Chickasaw owners because they had usually been owned by whites before being sold into the Chickasaw Nation. Of course, Christianity was present in Africa before the Transatlantic Slave Trade; therefore, some Africans already possessed Christian beliefs. Littlefield, *The Chickasaw Freedmen*, 89; Michael A. Gomez, *Exchanging Our Country Marks: The Transformation of African Identities in the Colonial and Antebellum South* (Chapel Hill: University of North Carolina Press, 1998), 59.

65. Littlefield, *The Chickasaw Freedmen*, 89.

66. Williams Reese, *Trail Sisters*, 126

67. Annual Reports of the Secretary of the Interior, Commissioner of Indian Affairs, and Secretary of War relating to Indian Affairs 1872–1875, Roll 7, MMF 610, 209.

68. Letter from the Secretary of the Interior, Office of Indian Affairs, May 8, 1888, DC Roll 051, Oklahoma Historical Society, 8.

69. Matilda Davis, 1904, Applications for Enrollment of the Commission to the Five

Civilized Tribes, Application 1026, 3–4; Lucy Varner, 1906, Applications for Enrollment of the Commission to the Five Civilized Tribes, Application 1027, 48; Marie Garland, "History Skips School Built by Miss Dawes," *Oklahoma's Orbit*, August 8, 1971.

70. Garland, "History Skips School Built by Miss Dawes."

71. Ibid.; figure acquired through the use of Measuringworth.com.

72. Garland, "History Skips School Built by Miss Dawes."

73. Ibid.

74. John Hope Franklin and John Whittington Franklin, eds., *My Life and an Era: The Autobiography of Buck Colbert Franklin* (Baton Rouge: Louisiana State University Press, 1997), 75.

75. Quarterly Report, Section X-Chickasaw Indians-Schools-Dawes Academy (Black), Oklahoma Historical Society.

76. Williams Reese, *Trail Sisters*, 121.

77. Ibid.

78. Ibid., 123.

79. Daniel F. Littlefield Jr., *The Cherokee Freedmen: From Emancipation to American Citizenship* (Westport, CT: Greenwood Press, 1978), 52–53.

80. M. Thomas Bailey, *Reconstruction in Indian Territory: A Story of Avarice, Discrimination, and Opportunism* (New York: Kennikat Press, 1972), 183; Zellar, *African Creeks*, 110.

81. Williams Reese, *Trail Sisters*, 126.

82. Zellar, *African Creeks*, 95.

83. "The Secretary of the Interior and the Choctaw and Chickasaw Treaty," *Cherokee Advocate* 5, no. 71 (1874).

84. When not actively comparing them to their former slaves, many governmental agents still spoke well of the Five Tribes—particularly when comparing them to other Indian people.

85. Williams Reese, *Trail Sisters*, 129.

86. Kristy Feldhousen-Giles, "To Prove Who You Are: Freedmen Identities in Oklahoma" (dissertation, University of Oklahoma, 2008), 104.

87. Ibid., 123–125.

88. Littlefield, *The Cherokee Freedmen*, 49; Smithers, *The Cherokee Diaspora*, 206; Patrick Minges, *Slavery in the Cherokee Nation: The Keetoowah Society and the Defining of a People, 1855-1867* (New York: Routledge, 2004), 152. Some Cherokee leaders used the fact that freedpeople often formed their own communities as evidence that they didn't want Cherokee citizenship.

89. Feldhousen-Giles, "To Prove Who You Are: Freedmen Identities in Oklahoma," 45–50, 57.

90. This was essentially a use-title arrangement. Zellar, *African Creeks*, 85.

91. May, *African Americans and Native Americans in the Creek and Cherokee Nations, 1830s to 1920s*, 179–180; Thomas Knight, "Black Towns in Oklahoma: Their Development and Survival" (dissertation, Oklahoma State University, 1975), 88.

92. Dawes sources, a mixture of letters and transcripts of verbal testimony, allow us

to see Indian freedpeople's economic motivations *and* their ideological and emotional connections to land. The Dawes sources are similar, in some ways, to the Federal Writers' Project Slave Narratives (the Federal Writers' Project was later renamed Works Progress Administration). Historians have used the Federal Writers' Project (FWP) interviews to discuss the creation of African American culture and the (after)effects of slavery. The Dawes Commission sought to extract specific facts from each application, so the resulting testimonies are not as varied and extended as the FWP interviews. And, of course, commissioners were not interested in cultural preservation. In this way, the Dawes testimonies are more similar to pension claims, as discussed by Elizabeth Regosin, in that both include strategic claims made by people of African descent. Dawes testimonies cannot serve the same function, then, as the FWP interviews. The Dawes records *can*, however, be used to create a portrait of patterns of movement, neighborhood politics, and interpersonal relationships. Elizabeth Regosin, *Freedom's Promise: Ex-Slave Families and Citizenship in the Age of Emancipation* (Charlottesville: University Press of Virginia, 2002), x, 15.

93. Theresa Gatewood, 1904, Applications for Enrollment of the Commission to the Five Civilized Tribes, Application 392, 3.

94. Ira Berlin, *The Long Emancipation: The Demise of Slavery in the United States* (Cambridge, MA: Harvard University Press, 2015). Ira Berlin explored emancipation as a process in the United States, but he looked at it as the eventual result of years of work by abolitionists and African Americans—which ended in 1865 with the end of the Civil War. Other scholars, such as Manisha Sinha, have added to this perspective. Throughout this book, I look at emancipation as a process in which people of African descent expressed freedom in various ways for decades *after* the Civil War.

95. I am able to reference only people who returned to speak with the Dawes Commission. The number of people who permanently left the Chickasaw Nation is likely higher, but it is impossible to ascertain.

96. Alice Bennett, 1902, Applications for Enrollment, Application 385, 5.

97. Ibid., 6.

98. Ibid., 4.

99. Among historians, David Chang has, in my opinion, most connected the land that Indian freedpeople sought to possess to the dispossessed Native Americans from whom it was taken. Chang, *The Color of the Land.*

100. Here, I am inspired by Stephanie Camp's theory of "rival geographies," which is the idea that white owners and Black slaves inhabited different spaces representing "rival geographies." By challenging white space and whites' control of Black bodies and space, enslaved people resisted white supremacy through mobility. Stephanie Camp, *Closer to Freedom: Enslaved Women and Everyday Resistance in the Plantation South* (Chapel Hill: University of North Carolina Press, 2004).

101. This also mirrors Stephanie Camps's idea of "rival geographies," wherein white owners' "social place" was situated upon their control of Black movement and their containment to certain places. Camp, *Closer to Freedom.*

102. Morris Sheppard, Federal Writers' Project: Slave Narrative Project, vol. 13, Oklahoma, Adams-Young, 288.

103. M234, Roll 837, NARA.

104. Ibid.

105. Annie Heloise Abel, *The American Indian Under Reconstruction* (Cleveland, OH: Arthur H. Clark Company, 1919), 288–289.

106. Address by P. P. Pitchlynn, Principal Chief of the Choctaw Nation, and Winchester Colbert, Governor of the Chickasaw Nation, to the Choctaws and Chickasaws, July 12, 1866, Chickasaw National Records, Box 6A, Doc. #7067, Oklahoma Historical Society. The Chickasaws and Choctaws alone had the choice to accept their former slaves as citizens and receive $300,000 as payment for the sale of their portion of the Leased District or to receive nothing if they did not adopt them as citizens. This choice likely affected Pitchlynn's and Colbert's rhetoric here.

107. Message of Gov. C. B. Burney to the Chickasaw Legislature, September 24, 1879, *Cherokee Advocate*, Oklahoma Historical Society.

108. Littlefield, *The Chickasaw Freedmen*, 70.

109. Reports of Agents in Indian Territory, Annual report of the commissioner of Indian affairs, 1888, 116.

110. Annual Message of Gov. D. H. Johnston, September 15, 1898, Litton, Gaston Collection M-2065 Box 2, Oklahoma Historical Society.

111. This chapter was written in the spirit of Leslie Schwalm's take on post–Civil War Black women "insisting on their right to live and work (without white supervision) on the land they and their ancestors had worked as slaves (often returning to these lands from being elsewhere)." In this chapter, I broaden this not just to women undertaking a gendered migration, but to men and women using movement to maintain ties to family and land. Schwalm, *A Hard Fight for We*, 5–6, 151–152, 154–160.

CHAPTER 3

1. Jackson Peters, 1898, Applications for Enrollment of the Commission to the Five Civilized Tribes, Application 219, 2.

2. Increasingly, historians have emphasized that Black political participation did not end with the Compromise of 1877. Especially at the local level, a number of African American communities continued to organize and vote, but they did not have the federal and legislative backing they had during the "Reconstruction" period. Karen Cook Bell, "Local Politics and Black Freedom After the Civil War," *Black Perspectives*, https://www.aaihs.org/local-politics-and-black-freedom-after-the-civil-war/, accessed 2019; Cook Bell, *Claiming Freedom*.

3. The original 1862 Homestead Act applied to 30 states, including midwestern states such as Michigan, Wisconsin, Ohio, and Indiana. The Southern Homestead Act of 1866 used this same idea of civilizing, recreating, and extending the American nation to rebuild the South after the war, and it included the states of Alabama,

Mississippi, Louisiana, Arkansas, and Florida. While the Civil Rights Act of 1866 gave freedpeople the right to homestead, and the Southern Homestead Act reduced the fee to prove a land claim, prohibited sale of homestead lands, and prohibited discrimination by race of color, among other things, most freedpeople were still too poor to partake, lacking the tools to cultivate land and to fight powerful corporate interests, like the timber industry. In addition, African Americans were subject to hostile violence from whites, and many had already signed labor contracts, which prevented them from homesteading. Thus, the failure of the Southern Homestead Act must also be looked at as a motivator for Blacks to go to the West. Richard Edwards, "African Americans and the Southern Homestead Act," *Great Plains Quarterly* 39, no. 2 (2019): 103–127.

4. "An Act to Secure Homesteads to Actual Settlers on the Public Domain," *A Century of Lawmaking for a New Nation: U.S. Congressional Documents and Debates, 1774–1875*, Library of Congress, https://memory.loc.gov/cgi-bin/ampage?collId=llsl&fileName=012/llsl012.db&recNum=423.

5. Ralph Ellison, *Going to the Territory* (New York: Random House, 1986).

6. While some enslaved people did allege that they were treated better by their Indian owners than their own white previous owners (many slaves of Indians were first owned by whites) or better than African Americans owned by whites (in general) were treated, enslaved people had a variety of experiences depending on their owner, where they lived, and their gender. This myth of large-scale benevolent Native slaveholding was a rumor largely spread by white abolitionists seeking to reconcile the tribulations of Native peoples (whom they also advocated for) with the fact that some Native women and men were involved in the practice of slavery, an institution these abolitionists found repugnant. Joy, "The Indian's Cause: Abolitionists and Native American Rights."

7. "Sherman's Special Field Orders No. 15," in *The War of the Rebellion: A Compilation of the Official Records of the Union and Confederate Armies*, series I, vol. 47, part II (Washington, DC: Government Printing Office, 1895), 60–62.

8. Cox, "The Promise of Land for the Freedmen," 414, 413.

9. "The First Confiscation Act," *Freedmen & Southern Society Project*, http://www.freedmen.umd.edu/conact1.htm, accessed 2019; "The Second Confiscation Act," *Freedmen & Southern Society Project*, http://www.freedmen.umd.edu/conact2.htm, accessed 2019; "Executive Order," *The American Presidency Project*, http://www.presidency.ucsb.edu/ws/?pid=72312, accessed 2019.

10. Containing the Debates and Proceedings of the First Session Fortieth Congress; Also Special Session of the Senate," *Congressional Globe*, 1867; Thaddeus Stevens, https://chnm.gmu.edu/courses/122/recon/stevens.htm, 204, accessed 2019.

11. Report of the Secretary of War, communicating, in compliance with a resolution of the Senate of the 26th of May, a copy of the preliminary report, and also of the final report of the American Freedmen's Inquiry Commission, 166.

12. Charles Sumner, "Further Guaranties in Reconstruction: Loyalty, Education, and

a Homestead for Freedmen; Measures of Reconstruction: Not a Burden or Penalty," in *The Works of Charles Sumner Vol. XI* (Boston: Lee and Shepard, 1875), 124.

13. Ibid.,128.

14. Ibid., 129.

15. Shirley Ann Wilson Moore, *Sweet Freedom's Plains: African Americans in the Overland Trails, 1841–1869* (Norman: University of Oklahoma Press, 2016). Shirley Ann Wilson Moore has shown that African Americans migrated to the far West beginning in the 1840s, using overland trails that took them to Oregon, California, Utah, New Mexico, and Idaho; African American migration westward escalated after emancipation.

16. United States, *U.S. Bureau of the Census, Extra Census Bulletin: The Five Civilized Tribes of the Indian Territory* (Washington, DC: Government Printing Office, 1894), 7–8; United States, *U.S. Bureau of the Census, Statistics for Oklahoma, Thirteenth Census of the United States, 1910* (Washington, DC: Government Printing Office, 1913), 695.

17. In *Dred Scott v. Sanford* (1857), the U.S. Supreme Court ruled that African Americans were not citizens. This would not be overruled on the federal level until the Fourteenth Amendment. "An Act to Secure Homesteads to Actual Settlers on the Public Domain." While (white) women had access to some privileges of citizenship, they could not yet vote. For more on the complexities of the variations in white women's citizenship before the Nineteenth Amendment, see Linda Kerber, *No Constitutional Right to Be Ladies: Women and the Obligations of Citizenship* (New York: Hill and Wang, 1998).

18. This does not mean I believe poor whites did not benefit from this legislation. I believe The Homesteading Project's assertion that land transfer through the Homestead Act was largely successful and that there was less fraud and transfer to big business than previously believed. Richard Edwards, "Changing Perceptions of Homesteading as a Policy of Public Domain Disposal," *Great Plains Quarterly* 29, no. 3 (2009): 179–202.

19. Joanne Turner-Sadler, *African American History: An Introduction* (New York: Peter Lang Publishing Inc., 2009), 82

20. "The Homestead Act of 1862," Library of Congress, https://blogs.loc.gov/law/2019/05/the-homestead-act-of-1862/, accessed 2019.

21. "Free Homes in Minnesota," *St. Cloud Democrat*, June 19, 1862, Chronicling America, Library of Congress.

22. "The Homestead Act," *Big Blue Union*, December 27, 1862, Chronicling America, Library of Congress.

23. "Negroes Among the Civilized Indian Tribes-Information Not Generally Known," *Freeman*, August 19, 1893, America's Historical Newspapers website.

24. Ibid.

25. "Negroes Among the Civilized Indian Tribes-Information Not Generally Known."

26. Ibid.; Saunt, "The Paradox of Freedom: Tribal Sovereignty and Emancipation During the Reconstruction of Indian Territory."

27. "Negroes Among the Civilized Indian Tribes-Information Not Generally Known."

28. "Millionaire Indian Slaves," *Washington Bee*, January 27, 1906, America's Historical Newspapers website.

29. Ibid.

30. Arthur Tolson, "The Negro in Oklahoma Territory, 1889–1907: A Study in Racial Discrimination" (dissertation, University of Oklahoma, 1966), 3.

31. Ibid.

32. Ibid.

33. "North Carolina Highway Historical Marker Program: John Williamson," North Carolina Department of Cultural Resources, http://www.ncmarkers.com/Markers.aspx?sp=search&k=Markers&sv=E-114.

34. Various parts of the West served as potential sites of an all-Black state, including Kansas and Indian Territory. Report and Testimony of the Select Committee of the United States Senate to Investigate the Causes of the Removal of the Negroes from the Southern States to the Northern States, Part II, 46th Cong., 2nd sess., Report 693, 1880, 304.

35. Report and Testimony of the Select Committee of the United States Senate to Investigate the Causes of the Removal of the Negroes from the Southern States to the Northern States. Part II, 46th Cong., 2nd sess., Report 693, 1880, 305. Elliott West's prescient article "Reconstructing Race" provided the lead for this source. West, "Reconstructing Race."

36. Frederick Douglass, "Let the Negro Alone: An Address Delivered in New York, on 11 May 1869," Frederick Douglass Papers, 206–207, https://frederickdouglass.infoset.io/islandora/object/islandora%3A2733#page/1/mode/1up.

37. Frederick Douglass, "Land for the Landless: The Record of Parties on the Homestead Principle No. 20," Frederick Douglass Papers, 4, Library of Congress, https://www.loc.gov/resource/mfd.41012/?sp=3, accessed 2019. Douglass also advocated for American governmental help in removing African Americans from the South to the North or the West due to the prejudice they faced in the South. Frederick Douglass, "The Negro Exodus from the Gulf States, A Paper Read in Saratoga, New York, on 12 September 1879," 519–521, https://frederickdouglass.infoset.io/islandora/object/islandora%3A3160#page/1/mode/1up, accessed 2019.

38. Linda Kerber and Natalie Joy have discussed the connections between abolitionism and Native advocacy, highlighting the often problematic ways in which white and Black abolitionists thought about Native Americans. For white abolitionists, white Americans' treatment of Native Americans competed with Black slavery as America's "original sin." In order to assuage their guilt about U.S. Indian policy, white abolitionists chose to believe that Native Americans had been improved by white civilization. Linda K. Kerber, "The Abolitionist Perception of the Indian," *Journal of American History* 62, no. 2 (1975): 271–295; Joy, "The Indian's Cause: Abolitionists and Native American Rights."

39. Crockett, *The Black Towns*, 21–25.

40. Nicholas Guyatt, *Bind Us Apart: How Enlightened Americans Invented Racial Segregation* (New York: Basic Books, 2016). For more information on lower-class southern African Americans' thoughts on racial separatism from the eighteenth century to the early twentieth century, see Selena Ronshaye Sanderfer, "For Land and Liberty: Black Territorial Separatism in the South, 1776–1904" (dissertation, Vanderbilt University, 2010).

41. Guyatt, *Bind Us Apart*, 217–224.

42. Abel, *The American Indian Under Reconstruction*, 271–273. Senator Doolittle's idea of creating colonists out of African Americans extended further than the boundaries of North America. In an 1862 speech on the Senate floor, he extolled the potential virtues of setting up voluntary Black colonies in places like Haiti, Guatemala, Venezuela, and other warm countries (to parallel African Americans' supposed warm blood). Doolittle saw this as a way to get whites to support emancipation and to foster economic ties with these countries. His motto was, "a generous homestead policy for both races, black and white. Homesteads for free white men in all the temperate territories of the United States, homesteads for all free colored men in the tropics and the islands of the Gulf of Mexico and the Caribbean sea." In Doolittle's mind, these Black colonists, composed of "the most enterprising, the most intelligent and aspiring among that people" would form the foundation of an "empire" and "republic" of Black people that would "grow up under" American protection, "support against foreign intervention," and "feel bound to us by interest, gratitude, and friendship forever." Doolittle felt that colonization elsewhere would most help African Americans because he had seen the negative effects of white–Indian interaction and felt that African Americans would not flourish if they were forced to stay in North America—they would wither in the company of a superior race, as had Indians. Speech of Hon. J. R. Doolittle of Wisconsin on Homesteads for white men in the temperate zone—homesteads for black men in the tropics—white immigration to and Black emigration from the United States—a continental policy, embracing all climes and races, bringing freedom and homes to all; delivered in the Senate of the United States, April 11, 1862 (Washington, DC: Printed at the *Congressional Globe* office, 1862), 11–12.

43. African Americans carved out Black spaces within the United States before and after slavery, outside of the West. For more information on this, see James Lockley, ed., *Maroon Communities in South Carolina: A Documentary Record* (Columbia: University of South Carolina Press, 2009).

44. Crockett, *The Black Towns*, 2.

45. This is the number I have approximated from my work on the Dawes Rolls testimony packets. Each packet can hold the testimonies and/or enrollments of multiple family members, however, so this number is likely higher. As none of these Chickasaw freedpeople distinguished between white or Black U.S. citizens, I assumed that their spouses were Black U.S. citizens; Black-white interracial marriage in Indian Territory at this time was quite low.

46. Tiya Miles and Sharon P. Holland, "Introduction," in *Crossing Waters, Crossing Worlds: The African Diaspora in Indian Country*, ed. Tiya Miles and Sharon P. Holland (Durham, NC: Duke University Press, 2006), 5; Williams Reese, *Trail Sisters*, 129.

47. Hollie I. West, "Boley, Oklahoma: Once a Town of Hope, Now a Fading Dream," *Washington Post*, February 9, 1975; Kenneth Marvin Hamilton, *Black Towns and Profit: Promotion and Development in the Trans-Appalachian West, 1877–1915* (Urbana: University of Illinois Press, 1991), 121, 124.

48. Chleyon Decatur Thomas, "Boley: An All-Black Pioneer Town and the Education of Its Children" (dissertation, University of Akron, 1989), 46–47.

49. Hamilton, *Black Towns and Profit*, 126.

50. Mark Jeffrey Hardwick, "Homesteads and Bungalows: African American Architecture in Langston, Oklahoma" (dissertation, University of Delaware, 1994), 37.

51. Crockett, *The Black Towns*, 16–22; Mary Jane Warde, *When the Wolf Came: The Civil War and the Indian Territory* (Fayetteville: University of Arkansas Press, 2013), 311; Miles and Holland, *Crossing Waters, Crossing Worlds*, 6; Wilson Moore, *Sweet Freedom's Plains*, 2–3; Crockett, *The Black Towns*, 1–7.

52. Hardwick, "Homesteads and Bungalows: African American architecture in Langston, Oklahoma," 36.

53. Crockett, *The Black Towns*, 23–24.

54. Hardwick, "Homesteads and Bungalows: African American architecture in Langston, Oklahoma," 21, 57.

55. Ibid., 40.

56. The only real southern parallel to this western opportunity might have been Mound Bayou, an all-Black community in Mississippi. Here, Black women and men opened their own businesses and farmed without much white harassment. Similar to many towns in the West, Mound Bayou sprang up in its chosen location due to the erection of a railroad line (the LNOT Railroad). However, an important difference seems to be that Mound Bayou was started by a group of Black leaders who largely controlled the cost of land (rather steep at $8–$9 per acre) and the social, economic, and political aspects of the community. On the other hand, in the West, African Americans could get cheaper land due to the Homestead Act, and there was enough "room" in the West to create one's own town or strike out on one's own if they disagreed with occurrences in a town. Milorad M. Novicevic, John H. Humphreys, Ifeoluwa T. Popoola, et al., "Collective Leadership as Institutional Work: Interpreting Evidence from Mound Bayou," *Leadership* 13, no. 5 (2017): 590–614.

57. A significant number of freedpeople in all of the Five Tribes, but especially in the Chickasaw and Choctaw Nations, filed lawsuits alleging that their Native ancestry was ignored by the Dawes commissioners or by the Indian nations themselves and that they deserved a larger land share, equal to that of people classified as Indians by Blood (rather than Freedmen). I have chosen not to document those lawsuits here, because in this work I focus on land and not necessarily the idea of racial ancestry in Indian nations (though my dissertation examined this in detail). The majority of books about Indian freedpeople focus on this issue of "blood," race, and identity. See Yarbrough, *Race and the Cherokee Nation*; Krauthamer, *Black Slaves, Indian Masters*.

58. I could say many things about the ways this process changed and continues to affect Native identity, tribal enrollment, and anti-Black racism in Native nations, but this is not my focus here, and other scholars have covered these topics. See Katherine M. B. Osburn, "'Any Sane Person': Race, Rights, and Tribal Sovereignty in the Construction of the Dawes Rolls for the Choctaw Nation," *Journal of the Gilded Age and Progressive Era* 9, no. 4 (2010): 451–471; Keneisha M. Green, "Who's Who: Exploring the Discrepancy Between

the Methods of Defining African Americans and Native Americans," *American Indian Law Review* 31, no. 1 (2006/2007): 93–110.

59. Although freedpeople typically received 40-acre lots and Indians received 120- or 160-acre lots, sizes varied.

60. "Treaty with the Choctaw and Chickasaw, 1866"; "Treaty with the Creeks, 1866," in Kappler, *Indian Affairs Laws and Treaties*, 931, https://dc.library.okstate.edu/digital/collection/kapplers/id/26772, accessed 2019; "Treaty with the Cherokee, 1866," in Kappler, *Indian Affairs Laws and Treaties*.

61. "Treaty with the Choctaw and Chickasaw, 1866."

62. Naylor, *African Cherokees in Indian Territory*, 165–168.

63. Ibid., 168–169.

64. Ibid.

65. Willard's Hotel, Washington, DC, May 14, 1897, Folder 4. Correspondence from Choctaw Nation Attorneys, January 10, 1897–June 5, 1897, Green McCurtain Papers, Oklahoma Historical Society.

66. McCurtain County Historical Society, https://www.facebook.com/341064668106/photos/ben-watkins-was-born-in-virginia-at-a-young-age-his-father-moved-his-family-to-m/10154822018448107/, accessed 2019; Ben Watkins to Green McCurtain, June 6, 1893, Folder 1, National Treasurer, 1890–1893, Green McCurtain Papers, Oklahoma Historical Society, 3–8.

67. Testimony of William Wilson, 74, former member of the Cherokee National Council. Quoted in "Conditions of the Indians in Indian Territory, and Other Reservations, Etc." Senate Report No. 1278, 1885/1886, 49th Cong., 1st sess. (Washington, DC: Government Printing Office, 1886), 73.

68. "Indian Territory Election," *New York Times*, August 2, 1887.

69. "Wake Up to Your Danger," *Cherokee Advocate*, October 17, 1894, 2. The other reason for the Five Tribes to worry about miscegenation and the Black presence in their nations revolved around the "one-drop rule." Though scholars believe that from approximately the seventeenth century on, Native peoples did not want to be associated with Black people (who, as slaves for the most part, had a lower status), these would not become serious, structural issues that influenced tribal sovereignty until the Jim Crow era. For more on this, see Maynor Lowery, *Lumbee Indians in the Jim Crow South*; Gabrielle Tayac, ed., *IndiVisible: African-Native Lives in the Americas* (Washington, DC: Smithsonian Institution, 2009).

70. Minges, *Black Indian Slave Narratives*, 101.

71. Lewis E. Lucky, Indian Pioneer papers.

72. Lindsay Baker and Julie P. Baker, eds., *The Oklahoma Slave Narratives* (Norman: University of Oklahoma Press, 1996), 83.

73. In this chapter, I engage with some of the questions raised by Stephanie Smallwood in her *William and Mary Quarterly* article. There, Smallwood hypothesizes that we might see birthright citizenship as "an extension of the settler colonial conceit of indigeneity." To answer one of the questions she poses in her article: I don't believe that enslaved African

Americans' labor necessarily gave them the right to land—particularly western land, which they had not lived on as slaves. Stephanie E. Smallwood, "Reflections on Settler Colonialism, the Hemispheric Americas, and Chattel Slavery," *William and Mary Quarterly* 76, no. 3 (2019): 415.

CHAPTER 4

1. Lillie Booker and Herbert Booker (family members), in discussion with author, August 12, 2013.

2. Keri Leigh Merrit discusses how increased economic inequality from the 1840s onward drove divisions between lower-class (usually landless) whites and middle-class and elite whites. For the planter aristocracy, poor whites did not embody the ideals of southern norms (slavery and property ownership). Keri Leigh Merritt, *Masterless Men: Poor Whites and Slavery in the Antebellum South* (New York: Cambridge University Press, 2017). Heather Cox Richardson makes a similar argument, contending that the Civil War had laid bare the fact that all white men were not, in fact, created equal, cementing class divisions and encouraging an exodus of poor whites to the West. Cox Richardson, *West from Appomattox*, 19–20.

3. Jason E. Pierce, *Making the White Man's West: Whiteness and the Creation of the American West* (Boulder: University Press of Colorado, 2016).

4. J. C. Gilbreath, Indian Pioneer papers.

5. "Immigration," Oklahoma Historical Society, https://www.okhistory.org/publications/enc/entry.php?entry=IM001, accessed 2019; "Asians," Oklahoma Historical Society, https://www.okhistory.org/publications/enc/entry.php?entry=AS006, accessed 2019. The 1910 census recorded 40,048 foreign-born individuals, constituting 2.8 percent of Oklahoma's population—far fewer than that of other western territories or states in the same year, such as Colorado (16.2 percent), Nebraska (14 percent), Kansas (8 percent), and Texas (6.2 percent). Christopher James Huggard, "The Role of the Family in Settling the Cherokee Outlet" (dissertation, University of Arkansas, 1987), 8.

6. George Elxander Lambe, Indian Pioneer Papers.

7. Report of the Secretary of the Interior, 1884, XI; "The Indian Territory," *New York Times*, December 5, 1884.

8. "Lawlessness in the Indian Territory," *New York Times*, August 31, 1873.

9. "Killed in Indian Territory," *New York Times*, September 5, 1883.

10. "Lawlessness in the Indian Territory."

11. "A Blot on the Map: Indian Territory Infested by Bands of Marauders," *Daily Public Ledger*, November 17, 1894, Library of Congress, Chronicling America.

12. "Our Indian Policy: Peace Policy of the Administration—Civilizing the Savage—Progress in the Indian Territory—The Indian as a Farmer—The Peace Mission to the Kiowas," *New York Times,* July 4, 1872.

13. Because Reconstruction is often considered the lone period in which the United States actually worked toward racial unity, it was long thought that white supremacist

violence ceased due to the military presence in the South. But the military in the South (and in Indian Territory) could not be everywhere at once, and individual soldiers themselves did not necessarily agree with racial equality. Shawn Leigh Alexander, "T. Thomas Fortune, Racial Violence of Reconstruction, and the Struggle for Historical Memory," in *Remembering Reconstruction: Struggles over the Meaning of America's Most Turbulent Era*, ed. Carole Emberton and Bruce E. Baker (Baton Rouge: Louisiana State University Press, 2017), 59–83; Hahn, *A Nation Under Our Feet*.

14. Evan Woodson, "Strange Fruit on the Southern Plains: Racial Violence, Lynching, and African Americans in Oklahoma, 1830-1930" (master's thesis, Oklahoma State University, 2015). Most of the other victims were white, while a minority were Native American, reflecting the fact that intraracial violence was the most prevalent before lynching took a white supremacist turn.

15. "Indian Territory Riot," *New York Times*, October 3, 1901.

16. Daniel F. Littlefield Jr., *Seminole Burning: A Story of Racial Vengeance* (Jackson: University Press of Mississippi, 1996).

17. "Burning of the Seminoles: Forty-Eight Persons to Be Arrested in Oklahoma Territory," *New York Times*, January 29, 1898.

18. Grant Foreman, *A History of Oklahoma* (Norman: University of Oklahoma Press, 1942), 279–80.

19. Joyce Ann Kievit, "Trail of Tears to Veil of Tears: The Impact of Removal on Reconstruction" (dissertation, University of Houston, 2002), 227–229.

20. Bailey, *Reconstruction in Indian Territory*, 105–106.

21. Kidwell, *The Choctaws in Oklahoma*, 89.

22. Bays, "A Historical Geography of Town Building in the Cherokee Nation, 1866-1906," 71.

23. Joanna Draper, Slave Narrative Project, 87.

24. Mary Lindsay, Slave Narrative Project, 186.

25. Annual Report of the Commissioner of Indian Affairs, 1887, 112, 204. The Five Tribes, led by Cherokee Elias Boudinot, even attempted, in 1867, to create their own railroad company (the Central Indian Railroad). Kievit, "Trail of Tears to Veil of Tears," 225–226.

26. Scholars such as Alessandra Link have used the 150th anniversary of the union of the Central Pacific and Union Pacific railroad tracks (2019) in Utah as a jumping-off point to revitalize discussions about the railroads' influence on Native peoples. See Alessandra Link, "150 Years After the Transcontinental Railroad, Indigenous Activists Continue to Battle Corporate Overreach," *Washington Post*, May 10, 2019, https://www.washingtonpost.com/outlook/2019/05/10/how-indigenous-activists-fought-transcontinental-railroad/.

27. "Reorganization of Indian Territory," *Washington Post*, February 9, 1897. Lighthorsemen (tribal police) and U.S. marshals operated to varying degrees as law enforcement in the Indian and Oklahoma territories.

28. Annual Report of the Commissioner of Indian Affairs, 1882, 88–89.

29. "The Indians: The Osage Reservations—Indians Assaulted by Lawless White Men—Affairs in the Indian Territory," *New York Times,* July 31, 1870.

30. "Indian Matters: Appropriations Wanted for Indians—White Settlers on Indian Territory," *New York Times*, March 18, 1872.

31. "Indian Territory Raiders," *New York Times*, December 22, 1880.

32. "Indian Territory Is for Indians," *New York Times*, July 31, 1881.

33. "War in the Indian Territory: The Oklahoma Boomers Ready to Fight the Troops Sent to Eject Them," *New York Times*, January 12, 1885.

34. "The Boomers: Another Immigration to Indian Territory Threatened," *Los Angeles Times*, February 1, 1885.

35. Annual Report of the Secretary of the Interior, 1884, XVIII.

36. "Indian Territory Raiders," *New York Times*, December 22, 1880; "The Indian Territory," *New York Times*, December 5, 1884.

37. William Foster, Indian Pioneer Papers, 344–345.

38. Yarbrough, *Race and the Cherokee Nation*, 27–29.

39. Fay Yarbrough, "Other Southerners: The Aftermath of the Civil War in the Cherokee Nation," in *Democracy and the American Civil War: Race and African Americans in the Nineteenth Century*, ed. Kevin Adams and Leonne M. Hudson (Kent, OH: Kent State University Press, 2016), 54; Yarbrough, *Race and the Cherokee Nation*, 29–30.

40. Regulating the Indian Department, 23rd Cong., 1st sess., University of Wisconsin libraries, http://images.library.wisc.edu/History/EFacs/CommRep/AnnRep2639/reference/history.annrep2639.i0010.pdf, 98.

41. Yarbrough, *Race and the Cherokee Nation*, 51–57.

42. Kurt Lively, "Where the Great Plains and the South Collide: A History of Farm Tenancy in Oklahoma, 1890–1950" (dissertation, Oklahoma State University, 2010), 65.

43. "Choctaw and Chickasaw Treaty of 1866."

44. An Act to Amend in Relation to Inter-Marriages Between Citizens of the Chickasaw Nation and Citizens of the United States, and for Other Purposes. An Act to Amend an Act in Relation to Intermarriages, etc., Box 6 Topical Files, 1795–1942 (M1982.105 Location: 0966.09) [1982.105], Lee Harkins Collection Manuscripts, Manuscripts/Vertical Files, Oklahoma Historical Society.

45. Report of the Commissioner of Indian Affairs, Annual Report of the Secretary of the Interior, Commissioner of Indian Affairs, and Secretary of War relating to Indian Affairs, 1899–1900 MMF 610 Roll 17, 116.

46. Charles Meserve, *The Dawes Commission and the Five Civilized Tribes of Indian Territory* (Philadelphia: Office of the Indian Rights Association, 1896), Western History Collections, 7.

47. Report of Commission to the Five Civilized Tribes, 1899, Annual Report of the Secretary of the Interior, Commissioner of Indian Affairs, and Secretary of War relating to Indian Affairs, 1899–1900 MMF 610 Roll 17, 15.

48. Ibid., 171.

49. Folder 5, Correspondence from Choctaw Nation Attorneys, July 22, 1897–December 30, 1897, Green McCurtain Papers, Manuscripts/Vertical Files, Oklahoma Historical Society.

50. OHS#12962 Special Message of D. H. Johnston, September 4, 1900, September 15, 1904, Douglas H. Johnston Collection Manuscripts, Manuscripts/Vertical Files, Oklahoma Historical Society.

51. Message of D. H. Johnston, September 15, 1904, Douglas H. Johnston Collection Manuscripts, Manuscripts/Vertical Files, Oklahoma Historical Society.

52. Stephen Kantrowitz explored this phenomenon in his "White Supremacy, Settler Colonialism, and the Two Citizenships of the Fourteenth Amendment," *Journal of the Civil War Era* 10, no. 1 (2020): 29–53.

53. "The Indian Territory," *New York Times*, August 13, 1864.

54. As politicians debated which persons the Civil Rights Act of 1866, and subsequently the Fourteenth Amendment, would apply to, they bandied about what language should be used to denote Native peoples and which Native peoples in which regions should be included. United States, Congress, February 1, 1866, *The Congressional Globe: Containing the Debates and Proceedings of the First Session of the Thirty-Ninth Congress* (Washington, DC, 1866), 571–572.

55. Christina Snyder, *Great Crossings: Indians, Settlers, and Slaves in the Age of Jackson* (New York: Oxford University Press, 2017), 294.

56. Chang, *The Color of the Land*, 74–89.

57. Creek followers of Chitto Harjo and Cherokee members of the Keetoowah band of Indians are notable for at least initially refusing to enroll and receive allotments. Some people never conceded, and their families never claimed land through the Dawes process. Chang, *The Color of the Land*, 84–90, 96–104; Stremlau, *Sustaining the Cherokee Family*. Julie Reed showed how some Cherokees protested allotment and statehood, as well as American citizenship, on the basis that it would disrupt the social welfare "safeguards" and "communitarian ethic" the Cherokee Nation had put in place to ensure that all tribal members were "shielded" from "individual suffering." Reed, *Serving the Nation*, 3–6.

58. For more on this see Chapter 1. Regulating the Indian Department, Annual Report of the Commissioner of Indian Affairs, for the Years 1826–1839, 1834, 101.

59. Kappler, Indian Affairs, Vol. II, 945–950; "A Historical Geography of Town Building in the Cherokee Nation," 60.

60. Phillip A. Lewis, Indian Pioneer Papers.

61. Angie Debo, *And Still the Waters Run* (Princeton, NJ: Princeton University Press, 1940), 160–161.

62. Address by P. P. Pitchlynn, Principal Chief of the Choctaw Nation and Winchester Colbert, Governor of the Chickasaw Nation, to the Choctaws and Chickasaws, 1866 (Doc. #7067), Chickasaw National Records, Box 6A, Oklahoma Historical Society. Pitchlynn had not immediately agreed to the land surveyance, but when the Chickasaw Council voted for it, he acquiesced. Kidwell, *The Choctaws in Oklahoma*, 85.

63. Kidwell, *The Choctaws in Oklahoma*, 82–85, 186–187; William H. Murray, "The Constitutional Convention," *Chronicles of Oklahoma* 9, no. 2 (1931): 126.

64. "Passing of Tribal Rule: Union of Indian Territory with Oklahoma," *Los Angeles Times*, March 3, 1907, VI15.

65. Gregory James Brueck, "Breaking the Plains: Indians, Settlers, and Reformers in the Oklahoma Land Rush" (dissertation, University of California, Davis, 2012), 1.

66. Lively, "Where the Great Plains and the South Collide," 65; Debo, *And Still the Waters Run*, 80–81.

67. Chang, *The Color of the Land*, 118.

68. The commission initially wanted this restriction to apply to all tribal citizens, but they were thwarted by politicians and land speculators. Debo, *And Still the Waters Run*, 32, 36. David Chang has covered the hearings (and associated testimony) that occurred before final decisions about restriction were made. Chang, *The Color of the Land*, 112–117.

69. Leslie Hewes, *Occupying the Cherokee Country of Oklahoma* (Lincoln: University of Nebraska Press, 1978).

70. Chang, *The Color of the Land*, 117–118. This also affected mixed-race white and Native peoples classified as "less than one-half Indian blood."

71. Debo, *And Still the Waters Run*, 93–100.

72. Ibid., 89, 103–104; Susan Work, "The 'Terminated' Five Tribes of Oklahoma: The Effect of Federal Legislation and Administrative Treatment on the Government of the Seminole Nation," *American Indian Law Review* 6, no. 1 (1978): 95.

73. Gabe James, January 14, 1899, Letters Sent and Received and Other Documents Chickasaw, Undated and January 15, 1899–April 28, 1899, DC Roll 051.

74. Chang, *The Color of the Land*, 117.

75. "Richest Colored Girl Forced to Live in Shack: Richest Colored Girl Forced to Live in Log Hut. White Guardian Who Controls Her Money a Real Southerner, It Is Said, Who Gets a Fabulous Sum of Money a Year for Being Her Guardian.—He Lives on the Fat of the Land with Her Money and Does Not Give His Colored Charge the Care He Would a White Girl. How Can Southern White Gentleman Fool with a 'Nigger'? Not Believing in Education for the Colored Boy or Girl, This Man Is Not a Fit Subject for the Position. The National Association for the Advancement of Colored People Should Take This Matter Out of This Man's Hands and See That This Little Girl and Her Ignorant Parents Are Not Robbed of Her Rightful Heritage. Steps to Stop This Wholesale Robbery Should Be Taken at Once," *Chicago Defender*, November 29, 1913.

76. "Richest Colored Girl Forced to Live in Shack."

77. Morris Sheppard, Federal Writers' Project, 292.

78. Mary Nevins, Indian Pioneer Papers.

79. Fannie Rentie Chapman, Indian Pioneer Papers.

80. Melinda Miller, "Essays on Race and the Persistence of Economic Inequality," *Journal of Economic History* 70, no. 2 (2010): 468–471.

81. Bonnie Lynn-Sherow, *Red Earth: Race and Agriculture in Oklahoma Territory* (Lawrence: University Press of Kansas, 2004), 3–19, 45.

82. Direct Examination by Charles von Weise, Folder 8, Dawes Commission, 1896–1907, Box 9 Native American Law: Citizenship, 1893–1918 (M1983.234 Location: 1034.05) [1983.234], John R. Thomas Collection Manuscripts, Oklahoma Historical Society; Hon. N. B. Ainsworth letter, Folder 2, Correspondence 1-1-1915 to 5-30-1915, Box 2 Correspondence 1914–1916 [1982.294], William H. Murray Collection Manuscripts, Oklahoma Historical Society.

83. Feldhousen-Giles, "To Prove Who You Are: Freedmen Identities in Oklahoma," 45–50, 60–61.

84. Work, "The 'Terminated' Five Tribes of Oklahoma," 81–141, 96. While this period is often called the "Termination Period," referring to the alleged termination of the governments of the Five Tribes and other Indian nations throughout North America, tribes such as the Seminoles immediately fought this interpretation of the act. A current Supreme Court case (*Sharp v. Murphy*) will determine whether the Treaties of 1866 and the Dawes Act actually discontinued tribal governments and "reservations."

85. "The constitution of Oklahoma," Article 1, Section 5, 1907, HathiTrust online database.

86. "The constitution of Oklahoma," Article XIII, Section 3, 1907, HathiTrust online database.

87. It was Paul Finkelman's chapter in *Black Americans and the Civil Rights Movement in the West* that brought this seemingly obvious timeline to my attention. Paul Finkelman, "Conceived in Segregation and Dedicated to the Proposition That All Men Were *Not* Created Equal: Oklahoma, the Last Southern State," in *Black Americans and the Civil Rights Movement in the West*, ed. Bruce A. Glasrud, Cary D. Wintz, and Quintard Taylor (Norman: University of Oklahoma Press, 2019), 216.

88. "Guinn & Beal v. United States," *Legal Information Institute*, Cornell Law School, https://www.law.cornell.edu/supremecourt/text/238/347#writing-USSC_CR_0238_0347_ZS.

89. Finkelman, "Conceived in Segregation and Dedicated to the Proposition That All Men Were *Not* Created Equal," 224.

90. "Grandfather Clause in Oklahoma! Wealthy Negroes Are Denied the Right of Franchise by Act of the New State," *Topeka Plaindealer* 12, no. 46 (November 18, 1910): 1.

91. Ibid.

92. Bert Luster, August 19, 1937, Federal Writers' Project, 205–206.

93. "Segregation," Oklahoma Historical Society, https://www.okhistory.org/publications/enc/entry.php?entry=SE006.

94. Paul R. Stevick to Hon. William H. Murray, November 12, 1915, Box 2 Correspondence, Folder 4 Correspondence, William H. Murray Collection Manuscripts, Oklahoma Historical Society; William H. Murray to Paul R. Stevick, November 27, 1915, Box 2 Correspondence, Folder 4 Correspondence, William H. Murray Collection Manuscripts, Oklahoma Historical Society.

95. "Murray, William Henry David," Oklahoma Historical Society, https://www.okhistory.org/publications/enc/entry.php?entry=MU014, accessed 2019.

96. Mrs. John Hawkins, Indian Pioneer Papers.

97. John Luther Branchcomb, Indian Pioneer Papers.

98. Hamilton, *Black Towns and Profit*, 131.

99. Rhonda M. Ragsdale, "A Place to Call Home: A Study of the Self-Segregated Community of Tatums, Oklahoma, 1894–1970" (dissertation, University of North Texas, 2005), 22, 41, 44, 62–63, 71, 74.

100. "Cora Gillam" in Patrick Minges, ed., *Black Indian Slave Narratives*, 23–24.

101. Although KKK activity was not particularly high in Oklahoma, especially relative to the South, a contingent of members terrorized African Americans there in the 1900s. Carter Blue Clark, "A History of the Ku Klux Klan in Oklahoma" (dissertation, University of Oklahoma, 1976); Alexander Charles Comer Jr., "Invisible Empire in the Southwest: The Ku Klux Klan in Texas, Louisiana, Oklahoma, and Arkansas, 1920-1930" (dissertation, University of Texas at Austin, 1962).

102. Untitled document, Indian Pioneer Papers.

103. Clark, "A History of the Ku Klux Klan in Oklahoma"; Comer, "Invisible Empire in the Southwest"; Woodson, "Strange Fruit on the Southern Plains"; Karen Sieber, "Visualizing the Red Summer," http://visualizingtheredsummer.com/?page_id=58, accessed November 3, 2019.

104. Glen Romaine Roberson, "City on the Plains: The History of Tulsa, Oklahoma" (dissertation, Oklahoma State University, 1977), 66–67, 88.

105. Ibid., 2, 65.

106. In their book *Tulsa: 1921*, Randy Krehbiel and Karlos K. Hill cast doubt on the well-told story that there was a newspaper editorial at the center of the massacre. Instead, they believe that the news spread orally. Krehbiel and Hill, *Tulsa 1921: Reporting a Massacre* (Norman: University of Oklahoma Press, 2019), 35–36.

107. B. C. Franklin, August 22, 1931, "The Tulsa Race Riot and Three of Its Victims," Smithsonian National Museum of African American History and Culture, https://nmaahc.si.edu/object/nmaahc_2015.176.1, accessed 2019; Buck Colbert Franklin, "Read an Eyewitness Account of the Massacre That Opens Watchmen," Slate.com, https://slate.com/culture/2019/10/watchmen-b-c-franklin-tulsa-massacre-account-full-text.html, accessed 2019.

108. Hirsch, *Riot and Remembrance*; Krehbiel and Hill, *Tulsa 1921*, 88.

109. Alfred Brophy, *Reconstructing the Dreamland: The Tulsa Riot of 1921—Race, Reparations, and Reconciliation* (New York: Oxford University Press, 2002), 160–180.

110. Rebecca Onion, "Photo Postcards Made to Celebrate the Ruins of Black Neighborhoods After the Tulsa Race Riot of 1921," Slate.com, https://slate.com/human-interest/2014/07/tulsa-race-riot-history-postcards-made-with-images-of-ruins-of-black-communities.html, accessed 2019.

111. "Denies Negroes Started Tulsa Riot: Head of Blood Brotherhood Defends the Purpose of the Organization," *New York Times*, June 5, 1921.

112. "85 Dead from Tulsa Race Riot," *Prescott Daily News*, June 2, 1921, Chronicling America, Library of Congress.

113. Hannibal B. Johnson, *Apartheid in Indian Country?: Seeing Red over Black Disen-franchisement* (Fort Worth, TX: Eakin Press, 2012), 83–84; Victor Luckerson, "Black Wall Street: The African American Haven That Burned and Then Rose from the Ashes," *Ringer*, https://www.theringer.com/2018/6/28/17511818/black-wall-street-oklahoma-greenwood-destruction-tulsa, accessed February 8, 2019.

114. Krehbiel and Hill, *Tulsa 1921*, xi.

115. Arrell M. Gibson, *Oklahoma: A History of Five Centuries* (Norman: University of Oklahoma Press, 1965), 8–9.

116. The other places that served a similar function for people of African descent were some northern spaces, like Canada, or ultra-southern places like Mexico—but there was no American governmental action in these spaces to make them particularly palatable for Black people, like there was in Indian Territory. In this respect, I do believe Indian Territory is unique.

EPILOGUE

1. This is six generations from me, which would be five generations from Travis.

2. Travis D. Roberts (family member) in discussion with author, September 2, 2013.

3. Steve Kantrowitz explores the ways in which the Civil War and Reconstruction affected (non–Five Tribes) western Indian nations. Stephen Kantrowitz, "'Not Quite Constitutionalized': The Meanings of 'Civilization' and the Limits of Native American Citizenship," in *The World the Civil War Made*, ed. Gregory P. Downs and Kate Masur (Chapel Hill: University of North Carolina Press, 2015), 75–105; Stephen Kantrowitz, "Citizens' Clothing: Reconstruction, Ho-Chunk Persistence, and the Politics of Dress," in *Civil War Wests: Testing the Limits of the United States*, ed. Adam Arenson and Andrew Graybill (Berkeley: University of California Press, 2015), 242–264.

4. Even literature often uses this idea of Black landownership as idealized autonomy, for the most part negating Native ownership and occupancy. Catherine Lynn Adams, "Africanizing the Territory: The History, Memory and Contemporary Imagination of Black Frontier Settlements in the Oklahoma Territory" (dissertation, University of Massachusetts, Amherst, 2010).

Index

Battle of Prairie Grove (1862), 34
Beams family, 26
belonging: as communitarian ethic, 146n9;
    and emancipation, 65; and Indian
    freedpeople's choice to stay in Indian
    Territory, 5–6, 44, 57, 65–66; and
    Indian Removal, 16; vs. United States
    citizenship, 5
Benezet, Anthony, 84
Bennett, Alice, 66
Bens, Jonas, 145n5
Berlin, Ira, 169n94
Berwyn, Oklahoma, 127
Black Codes, 13, 24–25, 27, 47, 150–51n23,
    157nn59,63
Black people. *See* African Americans
    (in United States); African American
    settlers; Five Tribes enslaved people;
    Indian freedpeople
Black towns, 62–63, 88, 120; and Five Tribes'
    hostility to Indian freedpeople, 67–68;
    founded by African American settlers,
    63, 72, 86–89, 88, 175n56; Robertsville,
    57–60, 72, 133, 167n63; and tribal
    citizenship, 168n88
"Black Wall Street" (Tulsa), 9, 70, 128, 132.
    See also Tulsa Race Massacre
Bloody Kansas, 2
Blue, William, 34
Boley, Oklahoma, 86–87, 88, 120, 126–27
Booker, Herbert, Jr., 96, 133
Booker, Lillie Roberts, 96–97, 133
Boomer movement, 105–6
Bottoms, D. Michael, 150n18
Bowes, John P., 152n2, 159n78
Branchcomb, John Luther, 126
Brashears, Richard, 54–55
Briggs, Cyril V., 130
Brown, Charley Moore, 58
Bruyneel, Kevin, 148n12
Buchanan, James, 49
Burney, B. C., 69

Byrd, Jodi, 145n5
Byrd, W. L., 69

Caddo Nation, 155n40
Calhoun, John C., 16–17
California, 148n13, 150n19
Calvary Baptist Church (Robertsville), 59,
    60, 167n63
Camp, Stephanie, 169–70nn100–101
Canadian Colored, Oklahoma, 63
Catawba Nation, 156n50
Centralia, Oklahoma, 101
Chandler, Cornelia, 15
Change, David, 147–48n12, 169n99
Chapman, Fannie Rentie, 118–19
Cherokee freedpeople: Dawes Act
    allotments, 50, 119–20; education, 61;
    government appeals by, 57; and tribal
    citizenship, 47, 91, 92, 168n88
Cherokee Nation: Black towns founded by,
    62–63, 168n88; and civilized/uncivilized
    rhetoric, 21, 151–52n2; and Civil
    War battles, 34; Civil War role of, 31;
    economic/social settlement, 22–23; and
    free Black people, 157n63; and grand
    council, 155n40; historical focus on, 45;
    Keetoowah Society, 28, 158n73, 180n57;
    miscegenation laws, 25, 157nn61,63; and
    mixed-race people, 26; Removal of, 15,
    152n13; resistance to Dawes Commission
    in, 180n57; slave ownership in, 24, 27,
    28, 143n3; treaty guarantees, 31, 159n86;
    white American settlers in, 105; white
    intergroup marriages within, 108–9; and
    Yamasee War, 156n50. *See also* Cherokee
    freedpeople; Five Tribes
Cherokee Nation v. Georgia, 145n5
Chickasaw freedpeople: Black towns
    founded by, 57–60, 62, 127; choice
    to stay in Indian Territory, 65–66,
    169n95; Dawes Act allotments, 50;
    education, 59–60; emancipation

of, 46–47; exploitation of, 53–54;
government appeals by, 47–48, 56–57,
59–60; informal settlement, 57–58;
intergroup marriages with African
American settlers, 86, 174n45; Native
ancestry among, 175n57; and Oklahoma
statehood, 124–25; and tribal citizenship,
45, 68–69, 91, 164n13, 170n106
Chickasaw Nation, 46; Black Codes,
47; Civil War military service, 34,
160n97; as Civil War refugees, 159n89;
Confederate alliance, 29–31, 32, 34,
165n35; economic/social settlement,
22; and grand council, 155n40; and
intertribal political efforts, 113–14;
Leased District, 30, 38, 39, 159n83,
163–64n12, 170n106; miscegenation
laws, 25, 157n61; and mixed-race
people, 26; and post-Reconstruction
racial order, 125–26; rewriting of
history, 20–21; slave ownership in, 24,
28, 34; treaty guarantees, 50, 165n35;
and tribal citizenship, 5–6, 45; and
tribal sovereignty destruction, 113–14;
and white intergroup marriages, 109–11.
See also Chickasaw freedpeople; Five
Tribes
Child, Lydia Marie, 158n77
Chinese immigrants, 151n26
Choctaw freedpeople: and African
American settlers, 91–92; Black towns
founded by, 62; Dawes Act allotments,
50; education, 60–61; government
appeals, 47–48; informal settlement, 58;
Native ancestry among, 175n57; and
tribal citizenship, 68–69, 91, 164n18,
170n106
Choctaw Nation: Black Codes, 47; and
civilized/uncivilized rhetoric, 152n4;
and Civil War battles, 34; Confederate
alliance, 29–30, 165n35; economic/
social settlement, 22–23; freedpeople in,

47, 164n18; and grand council, 155n40;
and intertribal political efforts, 113–14;
Leased District, 30, 38, 39, 159n83,
163–64n12, 170n106; miscegenation
laws, 25, 157n61; and mixed-race people,
26; and railroads, 103; Removal of, 15,
159n79; slave ownership in, 24, 28;
treaty guarantees, 50, 165n35; Treaty of
1855, 159n83, 161n114, 165n34; and tribal
sovereignty destruction, 113–14; white
economic exploitation of, 117; and white
intergroup marriages, 109, 110; and
Yamasee War, 156n50. *See also* Choctaw
freedpeople; Five Tribes
Chouteau, Peter, 21–22
Christianity, 59, 167n64
civilized/uncivilized rhetoric: African
American settlers use of, 73, 81–84; and
Dawes Act allotments, 44; and Indian
Removal, 16–17; and settler colonialism,
4, 18, 144–46n5, 151–52n2; and United
States policies, 16–17, 18, 19; and white
American settlers, 19, 98–100, 152n2. *See
also* Five Tribes civilized/uncivilized
rhetoric
Civil Rights Act (1866), 165n32, 171n3,
180n54
Civil War, 2; end of, 36–37, 161n110; and
Five Tribes enslaved people, 32, 34,
161n106; Five Tribes military service,
33–34, 160n97; Five Tribes refugees
from, 32, 159–60n89; Five Tribes roles
in, 29–34; and grand council, 155n40;
and Gullah Geechee land promise, 44,
75, 162n8; and settler colonialism, 36,
161n106; timetables for, 148n15; and
western expansion, 34–35
Clay, Henry, 94
Cohee, Charles, Jr., 26
Cohee, Charles, Sr., 26
Colbert, Holmes, 38
Colbert, Winchester, 68–69, 114, 170n106

Acknowledgments

FIRST, I MUST thank my favorite person in the world, my soul mate, Rob. Thank you for all you do to encourage me, support me, and accept me. Only you truly know the journey it took to get here: to the end of my graduate program, to a professorship at a research university, and to a published book. I am infinitely thankful that I had you as my partner on this trek. You are my everything.

This book would not exist in its present form without the counsel of Laura Edwards and Barbara Krauthamer through the support of the Penn State Richards Civil War Era Center. The Richards Center manuscript workshop where these two amazing scholars presented me with their feedback on my dissertation was nothing less than transformative. Before this, I thought of my work only as something that would add to the Black-Indian historiography. Afterward, I realized that my book project could connect my beloved field to broader Civil War and Reconstruction history and hopefully draw more historians' attention to the stories of Black and Native people that I was trying to tell. No doubt, the broadening of my project also made me a more compelling job candidate—a key concern in this market climate. I can say, then, that the year I spent in State College was essential to my personal and professional growth.

Thank you to Konstantin Dierks for so much. I've already thanked you privately, but it wouldn't feel right not to mention you here as well. Your graduate seminar at Indiana University forced me to use geography and space as categories of analysis, though I went kicking and screaming.

When I wrote a lackluster first draft of my final paper, your comments encouraged me to own my expertise and to work to become a better writer. I stopped procrastinating and became a morning person and never looked back. Thank you for the truly life-changing feedback.

Thank you to Dr. Reginald Hildebrand and Dr. John Bodnar (both of whom I would, still, never dare to call by their first names) for always believing in my project and in me, as a person, even when I had a hard time believing in either.

Thank you to Bob Lockhart at the University of Pennsylvania Press for your enthusiastic support for this book. You allowed me to write the book I wanted—no, needed—to write, and you came into my life at just the right time, offering me the perfect editorial home. Also at Penn Press, my book series editors, Steven Hahn and Brian DeLay, as well as my peer reviewers, offered great advice and encouragement.

Thank you to Christina Snyder, Greg Downs, Joe Genetin-Pilawa, Kelly Kennington, and Dave Prior for reading early drafts of this book and offering helpful observations.

Thank you to Steve Kantrowitz for supporting my work and serving as an amazingly meticulous reader in a number of different forms. Your feedback was so influential in shaping this book, and I will always remain thankful that our paths crossed as they did.

Thank you to Kathleen DuVal for thorough, wise, and kind feedback. I could not have known when we first met almost ten years ago that your work would inspire an important piece of this book.

Thank you to Tiya Miles for adopting me into what I like to call your "brood." The opportunities you've passed on to me have changed the course of my career. I'm also ever thankful for the example of success and generosity you represent for me and other Black women scholars.

Thank you to Kristin Oertel for the genius idea to release this book on the anniversary of the Tulsa Massacre as a way to contextualize this event and bring attention to the longer and broader history of many of the people who lived in Tulsa.

Thank you to Ebony Coletu for introducing me to Alyosha Goldstein and his work, which led me down the path to a focus on settler colonialism; thank you, Alyosha, for conversing with me and providing feedback on an early draft of this book.

Thank you to Daniel Littlefield for your trailblazing work in the field of Black-Indian history and also for being so kind and helpful when I stumbled into your research center in Arkansas. Your book on Chickasaw freedpeople, which I read as an undergraduate at UC Santa Barbara, shaped my path and helped light my way.

Thank you to Carla Swanson for being my personal cheerleader since the day we met. You helped me believe in friendship again.

Thank you to Roberta DeDonato for being the best personal trainer I've ever had and also for serving as a crucial source of emotional support during a difficult time.

Thank you to Alexa Woloshyn for being a wonderful and supportive friend and colleague who constantly challenges me to dive deeper into the field of Native American and Indigenous studies. You are a true example of an ally, and I treasure our relationship.

Thank you to Celia Naylor for being a source of reassurance and positivity.

Thank you to all the scholars who paved the way for academic monographs about (or including) one's own family. It was not so long ago that this was seen as self-indulgent and subjective (I know it still is by some). Now historians can call attention to their "biases" as their particular perspectives and use their family narratives to uncover truths and other ways of knowing. Thank you for enduring the naysayers to a degree that I won't have to.

A huge thank you to my department at the University of Pittsburgh. I came to you as a postdoctoral fellow and have never felt more welcomed and appreciated. I'm so glad that you chose me to become your more permanent colleague.

Last, but certainly not least, thank you to all of the organizations that funded the research that led to this book: the American Philosophical Society, the Richards Civil War Era Center at Penn State University, the Center for Research on Race and Ethnicity in Society at Indiana University, the Moore Undergraduate Research Apprentice Program at the University of North Carolina, Chapel Hill, the McNair Scholars Program at UC Santa Barbara, the history department at Indiana University, the University of Pittsburgh Dietrich School, and the Western History Association.

CPSIA information can be obtained
at www.ICGtesting.com
Printed in the USA
JSHW022120060423
40042JS00002B/4